PROCESS AND PERMANENCE IN ETHICS

PROCESS AND PERMANENCE IN ETHICS

Max Scheler's Moral Philosophy

by
Alfons Deeken, S.J.

PAULIST PRESS
New York, N.Y. / Paramus, N.J.

Library of Congress
Catalog Card Number: 73-87476

ISBN 0-8091-1800-9 (paper)
ISBN 0-8091-0179-3 (cloth)

Published by Paulist Press
Editorial Office: 1865 Broadway, N.Y., N.Y. 10023
Business Office: 400 Sette Drive, Paramus, N.J. 07652

Printed and bound in the
United States of America

ACKNOWLEDGMENTS

The author wishes to express his gratitude to the designated publishers
for their kind permission to quote from the following works:

Philosophical Perspectives by Max Scheler, translated by Oscar A. Haac.
Copyright 1958 by Beacon Press. Reprinted by permission.

Thus Spoke Zarathustra, from *The Portable Nietzsche,* translated and
edited by Walter Kaufmann. Copyright 1954 by The Viking Press, Inc.
Reprinted by permission of The Viking Press, Inc.

The Range of Reason by Jacques Maritain. Copyright 1952 by Charles
Scribner's Sons. Reprinted by permission.

Pascal for Our Time by Romano Guardini. Copyright 1966 by Herder
and Herder, Inc. Used by permission.

The Dynamic Element in the Church by Karl Rahner. Copyright 1964
Herder and Herder, Inc. Used by permission.

Ressentiment by Max Scheler, edited with an introduction by Louis A.
Coser and translated by William W. Holdheim. Copyright 1961 by The
Free Press, a division of The Macmillan Company. Reprinted by per-
mission of Francke Verlag, Bern, Switzerland.

Contents

Abbreviations

FORM   *Der Formalismus in der Ethik und die materiale Wertethik.*

UMST   *Vom Umsturz der Werte.*

VEIM   *Vom Ewigen im Menschen.*

Eternal   *On the Eternal in Man.*

SOZ   *Schriften zur Soziologie und Weltanschauungslehre.*

GES   *Die Wissensformen und die Gesellschaft.*

NACH   *Schriften aus dem Nachlass.* Band I: *Zur Ethik und Erkenntnislehre.*

SYM   *Wesen und Formen der Sympathie.*

Sympathy   *The Nature of Sympathy.*

PHIL   *Philosophische Weltanschauung.*

Perspectives   *Philosophical Perspectives.*

Introduction

With the publication of his Collected Works [1] projected in thirteen volumes—thus far seven weighty tomes have appeared—Max Scheler (1874-1928) clearly emerges as one of the most creative and ingenious moral philosophers of the twentieth century. The brilliant creativity of his fertile mind and the extraordinary richness of his philosophical insights make Scheler one of the major seminal thinkers of our time. If one had to characterize him in one word, 'genius' would seem to be the most appropriate term. Edith Stein who, as an assistant to Edmund Husserl, was personally acquainted with numerous leading European intellectuals of her time wrote of her encounter with Scheler: "The very first impression that Scheler made on me was overwhelming. Never again did I meet a person from whom shone forth in such pure form the 'phenomenon of genius'." [2] I. M. Bochenski, in his *Contemporary European Philosophy,* writes of Scheler that he was "beyond doubt the most brilliant German thinker of his day." Bochenski continues to describe him as "the most original figure in ethical studies during the first half of the twentieth century." [3]

[1] Max Scheler, *Gesammelte Werke,* 13 volumes (Bern: Francke Verlag, 1954-).
[2] Edith Stein, *Aus dem Leben einer jüdischen Familie,* edited by L. Gelber (Louvain: Nauwelaerts, 1965), p. 182.
[3] I. M. Bochenski, *Contemporary European Philosophy,* transl. by Donald Nicholl and Karl Aschenbrenner (Berkeley: University of California Press, 1961), p. 140.

Max Scheler established his place in contemporary European philosophy as one of the three founding fathers of the school of phenomenology. Edmund Husserl (1859-1938), Max Scheler (1874-1928) and Martin Heidegger (1889-) are generally considered to be the principal founders of phenomenological thought. Husserl's *Logical Investigations* (1900/01) and *Ideas* (1913), Scheler's *Formalism in Ethics and Non-Formal Ethics of Values* (1913), and Heidegger's *Being and Time* (1927) are landmarks in the development of phenomenology as well as of contemporary philosophy in general. The three phenomenologists knew each other personally. Husserl and Scheler first came into personal contact in 1901 in Halle, where they discussed the concepts of intuition and perception and discovered a close affinity between their philosophical insights. Scheler would later write about this encounter with Husserl:

> The author, dissatisfied with the Kantian philosophy, toward which he had tended to that time . . . had become convinced that the content of what is given in intuition is originally much richer than merely that which is covered by its sensible elements, their genetic derivatives, and the logical forms of unity connected with it. As he expressed his opinion in Husserl's presence and remarked that he saw in this view a new and fruitful principle for the construction of theoretical philosophy, Husserl remarked immediately that he, too, in his work on logic which was about to appear, had undertaken an analogous extension of the concept of intuition, applying it to the so-called 'categorical intuition.' From this moment on there grew up a spiritual relationship between Husserl and the author, which for the author has proved immeasurably fruitful.[4]

For both Husserl and Scheler objective essences can be

[4] Max Scheler, "Die deutsche Philosophie der Gegenwart," in *Deutsches Leben der Gegenwart,* edited by Philipp Witkop (Berlin: Wegweiser-Verlag, 1922), pp. 197-198. Transl. by Quentin Lauer in "The Phenomenological Ethics of Max Scheler," *International Philosophical Quarterly,* I (May 1961), pp. 287-288.

grasped in an intuition which comes at the end of a phenomenological investigation. The phenomenological method consists in the demonstration of that which is immediately and immanently "given" in human consciousness. The "phenomenon" is grasped within a stream of immanent experience of pure, intentional acts.

While Husserl laid the foundation for phenomenology and remained primarily concerned with philosophical method as such, Max Scheler applied phenomenological method to various philosophical themes, especially to the fields of values, ethics, and the philosophy of religion.

Husserl's spirit was that of the mathematician, and he considered his philosophical pursuit to be a "rigorous science." Scheler's spirit, on the other hand, was characterized by a loving, passionate endeavor to grasp the multidimensional richness of all reality. Scheler was an extraordinarily dynamic and vital personality who tried to live life to the utmost. "Overwhelmed by the wealth of his discoveries, he lived in a continuous haste of mind. He had to proclaim so many lucid insights that he staggered, bewildered by cognition and inebriated by truth." [5] The different personalities and divergent approaches to philosophy of Husserl and Scheler are strongly reflected in their respective writings. Quentin Lauer, the eminent Husserl scholar, admits that the reading of Husserl is, even for the most enthusiastic Husserlian a torture, while to read Scheler is a pleasure.[6] Scheler's brilliant and lively personality exudes, even through the pages of his books, such compelling force that one *wants* what he says to be true.

In his monumental work of applied phenomenology, *Der Formalismus in der Ethik und die materiale Wertethik*, Scheler developed a phenomenological theory of values and ethics based on a non-rational, intuitive grasp of values. It is one of the principal achievements of Max Scheler to have evolved a coherent theory of objective value and a corresponding theory of

[5] Alfred Schutz, "Max Scheler's Epistemology and Ethics I," *Review of Metaphysics*, XI (1957-58), p. 305.
[6] Quentin Lauer, "The Phenomenological Ethics of Max Scheler," *International Philosophical Quarterly*, I (May 1961), p. 276.

moral intuition. Thus he has laid a radically new foundation for a philosophical ethics. According to Scheler, the emotional experience of values is primordial to all experience of reality.

In the history of philosophical ethics few books have been acclaimed as highly as Scheler's major work on ethics. Manfred S. Frings writes that *Der Formalismus in der Ethik und die materiale Wertethik* "unquestionably represents the chief contribution to ethics in this century, and is along with Aristotelian Ethics and Kant's *Critique of Practical Reason* the most profound, erudite, and ingenious work on ethics to be found in the history of philosophy." [7]

Max Scheler's philosophical insights have deeply influenced a great number of contemporary minds, many of whom have become more widely known than the seminal thinker who inspired them. Among the men who came under Scheler's influence are Nicolai Hartmann and Ortega y Gasset, Merleau-Ponty and Sartre, Ernst Cassirer and Alois Dempf, Karl Mannheim and Jacques Maritain, Dietrich von Hildebrand and Bernhard Häring, Martin Heidegger and Gabriel Marcel. Nicolai Hartmann's three-volume *Ethics,* for example, is built upon Scheler's moral philosophy and cannot be understood without this foundation. Bernhard Häring, one of the best-known moral theologians today, wrote his first book as a dialogue with Max Scheler and his value ethics.[8] His numerous subsequent writings, too, attest to the fecundity of Scheler's inspiration. Of Heidegger's philosophical anthropology Scheler himself stated that he had influenced it. The young Heidegger spent several days as a guest at Scheler's home in Cologne. Scheler also supported in an important way the professional career of the young Heidegger.

Heinrich Fries has shown that Scheler is the founder of the modern philosophy of religion among contemporary German

[7] Manfred S. Frings, *Max Scheler: A Concise Introduction into the World of a Great Thinker* (Pittsburgh: Duquesne University Press, 1965), p. 103. This year, Northwestern University Press will publish an English translation of Scheler's major ethical work: *Formalism in Ethics and Non-Formal Ethics of Values.*

[8] Bernhard Häring, *Das Heilige und das Gute* (Munich: Erich Wewel Verlag, 1950).

Catholic thinkers.[9] Fries demonstrates that Scheler profoundly influenced the philosophy of religion of Karl Adam, Peter Wust, Johannes Hessen, Karl Rahner, Alois Dempf, Romano Guardini and Erich Przywara.[10] Scheler also made pioneering contributions to the field of sociology. He is credited with being "the founder of a new and purified sociology of knowledge." [11]

Max Scheler was born in Munich on August 22, 1874. His mother was Jewish and his father a Protestant who, for the sake of marriage, had adopted Judaism. Max Scheler attended a *Gymnasium* in his home town and, at the age of fourteen, converted to Catholicism. In 1893 he enrolled in the medical faculty at the University of Munich. The following year he transferred to the University of Berlin where he studied philosophy and sociology and attended the stimulating lectures of Georg Simmel and Wilhelm Dilthey. In 1895, Scheler entered the University of Jena and studied under the famous philosopher Rudolf Eucken. After his *Habilitation* he assumed a teaching position in Jena where he taught ethics and the history of philosophy. Gradually he turned away from the neo-Kantianism of his teacher Eucken and developed his own phenomenological approach to philosophy. His acquaintance with Edmund Husserl helped him to clarify his own phenomenological method, especially the role of intuition in philosophical inquiry. In 1907 Scheler returned to his home town of Munich, then an important center of phenomenological studies. There he lectured at the University of Munich on ethics and psychology. By 1910 he had retired from teaching and launched a new career as a free-lance writer in Göttingen and Berlin. An ardent nationalist and supporter of the war during the first year of World War I, Scheler soon became disillusioned with the militant temper of his time and turned into an influential spokesman for peace and for the spiritual renewal and unification of war-torn Europe. Rejecting nationalism,

[9] Heinrich Fries, *Die Katholische Religionsphilosophie der Gegenwart* (Heidelberg: Kerle, 1949), p. 33.

[10] *Ibid.*, pp. 157-377.

[11] Werner Stark, "Introduction" in Max Scheler, *The Nature of Sympathy* (London, Routledge & Kegan Paul), p. xxxv.

Scheler expounded his ideas on Christian solidarity and brotherhood as the foundation for European cooperation and unity. He presented Christian solidarism as a golden mean between the extreme individualism of capitalism and the collectivism of socialism. Pointing to the community-building potential of Catholicism, Scheler made European Catholics aware of their social responsibility and the important contribution they could make toward the reconciliation and unification of all nations.

In 1919, Scheler assumed a teaching position at the Sociological Institute of the University of Cologne. From that point on, his interests centered around sociology, philosophical anthropology and metaphysics. Through his pioneering "sociology of knowledge," he made a lasting contribution to the field of substantive sociology.

After 1922, Scheler's metaphysics and philosophy of religion underwent an abrupt and radical transformation. Moving gradually away from a theistic position, Scheler abandoned Catholicism and began to develop a dynamic pantheism according to which God realizes himself in man and history. The birth of man and the birth of God are explained as reciprocally dependent upon each other. Man becomes the *locus* of deification: God becomes aware of himself only in man.

This last phase of Scheler's philosophy remained an unfinished project. In 1928 he accepted a professorship at the University of Frankfurt but before resuming his teaching died of a severe stroke on May 19, 1928. He was 54 years old.

As is evident from this brief outline of Scheler's life and philosophical career, there are three distinct periods in his philosophy. During the first period which ends about 1912, Scheler was primarily occupied with Kant, Eucken, and Dilthey. The main works of this period are: *Über Ressentiment und moralisches Werturteil, Versuche einer Philosophie des Lebens, Zur Rehabilitierung der Tugend.* In his second period (1912-1921) —the most creative and productive years of his life—he developed his phenomenological value-philosophy, his moral philosophy, his philosophy of religion, and his theory of sympathy and love. The major works of this period are: *Zur Phänome-*

nologie und Theorie der Sympathiegefühle und von Liebe und Hass (the second edition is entitled: *Wesen und Formen der Sympathie*), *Der Formalismus in der Ethik und die materiale Wertethik,* and *Vom Ewigen im Menschen.* Scheler's last period, the beginning of which coincides with his divorce from his second wife and his contraction of an unhappy third marrriage, covers the years 1922 till 1928.

Since most of Scheler's ethical writings originated during the fertile second period, this study will concentrate primarily on the philosophy of this middle period. Even in his later period, Scheler never retracted the basic moral insights of his middle years.

Scheler's insights on ethics are immensely rich and illuminate a multiplicity of problem areas. In order to discover some unity in the plentitude of his ethical insights and to present his moral philosophy in a certain focus, I have centered my study on Scheler's basic quest to achieve a synthesis between the developmental and the permanent dimensions in ethics. In this way, I hope to make a contribution towards the ongoing discussion concerning the changeable and unchangeable elements in ethics. The book attempts to show how, according to Max Scheler, the historicity of value comprehension, of ethos forms and of man, offers an important key to an understanding of the complex question of absoluteness and relativity in ethics. By his reflections on the historical and developmental aspects of ethics, Scheler has made a contribution which should prove valuable to the current debate on situation-ethics and the so-called new morality.

The traditional constructivist approaches to ethics, especially Kant's moral philosophy, rightly emphasized the universality and absoluteness of ethics, but did not pay sufficient attention to the concrete richness of moral values as revealed among different peoples and in different periods of history. Thinkers like Nietzsche and Dilthey, on the other hand, stressed the historical aspect of ethics and tried to capture the rich variety of moral values but fell into the pitfall of relativism. Max Scheler has attempted a synthesis of traditional ethics with its concern for the unchangeable dimension in morality and of modern ethics with its concern for the developmental aspect of morals. In this synthesis Scheler tries to preserve the absolute character of morality and at the same time to integrate into his ethics the richness of all the manifold forms of ethos which had developed in different historical periods and geographical settings, in different nations and social groupings.

In this book I will try to show that Scheler greatly enriched moral philosophy by breaking out of the narrow mold of ethical constructivism and reopening the vistas toward a richer multiplicity of ethically significant phenomena. The various forms of constructivism, in their attempt to derive all ethical phenomena from a single principle, had lost sight of numerous aspects in ethics which they could not fit into the Procrustean bed of their systematic constructions. Scheler, with his new sense of history and his openness to the multiplicity of moral phenomena, has recovered and redeemed many aspects of morality and moral values.

The foundation of Scheler's moral philosophy is to be found in his theory of material value ethics. He establishes the absolute character of the hierarchy of values and refutes any relativism of values and of the hierarchy of values (chapter I).

Though moral values as such are not subject to historical change, man's understanding of values is historically contingent. As a result the particular ethos of a given people differs from age to age. The reason for the evolution of man's value comprehension must ultimately be seen in the richness of the realm of values, which constitutes a wealth of such proportions that no one historical period or one particular people could completely grasp and realize it. Rejecting relativism, Scheler develops the idea of an historical value perspectivism. The mountain range of eternal and immutable values towers high above the valleys in which humans live. Every age and every people see, acccording to their respective limited points of view, different aspects of the abundant realm of values (chapter II).

Each nation and each age have a proper ethos, and it is only through the cooperation of all nations and all historical periods that the fullness of the moral good comes to the fore. Scheler compares the structure of history to a river system in which a great number of rivers continue their particular courses for centuries. Nourished by innumerable tributaries, these rivers finally tend to converge and to unite in one great river. The different ethos forms in history should not be seen as a falling short of an ideal ethic but rather as manifesting the infinite richness and variety of goodness (chapter III).

Consideration will be given to a point that would later be more fully developed by Scheler's disciples and would prove particularly fruitful in the works of recent moral theologians, i.e. the idea of kairos, the ethical demand of the present hour (chapter IV). A moral imperative can be directed to one individual alone and can, without becoming universal law for all men, be binding on this individual person in a specific historical life situation. Kairos as a unique opportunity and a specific call of the present moment in history can be a challenge to one individual as well as to a particular community or nation. In Scheler's moral system, kairos takes on the characteristics of an essential category of ethics. Heidegger, Rahner, Tillich, Schillebeeckx and others later appropriated and developed the idea of kairos as the demand of the present hour.

In his discussion of the historical dimensions of ethics Scheler is primarily concerned with the growth and development of ethos, with the discovery of new values and the unique opportunities that each historical situation presents to man for the realization of moral goodness. However, history also manifests frequent falsifications of the hierarchy of values and basic distortions of man's moral outlook. Of the many possible forms of value-deception, Scheler studies *one* in particular depth, namely "resentment." Resentment is a self-induced poisoning of the mind which leads to a devaluation of values. It usually originates from a sense of moral weakness and its consequent tendency to downgrade genuine values to the level of one's own actual moral condition (chapter V).

History discloses the frequent failure of man to correspond in his moral quest to the objective hierarchy of values. But as man can fail morally, so he can also rise again and ascend to new moral heights. Scheler describes repentance as the ever-present dynamic of the moral world for self-renewal. Although man cannot alter the physical fact of his past deeds he still has the power to alter their internal meaning and value. Through the act of repentance man can reappraise his past life and give it a new worth and significance. Man's historicity and its moral significance especially manifest themselves in the fact that man's past history remains redeemable through the process of repentance and moral rebirth. Scheler applies the idea of repentance to the individual person as well as to whole social groups and historical epochs (chapter VI).

The objective order of values is reflected in every man's heart. The human heart is the seat of the *ordo amoris* and, as a result, a kind of microcosm of the whole objective world of values. In its genuine form, man's love is an ordered counterpart of the hierarchy of values. Love, however, is not a static state of feeling but a dynamic movement toward higher values. Here again man's historical nature is revealed through this dynamism of love. Love is a creative discoverer of new values and the principal driving power in man's continuous quest for self-transcendence. Scheler maintains the primacy of love over knowledge. "Man is first and foremost a loving being (*ens amans*) before he is ever a knowing (*ens cogitans*) or willing being (*ens volens*)." The prototype and apex of all personal love are to be found in man's participation in the divine love (chapter VII).

Scheler developed a value-personalism in order to give a concrete status to the otherwise abstract values (chapter VIII). In his personalist philosophy, values are concretized and incarnated in the person as the bearer of values. Scheler established a hierarchy of value-person-types or ideal model persons which corrresponds to the hierarchy of higher and lower values. People must see the eternal values embodied in model persons whom they will be inspired to imitate. Thus, the model is the most efficacious stimulus to good and the most important source of development and growth in the moral cosmos. Man is formed and molded in his moral behavior and being more by following an example than by following norms. Scheler attaches central importance to value-person-types and historical model persons. He characterizes the history of ethics as a history of value-person-types. Model persons are the principal instruments in all historical change. According to Scheler, the very meaning of history lies in the continuously growing and developing concrete models of humanity.

In various contexts, Scheler develops his thesis that history is moving toward an "era of harmonization" (chapter IX). This emerging historical epoch will achieve a mutually fulfilling balance of the three types of knowledge, a harmonization of man's emotional powers and a convergence of mankind's divergent thought patterns, ideas and ideals. The thesis of a dawning era of harmonization, with its multiple ethical implications, emphasizes the dominant role which the historical dimension plays in Scheler's moral philosophy. With these insights, Scheler presents us with valuable building stones for the ethical, social and cultural foundation of a future world civilization.

I
Material Value Ethics

The title of Scheler's major ethical work, *Der Formalismus in der Ethik und die materiale Wertethik*,[1] clearly indicates a twofold theme and purpose. First, Scheler intended to submit the formalistic ethics of Kant to a critical appraisal. Secondly, he endeavored to go beyond Kant's formalism and to establish a new material value ethics.[2]

I
FOUNDATIONS OF A MATERIAL VALUE ETHICS

Scheler's *Formalismus* may be seen as a continuing dialogue with Kant. As a leitmotiv, the critique of Kantian ethics permeates the whole work and emerges as a major unifying theme. However, already in the preface Scheler states that this is not meant to be an "anti-Kantian" book nor a return to a pre-Kantian position. Scheler is, in fact, quite generous in his praise of Kant's achievement, acclaiming his ethics as the most perfect philosophical ethics designed by man till now.[3] Thus, in his

[1] Max Scheler, *Der Formalismus in der Ethik und die materiale Wertethik* (5th ed. rev.; Bern: Francke Verlag, 1966). (Hereinafter referred to as FORM.)

[2] The adjective "material" connotes "content" and is to be understood in contrast to Kant's "formal." Scheler's phrase *materiale Wertethik* is sometimes translated as "non-formal ethics of values" but since this sounds rather awkward we shall adhere to the literal translation "material value ethics."

[3] FORM, p. 9.

13

new material value ethics Scheler presupposes the valid insights of Kant but "wishes . . . . to go beyond Kant." [4]

Scheler agrees with Kant that one must reject any ethics of goods (*Güterethik*), that is, any ethics which bases moral goodness on its relationship to a world of existing goods (*Güter*).[5] Goods, for example, social welfare, the state, or culture, are in a constant state of change. If one were to base morality on such transitory foundations one would inevitably fall into ethical relativism.

Goods (*Güter*) are, according to Scheler, essentially value-*things* or things of value (*Wertdinge*).[6] Value-things must, however, be clearly distinguished from values. Kant went wrong precisely because he falsely equated goods and values.[7] Goods, according to Scheler, are the bearers of value in a similar way as things are the bearers of color. Values are qualities experienced *in* things but they are not identical with them. We can conceive values without reference to their respective bearers just as we can think of a certain color independently of its bearer. For example, values like the "whole," the "sublime," the "beautiful," and the "charming" are conceivable without necessarily thinking of them as properties of men or of things.[8] Again, agreeableness is an authentic characteristic of any savory fruit, yet the value quality "agreeable" is not simply reducible to the taste-sensations of the fruit. Rather it retains a certain distinctness from, and independence of its bearer. This independence and irreducibility is even more evident in the sphere of higher values, for example, in the realm of esthetics and ethics.

According to Scheler, all values are material qualities (*materiale Qualitäten*) which are independent of the different forms in which they present themselves to us:

All values (including the values "good" and "bad") are

---

[4] FORM, p. 20: "Sie wünscht nicht, 'antikantisch' zu sein oder hinter Kant zurückzugehen, sondern über Kant 'hinauszugehen.' "
[5] FORM, p. 32.
[6] *Ibid.*, pp. 32-51.
[7] *Ibid.*, p. 32.
[8] *Ibid.*, p. 35.

material qualities which exist in a certain hierarchical order of "high" and "low." They are independent of the form of being (*Seinsform*) into which they enter, for example, whether they present themselves to us as purely objective qualities, or as members of value-structures (for example, the being agreeable or the being beautiful of something), or again as partial elements belonging to goods, or finally as the value which "a thing has." [9]

Scheler demonstrates again the difference between values and goods (the bearers of values) by offering a series of examples which all show that "neither the experience of a value . . . nor its evidence . . . depend in any way on the experience of the bearer of the value (*Wertträger*)." [10] It would seem that often the value-dimension of an object is the primary and most original knowledge we have of it and that all subsequent knowledge of the object comes to us through the value as a medium. The value precedes the thing and is, so to speak, the first "messenger" of its specific nature. In the cognitive perception of a total milieu we first grasp the totality and its value and only then the distinct elements of the milieu. [11]

Value qualities do not alter when their bearers change nor are they destroyed when the bearers are extinguished. [12] This shows again that there is a clear difference between values and their bearers. The color blue does not become red when a blue object is painted red. Similarly, a certain value does not alter when its bearer undergoes a transformation. The value of friendship is not nullified when an assumed friend reveals himself to be false.

To understand Scheler's view on the objectivity of values we must consider his interpretation of the relationship between mind and world, or between subjectivity and objectivity. There exists, according to Scheler, a certain "essential constitutional relationship (*konstitutives Wesensverhältnis*) between mind

9 *Ibid.*, pp. 39-40.
10 *Ibid.*, p. 40.
11 *Ibid.*, p. 40.
12 *Ibid.*, p. 41.

and world." [13] This relationship pertains to the "eternal essence of the mind" and is valid for any possible world. Scheler characterizes it as follows:

> It is . . . evident that every possible extramental reality stands in mutual dependence on a possible mind. To all knowledge (and indeed all intentional acts) a being must correspond, and to every being a possible knowledge. Similarly, to all love and preference there must correspond a value, and to every value a love and preference. That is the essential relationship which subsists between the act qua merely performable-being and the object qua existent-being. . . . It is a relationship which I have developed elsewhere as one of philosophy's most fundamental insights.[14]

The objectivity of values would seem to be closely linked to the "essential constitutional relationship" that exists between the subject that perceives and realizes values, and the corresponding values themselves.

Scheler's discussion of this question remains rather sketchy and incomplete. Quentin Lauer, in his essay "The Subjectivity of Objectivity," [15] has developed more systematically a theory on the close interrelationship between subjectivity and objectivity. Lauer shows that one can avoid the dead-end street of the subject-object dichotomy by attempting "to see all being as neither subjective nor objective, precisely because it is both." [16]

[13] Max Scheler, *Vom Ewigen im Menschen* (5th ed. rev.; Bern: Francke Verlag, 1968), p. 181. (Hereinafter referred to as VEIM.) English translation: *On the Eternal in Man*, trans. by Bernard Noble (New York: Harper & Brothers, 1960), p. 185. (Hereinafter referred to as *Eternal*.) Whenever a particular work of Scheler exists in English translation, the translated version will be used except in cases when the writer has considered it necessary to amend the translation. In the footnotes reference will always be made to both the original German and English translations.

[14] VEIM, p. 181; *Eternal*, p. 184.

[15] Quentin Lauer, "The Subjectivity of Objectivity," in *Edmund Husserl 1859-1959* (The Hague: Martinus Nijhoff, 1956), pp. 167-174.

[16] *Ibid.*, p. 173.

According to Lauer, there can be no objectivity without subjectivity and vice versa. It is only through man, i.e. through subjectivity, that the world makes sense. Without him there would only be chaos without significance. "An object *is* in eliciting a response from a subject; the subject *is* in responding to objects." [17]

Scheler places the ultimate metaphysical foundation of values and the ground of their objectivity in the supreme value of a personal God. "All possible values are founded upon the value of an infinite personal Spirit and of the world of values which stands before Him." [18] All values and value-person-types are, in fact, "co-contained" (*mitenthalten*) in the essential goodness of God.[19] It is, therefore, a serious misinterpretation of Scheler to read his ethics as a doctrine of abstract values, or to equate it simply with the impersonal and atheistic value ethics of Nicolai Hartmann. For Scheler, values are manifestations of the divine essence, and they reflect in a fragmentary way the supreme value of God.

Erich Przywara has pointed out that the idea of participation (*Teilnahmegedanke*) is a "basic element in Scheler's thinking." [20] It is this theory of participation which illuminates most clearly the ontological status of values. God and the emerging "kingdom of God" are the foundation and source of such values as love, community and human solidarity.[21] These values which man realizes participate in the supreme values of God himself and of his kingdom and find here their deepest ontological foundation. The value-realizing human person is ultimately "constituted by participation in the kingdom of God." [22]

Through participation in God's own volition and love (*velle*

---

[17] *Ibid.,* p. 171.

[18] FORM, p. 113.

[19] FORM, p. 573.

[20] Erich Przywara, *Religionsbegründung. Max Scheler-J. H. Newman* (Freiburg: Herder, 1923), p. 2.

[21] Max Scheler, *Vom Umsturz der Werte* (4th ed. rev.; Bern: Francke Verlag, 1955), pp. 89-90. (Hereinafter referred to as UMST.)

[22] *Ibid.,* p. 110: " . . . sich in der Teilnahme am Gottesreich konstituieren soll."

in Deo, amare in Deo) [23] man co-realizes (*mitvollzieht*) [24] the divine acts in which God loves himself and the world. Genuine love of other men is ultimately rooted in the act of loving all things in God (*amare in Deo*) and is thus mediated through God.[25] Bernhard Häring has called this grandiose vision of man's ethical life as co-realization (*Mitvollzug*) of the divine love for all persons "a central doctrine of his [Scheler's] personalism, of his value philosophy and especially of his whole philosophy of religion." [26]

In chapter VIII we shall discuss in greater detail the question of the "concretization" of values in value-person-types. It suffices here to note that Scheler always considers values as functioning within a personal framework. This personal dimension of values manifests itself in three ways. First, personal values occupy the highest place in the hierarchy of values; secondly, values disclose themselves through value-person-types or ideal model persons; and thirdly, as we have shown above, all values are ultimately rooted in an infinite Divine Person. It is this value-personalism that distinguishes Scheler's value philosophy most clearly from that of Nicolai Hartmann who by his rejection of a personal God severs the very foundation upon which Scheler grounds all values.[27]

The concretization or "incarnation" of values in concrete existents, especially in persons, is underlined again in Scheler's discussion of love and hatred. In *The Nature of Sympathy* he writes: "There is no such thing as love and hatred for values or

[23] Max Scheler, *Wesen und Formen der Sympathie* (5th ed. rev.; Frankfurt: Verlag G. Schulte-Bulmke, 1948), pp. 181, 205, 241. (Hereinafter referred to as SYM.) English translation: *The Nature of Sympathy*, trans. by Peter Heath, with a general introduction by Werner Stark (London: Routledge and Kegan Paul, 1958), pp. 168, 191, 224. (Hereinafter referred to as *Sympathy*.) Cf. also FORM, p. 396.

[24] SYM, p. 241; *Sympathy*, p. 224.

[25] SYM, p. 205; *Sympathy*, p. 191.

[26] Bernhard Häring, *Das Heilige und das Gute* (Munich: Erich Wewel Verlag, 1950), p. 210.

[27] For a discussion of the differences between the value philosophy of Scheler and Nicolai Hartmann see Ricardo-Guillermo Maliandi, *Wertobjektivität und Realitätserfahrung* (Bonn: H. Bouvier Verlag, 1966); see also Johannes Messner, *Kulturethik* (Innsbruck: Tyrolia Verlag, 1954), pp. 104-110.

ideas of value as independent objects. Love and hatred invariably relate to concrete existents [i.e. bearers of values]." [28]

II

THE RICHNESS AND DIVERSITY OF THE VALUE-COSMOS

In his critique of Kant, Scheler points out that Kant's preoccupation with the formal element in ethics fails to do justice to the richness and diversity of the concrete moral life. His moral imperative suggests a uniformity in good actions but it cannot account for a multitude of richly varied moral phenomena, especially for the morality of unique acts in particular historical circumstances and for the moral significance of historically changing types of ethos. According to Scheler, ethics must not only be concerned with universal laws but must also help man to discover the rich variety of moral growth in space and time both for the individual and for mankind. It is, therefore, insufficient to define good volition in formal terms alone; it must also be described in terms of its content, that is, in its material dimension. It is within this context that Scheler develops his material value ethics.

Otto Friedrich Bollnow, the distinguished moral philosopher of Tübingen, has offered a valuable and incisive interpretation of Scheler's ethics, and especially of his main objection to both Kant and modern ethics in general. Bollnow attaches extraordinary importance to Scheler's value-ethics, calling it "the most important event in philosophical ethics in our century." [29] Scheler's attack, according to Bollnow, is directed not only against the formalism of Kant's ethics but in a more general way against the "constructivism" (*Konstruktivismus*) that is prevalent in most forms of modern ethics.[30] Constructivism is defined as "the tendency to derive the multiple variety of moral

[28] SYM, p. 175; *Sympathy*, p. 163.
[29] Otto Friedrich Bollnow, "Konkrete Ethik. Vorbetrachtungen zu einer philosophischen Tugendlehre," *Zeitschrift für philosophische Forschung*, VI (Winter, 1952), p. 321.
[30] *Ibid.*, p. 322.

phenomena from one uniform principle." [31] Examples of such principles are the good of society, the "will to power" (Nietzsche), compassion (Schopenhauer), or duty (Kant). All constructivist approaches, however, no matter how much they may differ in what they choose as their specific basic principle, have one trait in common, namely, the tendency to reduce the rich totality of moral phenomena to one common origin and principle. Man's vision of the full richness and abundance of values has been partially blocked by the various restricting "constructivist" principles, each of which reduces everything to a "nothing but." Even Bergson, who acknowledges "two sources of morality"—one more than most other modern philosophers would accept—remains basically trapped within a "constructivist" mentality.

Bollnow recognizes the immense achievement of Max Scheler in breaking free from a narrow "constructivist" mentality and in refocusing man's vision on the rich variety and the abundant wealth of all morally relevant phenomena, namely on the total realm of values.[32] Scheler inaugurated a new open-minded, phenomenological approach to ethics which takes into account all values as well as the full breadth of moral possibilities that exist both in the individual and in mankind as a whole.[33]

In his discovery of the plenitude and diversity of values, Scheler was greatly inspired by the philosophy of Friedrich Nietzsche. Ernst Troeltsch noted such a remarkable intellectual affinity between these two thinkers that he did not hesitate to refer to Scheler as "the Catholic Nietzsche." [34] In a time when

[31] *Ibid.*: "Wir verstehen dabei unter Konstruktivismus das Bestreben, die Mannigfaltigkeit der sittlichen Erscheinungen von einem einheitlichen Prinzip aus abzuleiten."

[32] *Ibid.*

[33] *Ibid.*, pp. 321-322. Cf. also Otto Friedrich Bollnow, *Wesen und Wandel der Tugenden,* Ullstein Bücher (Frankfurt: Ullstein Verlag, 1958), pp. 16-19. In several books Bollnow has taken over some basic insights of Scheler and developed them more systematically. A fine example is Bollnow's essay "Einfache Sittlichkeit" which is reprinted in his book *Einfache Sittlichkeit* (3rd ed. rev.; Göttingen: Vandenhoeck & Ruprecht, 1962), pp. 20-30.

[34] Ernst Troeltsch, *Der Historismus und seine Probleme,* in *Gesammelte Schriften* (2nd ed.; Tübingen: Scientia Aalen, 1961), III, p. 609.

most Europeans took the limited and often narrow ethos of their time and place for the whole of morality, it was Friedrich Nietzsche who rediscovered the historical wealth of moral values. The reading of Nietzsche's powerful descriptions of the manifold moral ideas and ideals contained in history made Scheler more alert to the multiplicity and variety of values which had been overlooked and neglected by generations of reductionist ethicians.

On two points, however, Scheler sharply disagrees with Nietzsche. For Nietzsche, the multiformity of moral values and ideals leads to ethical relativism; values are not perceived by man, but man rather creates them. For Scheler, as we shall show later in greater detail, a change of ethos can be explained without accepting a relativistic position. Furthermore, man is the discoverer or recipient of values, not their creator.

In an important passage of *Thus Spoke Zarathustra,* Nietzsche develops, among other things, his idea of the richness of moral values and the change of ethos in history and place:

On the Thousand and One Goals.
Zarathustra saw many lands and many peoples: thus he discovered the good and evil of many peoples. . . . No people could live without first esteeming; but if they want to preserve themselves, then they must not esteem as the neighbor esteems. Much that was good to one people was scorn and infamy to another; thus I found it. . . . A tablet of the good hangs over every people. Behold, it is the tablet of their overcomings; behold, it is the voice of their will to power.[35]

Nietzsche then offers four examples of different ethos forms: the aristocratic ethics of early Greece, truthfulness and bravery as the ethos of the ancient Persians, filial piety as the characteristic of Jewish morality, and, finally, loyalty as the ethos of the ancient Germans:

[35] Friedrich Nietzsche, *Thus Spoke Zarathustra,* trans. by Walter Kaufmann (New York: The Viking Press, 1970), p. 58.

You shall always be the first and excel all others: your jealous soul shall love no one, unless it be the friend—that made the soul of the Greek quiver: thus he walked the path of his greatness.

To speak the truth and to handle bow and arrow well—that seemed both dear and difficult to the people who gave me my name—the name which is both dear and difficult to me.

To honor father and mother and to follow their will to the root of one's soul—this was the tablet of overcoming that another people hung up over themselves and became powerful and eternal thereby.

To practice loyalty and, for the sake of loyalty, to risk honor and blood even for evil and dangerous things—with this teaching another people conquered themselves; and through this self-conquest they became pregnant and heavy with great hopes.[36]

Nietzsche shows different forms of ethos in history but he does not analyze them phenomenologically as Scheler and Nicolai Hartmann were later to do. In Nietzsche's philosophy, the ethos forms are ultimately degraded to a simple mirroring of the vitality of peoples and of historical periods, thus playing a somewhat analogous role to superstructure in the thought of Karl Marx. Consequently, Nietzsche fails to harvest the fruit of his rich discoveries in the realm of values. While attempting to develop an appreciation of vital values in the ethical sphere, he reduces the richness of moral values to an impoverished ethical system which is judged and evaluated according to the norms of the superman and the will to power.

Scheler integrated into his moral philosophy Nietzsche's discovery of the plenitude of values, but he was equally concerned with preserving the valid ethical ideas of Kant. Scheler's value philosophy has, indeed, been characterized as a synthesis of Kant and Nietzsche.[37] From each of these two thinkers,

---

[36] *Ibid.*, pp. 58-59.
[37] Nicolai Hartmann, *Kleinere Schriften* (3 vols.; Berlin: Walter de Gruyter, 1958), III, p. 353.

Scheler appropriated a basic insight and purified it from its accompanying flaw. From Kant, he took over the apriority of the moral law and the absolute character of ethics but detached it from the formalism. From Nietzsche, he adopted the richness and multiplicity of values but dissociated them from the defect of relativism.

In a tribute to the achievement of Max Scheler, Nicolai Hartmann writes:

> Material value ethics, by opening to our vision the gates of the kingdom of values, achieved the synthesis of two fundamental insights which had historically grown up in very different fields, and in sharp contrast to each other. One was the Kantian apriority of the moral law and the other the manifoldness of values which Nietzsche—though only from a distance—had discerned. Nietzsche was the first to see the rich plenitude of the ethical cosmos, but with him it melted away in historical relativism. On the other hand, Kant had, in the apriority of the moral law, a well-considered and purified knowledge of the absoluteness of genuine ethical standards. He lacked, however, the perception of the concrete content and the breadth of heart which would have given his knowledge its true value. The material value ethics is the historical reunion of factors which belonged together from the beginning. . . . It gives back to ethical apriorism its original richness of content, while to the consciousness of value it gives the certainty of an unchangeable reality in the midst of the relativity of human valuations.[38]

The fact that Scheler was profoundly preoccupied with the idea of bringing about a synthesis between Kant and Nietzsche has been corroborated by one of Scheler's most outstanding disciples, Werner Schöllgen. Schöllgen participated in several seminars directed by Scheler. During these seminar exercises, Scheler emphasized time and again that he had developed his

[38] Nicolai Hartmann, *Ethik* (4th ed.; Berlin: Walter de Gruyter, 1962), pp. V-VI.

value ethics in order to escape from the relativism of cultural history.[39] He acknowledged Kant's achievement in having overcome the utilitarianism of the enlightenment. Equally, he welcomed Nietzsche's rediscovery of the multiplicity and richness of human community life. However, the main task had still to be performed, namely to bring about a systematic synthesis between the rigor of Kantian ethics and the content-rich ethics of Nietzsche, without falling into the error of relativism.[40] According to Schöllgen's account, Scheler considered the attempt to achieve such a synthesis the basic problem-approach (*Problemansatz*) for any modern ethics. His own value ethics was intended as an important step toward this synthesis.

It is significant to note that Scheler inspired several disciples to explore further this issue in their own research. Werner Schöllgen, for example, in one of his major works, *Die soziologischen Grundlagen der katholischen Sittenlehre*,[41] explicitly deals with Scheler's idea of a synthesis between Kant and Nietzsche and investigates the problem from the point of view of a sociology of culture. Beginning with a sociological perspective, he tries to achieve the same goal as Scheler, namely, to establish a formal framework for a universally valid ethics and to identify and explore within that framework the scope of ethos forms which may be valid only for certain social groups and historical periods.[42]

Time and again Scheler describes his moral philosophy as an

[39] Werner Schöllgen, *Die soziologischen Grundlagen der katholischen Sittenlehre* (Düsseldorf: Patmos, 1953), p. 276.

[40] *Ibid.:* " . . . die wesentliche Aufgabe . . . die Strenge eigentlicher Ethik bei Kant mit der inhaltlichen Gefülltheit bei Nietzsche systematisch so zu vereinen, dass trotzdem der Absturz in den Relativismus vermieden würde."

[41] Werner Schöllgen, *Die soziologischen Grundlagen der katholischen Sittenlehre* (Düsseldorf: Patmos, 1953).

[42] *Ibid.*, p. 276. This Scheler-inspired basic concern of Werner Schöllgen is manifest in many of his works. Cf. Werner Schöllgen, "Ethik und Ethos," in *Aus Theologie und Philosophie. Festschrift für Fritz Tillmann*, ed. by Theodor Steinbüchel und Theodor Müncker (Düsseldorf: Patmos, 1950), pp. 419-437; *Aktuelle Moralprobleme* (Düsseldorf: Patmos, 1955); *Konkrete Ethik* (Düsseldorf: Patmos, 1961); "Ethos," *Staatslexikon*, 6th ed., III, 56-58; "Moralsoziologie," *Lexikon für Theologie und Kirche*, 2nd ed., VII, pp. 609-611; "Das Prinzip Gegen-

attempt to unfold and demonstrate the rich dimensions of values and of moral phenomena. In the preface to the second edition of his *Formalismus,* he defines the overall goal he is trying to achieve in this, his major work on ethics. Three key issues are brought together in an impressive and coherent vision, namely, personalism, a philosophy of plenitude, and a dynamic, history-oriented moral philosophy.

> The most essential and important proposition which this work wants to defend and to convey as completely as possible is this: that the ultimate meaning and value of this whole universe is in the last resort to be measured by the amount of pure being (not of achievement) present in personalities (*Personen*), by their greatest possible goodness, by their maximum abundance, by their most complete development, and by their purest beauty and inner harmony—personalities upon whom all the energies of the cosmos at times converge and to whom they surge.[43]

First, Scheler describes his main work on ethics as being primarily concerned with the person. This statement may have been intended as a response to critics who falsely construed Scheler's ethic as a one-sided preoccupation with abstract values. The subtitle of the *Formalismus* should, of course, have cautioned these critics, for it clearly states that this is "A New Attempt at Establishing an Ethical Personalism." [44] A second point that stands out in the above proposition is the idea that human fulfillment, plenitude and inner harmony of the person are essential goals of man's ethical striving. A third prominent point is Scheler's emphasis on the dynamic, historical dimension of eth-

---

wart. Naturrecht und Geschichte im Widerstreit menschlicher Grundhaltungen," *Wort und Wahrheit,* XVIII (March, 1963), pp. 176-186; "Wertethik und Kultursoziologischer Pluralismus," in *Die Rolle der Werte im Leben. Festschrift für Johannes Hessen,* ed. by Cornel J. Bock (Cologne: Wienand Verlag, 1969), pp. 103-126; "Friedrich Nietzsche und Thomas Aquin als Deuter christlicher Lebensideale," *Theologie und Glaube,* XXXV (Spring, 1943), pp. 61-73.

[43] FORM, p. 16.

[44] "Neuer Versuch der Grundlegung eines ethischen Personalismus."

ics. The energies of the cosmos converge and then surge forward toward the most complete development and growth of the human person.

Scheler's openness toward the plenitude of the value-cosmos must ultimately be seen as an expression of his new attitude toward reality and philosophy. In an essay published in 1913, entitled "Reflections on a Philosophy of Life," he calls attention to some new insights that originated in the philosophies of Nietzsche, Dilthey and Bergson.[45] "Philosophy of Life," according to Scheler, does not mean a philosophy "applied to practical life." Rather, life is here used as a subjective genitive, and' hence, a philosophy of life means a "philosophy emerging from the fullness of life, or more precisely, a philosophy emerging from the full experience of life." [46]

Scheler makes his own the new conception of philosophy as a "philosophy of life" [47] and in an eloquent passage he sums up his own new philosophical attitude, contrasting it with that of Kant and Descartes:

This new attitude might first of all be characterized vaguely enough from the emotional point of view as a surrender of self to the intuitional content of things, as a movement of profound trust in the unshakeableness of all that is simply and evidently "given," as a courageous letting-oneself-go in intuition and in the loving movement toward the world in its capacity for being intuited. This philosophy faces the world with the gesture of the outstretched open hand, with

[45] "Versuche einer Philosophie des Lebens," in *Vom Umsturz der Werte*, pp. 311-339.

[46] *Ibid.*, p. 313: " . . . eine Philosophie aus der Fülle des Lebens heraus, ja–schärfer gesagt–eine Philosophie aus der Fülle des Erlebens des Lebens heraus."

[47] Friedrich Kreppel calls the "philosophy emerging from the fullness of experience and from the fullness of life" the *Grundmotiv* of Scheler's philosophical endeavor. Cf. Friedrich Kreppel, "Max Scheler und das Philosophieren," *Zeitschrift für Religions- und Geistesgeschichte*, XI (Fall, 1959), p. 384: " 'Philosophie aus der Fülle des Erlebens, des Lebens heraus'–darauf kommt es Scheler an. . . . Wir erwähnen es hier, weil uns dieser Satz das Grundmotiv des Schelerschen Philosophierens zu sein scheint, das selbst in seinen erkenntnistheoretischen Überlegungen immer durchklingt."

open-eyed gaze. This is not the squinting, critical gaze
which Descartes—beginning with the universal doubt—
casts upon things; not the eye of Kant, from which comes
a spiritual beam so alien, as though from another world,
in its own dominating fashion illuminating and penetrating
the world of things. He who philosophizes here has neither
the anxiety which belongs to modern calculation and to the
modern desire to verify things, nor the proud sovereignty of the "thinking reed," which is in Descartes and
Kant the original source—the emotional a priori—of all
theories. Rather the stream of being flows in on him and
down to his spiritual roots as a self-evident stream of being
and simply as that—apart from all content—a benevolent
element. It is not the will to "dominate," to "organize," to
determine unequivocally and to fix, which animates each
thought, but rather a movement of sympathy, of not be-
grudging being, of welcoming an increase in the fullness
with which for a gaze of contemplative recognition the
contents of the world is constantly disengaging itself from
the invasion of human understanding, exceeding as it does
the limits of mere concepts.[48]

Scheler's basic philosophical attitude is characterized by a
trusting, loving and wondering openness to the richness of human experience and knowledge. When he speaks of his intention "to go beyond Kant," he means the desire to rediscover
dimensions of reality that Kant had ignored or overlooked. In
his essay on the philosophy of life, he likens the epistemological
confines of the rationalists to the walls of a dark prison and he
expresses the hope that his new philosophical attitude will help
modern man to break out of that prison and to discover again
the "flowering garden . . . of God's colorful world which we see
opening before us and greeting us brightly, if only from a
distance." [49]

[48] *Ibid.*, p. 325. English translation by Quentin Lauer, S.J. Cf. Quentin
Lauer, S.J., "The Phenomenological Ethics of Max Scheler," *International Philosophical Quarterly,* I (May, 1961), p. 277.
[49] UMST, p. 339.

28   PROCESS AND PERMANENCE IN ETHICS

Nicolai Hartmann, who in his monumental *Ethik* [50] appropriated and creatively advanced the Schelerian value ethics, has
restated forcefully and perceptively Scheler's basic insight concerning the poverty as well as the potential plenitude of modern
man's value-cosmos. In an incisive introductory chapter of his
Ethics entitled "On Passing-by" (*Vom Vorbeigehen*) [51] he de-
picts the foibles of modern man who "passes by" the richness
and depth of human values without looking, without noticing,
and of course, without appreciating their abundant wealth.
This inability to "see," the narrowness of the value-horizon, the
blindness toward the abundance of higher values, and the
poverty of moral perception—these are the weaknesses of
modern man that make him pass by the riches of the moral
cosmos and prevent him from living a fully human life. Even in
meeting other human beings, he seldom truly "sees" nor does
he encounter them in the ethical sense. He seldom gives them a
sympathetic, loving glance in which he tries to discover and
appreciate their unique value. He frequently passes by the
other person. Although superficially he may face him, yet in the
depth of his being he remains untouched; he remains isolated in
his solitude, and then departs again. Afflicted with moral blindness, he fails to perceive the value of the other person and is
incapable of entering into a genuine interpersonal dialogue
with him.

Modern philosophy in general, and modern ethics in particular suffer from the hazards of myopic vision and consequently
pass by the richness of the moral cosmos without averting
to it or appreciating it.

A narrowing of the field of vision is the inveterate vice of
philosophy. The defect in all "isms"—whether rationalism,
empiricism, sensualism, materialism, psychologism or log-
icism—is narrowness in the mapping out of the problem.
Everywhere the manifoldness of the phenomena is mis-

[50] Nicolai Hartmann, *Ethik* (4th ed.; Berlin: Walter de Gruyter,
1962). English translation: *Ethics,* trans. by Stanton Coit (3 vols.; 3rd
ed.; New York: The Macmillan Company, 1958-1963).
[51] *Ethik,* pp. 13-16; *Ethics,* I, pp. 41-44.

judged and varieties are erroneously treated as if they were all alike. In ethics, it is not otherwise. Eudaemonism and utilitarianism, individualism and ethical socialism, express precisely such one-sided views. They contain errors due to a too-narrow understanding of the problem—errors caused by a selection of ethical phenomena which arbitrarily restricts the field of investigation.[52]

What modern ethics needs, according to Nicolai Hartmann, is an awakening, a deepening and a broadening of value-consciousness. He commends Scheler for having undertaken the important task of drawing into the circle of ethical reflection the whole universe of values. Following in the footsteps of Scheler, Hartmann considers it his task to convey to modern man a new sense of wonder, amazement and respect for a cosmos rich in values. It is the task of philosophical ethics to develop in man a new awareness of his "moral faculty" (*moralisches Organ*), and to open up to him the diversity and plenitude of the realm of values from which man has isolated himself. Man must become once again a seer of values, a *sapiens* in the original sense of the word, a "taster," one who can savor the rich flavor of the important values in life.[53]

At the end of a chapter entitled "Plenitude" (*Die Fülle*), Hartmann sums up his reflections on the new "ethos of plenitude":

Ethical reality is richer than all human fantasy, richer than dream and fiction. To live apathetically from moment to moment amid such abundance, is nothing short of sin. The narrowness of a man's sense of value makes him poor. It is because of his prejudice and blindness that he does not see the abundance, in the midst of which he stands. The ethos of openness-to-all-values is the tendency to do inward justice to life, to win from it its greatness. Its passion springs from reverence for the unbounded abundance of

[52] *Ethik*, p. 63; *Ethics*, I, p. 106.
[53] *Ethik*, p. 17; *Ethics*, I, pp. 44-46.

the things that are of worth, it is knowledge filled with gratitude; and, where knowledge fails, it is the presentiment that the values of existence are inexhaustible. Whoever lives in this frame of mind, recognizes every restriction of experience as superficiality, dullness, barrenness, a waste of life . . . and a moral ingratitude.[54]

III
THE ROLE OF INTENTIONAL FEELING
AND AFFECTIVITY IN ETHICS

In contrast to Kant's one-sided intellectualism, Scheler reemphasized the emotional aspect of man and elucidated its function in the process of moral knowledge and moral action. According to Scheler, we are primarily related to the world not by way of intellectual perception but through value-feeling. Our emotional relationship precedes our intellectual operations:

All primary relations to the world, not only to the outer world, but also to the inner world, not only to others but also to our own selves, are not conceptual, not a relationship of perception, but always . . . primarily emotional and value-realizing.[55]

The world of reality is revealed in its value-dimension in and through the dynamic process of intentional feeling.[56] Intentional feeling or "feeling of something" (*Fühlen von etwas*) is, of course, essentially distinct from nonintentional "feeling-states" (*Gefühlszustände*). In our present discussion we are referring only to intentional feelings. The correlation of intentional feeling and values constitutes man's original participation in being.

[54] *Ethik,* p. 406; *Ethics,* II, p. 210.
[55] FORM, p. 206.
[56] *Ibid.,* p. 265: "Im Verlauf des intentionalen Fühlens 'erschliesst' sich uns vielmehr die Welt der Gegenstände selbst, nur eben von ihrer Wertseite her."

The cognitive dimension of value-feeling is unique and therefore irreducible to the intellect or any other human faculty.

There is a type of experience whose objects are completely inaccessible to the understanding (*Verstand*), for which the understanding is as uncomprehending as the ear and the auditory sense are blind to color; a type of experience, however, which provides us with truly objective objects ranged in a fixed order; these are values and the hierarchy that exists among them.[57]

Kant had relegated human feelings, even love and hatred, to the realm of sensuality. The extreme dualism of *Vernunft* and *Sinnlichkeit*—Scheler calls it a *grundfalscher Dualismus*—manifests a false conception of the true nature of the emotional side of man, especially of love. Scheler affirms the existence of acts of pure feeling and pure love which are as independent of the psycho-physical structure of the human being as is pure thinking. "Those acts of the spirit, such as feeling, preference, subordinating, love and hate, have their own a priori content which is as independent of inductive experience as are the pure laws of thought." [58] Consequently, Scheler's "emotive ethics" is not a form of "empiricism" for it is based on intuition of essences (*Wesensschau*) and on strict phenomenological evidence.[59] Scheler claims that Kant's equation of "a priori" and "rationalism" is false, for there exists also an "emotive a priori" (*ein Apriorismus des Emotionalen*).[60]

The emotional dimension of the mind—feeling, preference, love, hate, volition—also has its own unique a priori content which it does not borrow from thought, and which ethics must explore and unfold quite independently of logic. There is an a priori *ordre du coeur,* or *logique du coeur,* as Blaise Pascal tellingly puts it.[61]

[57] FORM, p. 261.
[58] *Ibid.,* p. 84.
[59] *Ibid.*
[60] *Ibid.*
[61] *Ibid.,* p. 82.

The true source of every "value a priori" (*Wertapriori*) is the value-perception stemming from feeling, preference and love.[62] The values and their hierarchical order blaze forth (*blitzen auf*) *in* the experience of an emotional relationship with the world and *in* the exercise of intentional acts of feeling, preferring and loving.

In a later chapter I shall show in greater detail the important role of love in the process of value-perception. It suffices at this point to call attention to one interesting aspect of Scheler's doctrine of love. Through love man does not merely respond to values he already knows but rather he discovers new values. Love, therefore, precedes value-feeling; it is a dynamic force driving man to seek out ever new and ever higher values.

> Love . . . plays the role of a discoverer in our perception of values. Love is a movement in the course of which new and higher values flash forth and reveal themselves, i.e. values hitherto unknown to this person. Hence, love does not follow after value-feeling or value-preference, but precedes them as their pioneer and leader.[63]

At the beginning of his essay "Love and Knowledge" Scheler quotes Goethe in support of his own theory on the relationship between love and knowledge. It was Goethe who against the rationalists reemphasized the cognitive function of love. Goethe wrote: "One can know nothing except what one loves; and the deeper and more complete one desires the knowledge to be, the stronger, more powerful and dynamic must the love, indeed, the passion be." [64]

[62] *Ibid.*, p. 87.
[63] *Ibid.*, pp. 266-267.
[64] Max Scheler, "Liebe und Erkenntnis," in *Schriften zur Soziologie und Weltanschauungslehre* (2nd ed. rev.; Bern: Francke Verlag, 1963), p. 77. (Hereinafter referred to as SOZ.) Goethe: "Man lernt nichts kennen, als was man liebt, und je tiefer und vollständiger die Kenntnis werden soll, desto stärker, kräftiger, lebendiger muss die Liebe, ja Leidenschaft sein." As is often the case, Scheler does not seem to be quoting exactly. But in one form or another this thought appears frequently in Goethe's writings. Cf. John M. Oesterreicher, *Five in Search of Wisdom* (Notre Dame: Notre Dame University Press, 1967), p. 279.

The theory of an emotional a priori is one of the most original contributions of Scheler to moral philosophy. Of course, many other philosophers before him had emphasized the importance of the emotions in ethics. What characterizes Scheler's approach—and here he would seem to far surpass all previous attempts—is the close correlation that he establishes between the theory of an emotional a priori and the theory of objective values. The heart of man is not a chaos of blind feelings but an ordered counterpart to the cosmos of values.[65] There is a correspondence between man's heart and the cosmos of values, or a strict parallel between the a priori *ordre du coeur* and the objective hierarchical order of higher and lower values.

> The heart possesses, within its own realm, a strict analogue to logic, which it does not, however, borrow from the logic of the intellect. As the ancient doctrine of *Nomos Agraphos* can already teach us, there are laws written into the heart which correspond to the plan according to which the world, as a world of values, is built up. It can love and hate blindly or with evidence, just as we can judge blindly or with evidence.[66]

This theory may seem both naive and improbable. For the experience of mankind would seem to warn us against putting too much trust in the human heart. Experience teaches us that the heart is easily deceived by passions and prejudices. Scheler is fully aware of the numerous self-deceptions of the human heart and he has even done extensive research in the falsifications of value-perception. In a later chapter we shall discuss resentment as one such cause of the dwarfing of man's value-cosmos. Concern with the possibility and reality of sickness and abuse, however, should not blind us to the other possibility and reality that a man's "heart" can also be "healthy" and be a pure and true mirror of the objective cosmos of values. Scheler displays a firm trust in the basic goodness of the human heart and

[65] FORM, pp. 62-64.
[66] Max Scheler, *Schriften aus dem Nachlass*. Band I: *Zur Ethik und Erkenntnislehre* (2nd ed. rev.; Bern: Francke Verlag, 1957), p. 362. (Hereinafter referred to as NACH.)

its capacity for knowing the objective order of values. One might see this as a healthy antidote to the basic distrust of feelings in Kant and other philosophers of a rationalist persuasion.

Scheler quotes St. Augustine and Blaise Pascal to support his thesis that the emotions have a cognitive structure and that there can be an ethics that is both emotive and absolute. In the history of ethics, he says, there was usually a false dualism between an absolute, a priori, rational ethics and a relativist, empirical, emotive ethics. The question was scarcely raised whether there could not be an ethics which is both absolute and emotive.[67] Few thinkers surmounted this prejudice and among these few were Augustine and Pascal.[68]

For a deeper understanding of Scheler's emotive ethics it might be helpful to glance briefly at the ideas of *cor* in St. Augustine and *coeur* in Pascal which Scheler acknowledges as the foundation of his own thinking.[69]

Anton Maxsein in his study on the "philosophy of the heart" in St. Augustine [70] has shown that *cor* for Augustine is the "personal center and the organ of the substantial unity of man." [71] The idea of love occupies a central place in Augustine's basic philosophical attitude, and that enables Maxsein to characterize Augustine's philosophy as a "philosophy of the heart." [72] The Augustinian "heart" plays a crucial role in the cognitive process of man, especially in his religious and moral knowledge. The *cor inquietum* reveals the personal dynamism of man in his search for God and for moral goodness. God as the supreme good manifests himself in the human heart and draws it

[67] FORM, p. 260.
[68] *Ibid.*
[69] FORM, pp. 260-261: " . . . ordre du coeur . . . logique du coeur. . . . Le coeur a ses raisons. . . . An diese Idee Pascals knüpfen wir hier an."
[70] Anton Maxsein, *Philosophia Cordis: Das Wesen der Personalität bei Augustinus* (Salzburg: Otto Müller Verlag, 1966). Maxsein has also published an earlier shorter version of the same study: Anton Maxsein, "Philosophia Cordis bei Augustinus," in *Augustinus Magister*. Congrès Internationale Augustinienne Paris, September, 1954. Communications (3 vols.; Paris: Etudes Augustiniennes, 1954), I, pp. 357-371.
[71] *Philosophia Cordis: Das Wesen der Personalität bei Augustinus*, p. 14.
[72] *Ibid.*, p. 23.

in loving dialogue to ever greater moral, religious and mystical heights. This theophany in man's heart is intimately linked to the cognitive process of *memoria* and *recordari*. In the act of *recordari* the treasures of the *memoria* are raised to full awareness in man's conscious life and become fully operative.[73] The verb *recordari* contains the noun *cor* and indicates again the crucial role of the "heart" in Augustine's theory of knowledge.

The human heart can, of course, go astray and Augustine knew from personal experience the aberrations of the heart. He discovered, however, also the other dimension, the *cor rectum*, the straightforward, orderly and pure heart which mirrors the objective order of things and can, therefore, function as the norm and rule for man's moral life. Transformed by love this *cor rectum* can become an objective organ for the cognition of values and a trustworthy guide for moral choices.[74]

This brief exposition of one aspect of Augustine's "philosophy of the heart" explains sufficiently why Max Scheler could rightly be referred to as a philosopher with an "anima naturaliter augustiniana." [75] Scheler does not enter into any critical discussion of the relationship between love and intellectual knowledge in Augustine. He simply interprets Augustine as defending a primacy of love [76] and sees his own thinking as a continuation and advancement of the Augustinian tradition. Approvingly he relates: "In the sphere of Christian morality . . . love is explicitly placed above the rational domain—love 'that makes more blessed than all reason' (Augustine)." [77] Adolf von Harnack and Josef Mausbach are called as witnesses that Augustine was a predecessor of the type of emotive ethics which Scheler himself proposes.[78]

In developing his emotive ethics, Scheler frequently refers to

[73] *Ibid.*, pp. 177-193.
[74] *Ibid.*, pp. 70-151.
[75] Johann Grooten, "L'augustinisme de Max Scheler," in *Augustinus Magister* (3 vols.; Paris: Etudes Augustiniennes, 1954), II, 1111.
[76] Max Scheler, *Liebe und Erkenntnis* (Bern: Francke Verlag, 1955), pp. 8, 21, 24.
[77] UMST, p. 71.
[78] FORM, p. 260: "Für Augustinus verweise ich auf A. v. Harnacks Dogmengeschichte und 'Die Ethik des hl. Augustinus' von J. Mausbach."

Blaise Pascal and his philosophy of the *coeur*. It was the writings of Pascal, Scheler acknowledges, which inspired him and on which he based his own philosophy of feelings and his emotive ethics.[79] In Pascal he admired especially the attempt to develop an ethics that is a priori and absolute and at the same time emotive—a type of ethics that Scheler himself was trying to establish. Scheler pointed to one recurring theme in Pascal's works which is sometimes expressed as *ordre du coeur,* in other places as *logique du coeur,* and again in the famous phrase *le coeur a ses raisons*. Pascal means by this, in Scheler's interpretation, "an eternal and absolute order (*Gesetzmässigkeit*) of feeling, love and hate which is as absolute as the order of pure logic, which is, however, not reducible to the order of reason." [80] When Pascal says that "the heart has its reasons which reason does not know" he refers to a unique mode of experience and knowledge which is inaccessible to the intellect. An objective, absolute and eternal order of values and their hierarchical ranking is disclosed to the intentional feelings of the heart. The intellect is as blind to these objects as the ear and the auditory sense are to color.[81] The emotive acts of intentional feeling, preferring and love possess an original a priori content which is independent of thinking (*Denken*).[82] Consequently, the order and the laws of the experience of the heart are as exact and as evident as those of logic and of mathematics.

Scheler was not noted for his careful reading and analysis of the history of philosophy and his interpretation of Pascal is no exception. In the light of recent Pascal scholarship one might doubt whether Scheler was justified in his interpretation of Pascal's *coeur* and whether the latter's philosophy does, indeed, support the theory that the emotions possess a cognitive structure in the sense Scheler attributes to them. Moreover, Pascal was not too clear himself in this particular question and the precise meaning of his *ordre du coeur, logique du coeur* and *le coeur a*

[79] FORM, p. 261: "An diese Idee Pascals knüpfen wir hier an."
[80] *Ibid.,* p. 260.
[81] *Ibid.,* p. 261.
[82] *Ibid.,* p. 82.

ses raison remains controversial.[83] Romano Guardini, one of the most respected Pascal scholars, rejects the idea that there exists a strict antithesis in Pascal between heart and intellect. On the other hand, he agrees with Scheler that certain objects are only accessible to the heart—although through the heart these objects also become accessible to rational penetration—and that the heart is, for Pascal, preeminently the organ which grasps the value-dimension of being.

What is the heart in the Pascalian sense? One thing above all: It is not the expression of the emotional in opposition to the logical, not feeling in opposition to the intellect, not "soul" in opposition to "mind." "Coeur" is itself mind: a manifestation of the mind. The act of the heart is an act productive for knowledge. Certain objects only become given in the act of the heart. But they do not remain there in a-rational intuition, but are accessible to intellectual and rational penetration.[84]

Guardini confirms Scheler's interpretation that the heart, according to Pascal, fulfills a unique and irreducible cognitive function with regard to values. To values, or the "preciousness of things," corresponds a specific mode of experience in man. This experience is an irreducible sensibility and a vibration of the mind at the contact of the value, not of the theoretical mind or reason, but of the mind which appreciates and values. This is what Pascal means by heart.

"Heart" is the mind, so far as it gets into proximity of the blood, into the feeling, living fibre of the body—yet without becoming torpid. Heart is the mind rendered ardent and

[83] Anthony Levi, "The Heart's Reasons: Pascal and the Rationalist Dilemma," *The Month,* CCVIII (August, 1959), pp. 92-101. William Walter Goodhue, "Pascal's Theory of Knowledge: A Reaction to the Analytical Method of Descartes," *The Modern Schoolman,* XLVII (November, 1969), pp. 15-35.

[84] Romano Guardini, *Pascal for Our Time* (New York: Herder and Herder, 1966), p. 129.

sensitive by the blood, but which at the same time ascends into the clarity of contemplation, the distinctness of form, the precision of judgment. Heart is the organ of love—of that love from which arose Platonic philosophy, and then, newly fructified by Christian Faith, the *Divine Comedy*. This love implies the relationship of the center of man's desires and feelings to the idea; the movement from the blood to the mind, from the presence of the body to the eternity of the mind. It is what is experienced in the heart.[85]

It should be evident from our brief reflections on Pascal's understanding of *coeur* and Augustine's *philosophia cordis* that Max Scheler, besides being a true pioneer in the development of an emotive ethics, is at the same time the guardian and creative developer of a noble tradition in Western philosophy. Plato prepared this tradition, Augustine developed it and Bernard of Clairveaux enriched both its experience and expression. Francis of Assisi became a powerful witness to this tradition of the "heart" and St. Bonaventure created a philosophical system of the Franciscan spirit. Dante expressed the same spirit in poetry, Francis de Sales in spiritual writings. In modern times the "philosophy of the heart" was powerfully revived and developed by such diverse thinkers as Newman and Pascal, Soloviev and Kierkegaard, Nietzsche and Scheler, Hessen and Guardini.

In chapter VII we shall return to the question of a "philosophy of the heart" and show how Scheler creatively advanced this philosophical tradition in his philosophy of love. We shall conclude by pointing to one important creative addition of Scheler to Pascal's *ordre du coeur* which is of particular interest to the investigation of this book, namely historicity and ethics. The *ordre du coeur,* Scheler says, is unchanging and eternal, but man's knowledge of it develops only gradually in steps and in history. "There does exist an *ordre du coeur* and *logique du coeur* (in Pascal's words) which the moral genius gradually uncovers in history, and it is eternal—only its apprehension and acquisition is 'historical.' " [86]

[85] *Ibid.,* p. 130.
[86] UMST, p. 63.

Scheler's affirmation of the role of affectivity in ethics has exercised a profound influence on numerous philosophers and psychologists. During the past few decades many authors have taken up the insights of Scheler and further explored the emotive side in man and its bearing on the moral growth of a person. Ludwig Binswanger, for example, starting from a neo-Kantian background, came under the influence of Scheler's writings and applied in a creative way Scheler's ideas on feelings, love and sympathy to psychiatry. Many insights of Scheler were incorporated in Binswanger's philosophical anthropology and phenomenological psychoanalysis.[87]

Arthur Luther, in a comparative study of Scheler and W. E. Hocking,[88] has ascertained a considerable affinity between both thinkers in their theories of feeling. Feeling, according to Hocking, is the "initial directed 'outpushing' towards value." [89] The self's total response to the world of reality is primarily one of feeling. Feeling has a cognitive aspect, especially with regard to the realm of values. Both Scheler and Hocking are deeply concerned with the essential relatedness of man and world and with the concrete, lived experience of this relational unity. For both thinkers, feeling is the lived experience of man's direct personal response to world and values.

Both for Hocking and for Scheler, feeling indicates the whole man as directed towards the total real. From the side of world, feeling indicates the inexhaustibly rich structure of

[87] Ludwig Binswanger, *Grundformen und Erkenntnis menschlichen Daseins* (2nd ed.; Zürich: Niehaus Verlag, 1953). Ludwig Binswanger, *Ausgewählte Vorträge und Aufsätze,* Vol. I (Bern: Francke Verlag, 1947). Ludwig Binswanger, *Ausgewählte Vorträge und Aufsätze,* Vol. II (Bern: Francke Verlag, 1955). William A. Sadler, *Existence and Love: A New Approach in Existential Phenomenology* (New York: Charles Scribner's Sons, 1969). Sadler, who wrote his doctoral dissertation about Binswanger, has also a fine chapter on Binswanger in his book *Existence and Love* (pp. 115-142). He points out repeatedly Binswanger's intellectual indebtedness to Scheler. Cf. *Existence and Love,* p. 124: "The influence of Scheler and of Binswanger's friend, the Swiss philosopher Paul Häberlin, was extremely marked. Like Scheler, Binswanger put tremendous emphasis upon feelings. . . ."

[88] Arthur Luther, "Hocking and Scheler on Feeling," *Philosophy Today,* XII (Summer, 1968), pp. 93-99.

[89] *Ibid.,* p. 95

the total real as it reveals itself to man in its value dimension. In short, feeling describes the concrete unity of man's existential situation. . . . The structure of this value experience or perception is in the fullest sense dynamic. Man is "in" the total real from the beginning. . . . Man discovers himself historically as much as the world reveals itself historically. . . . Feeling describes this living exchange primordially and at a metaphysical level.[90]

One might also point to an interesting parallel between Scheler and Abraham H. Maslow.[91] Maslow studies the highest moments or peak experiences in human life and he argues that it is love and other peak experiences that change man's *Weltanschauung* and transform the whole dimension and character of one's life. Maslow reiterates, within the framework of psychology, one of the key insights of Scheler, that we must look at man in his elevated or ecstatic experiences (*Aufschwung*) in order to discover the fullest possible picture of man and that the affective dimension is an essential part of man as a human being and as a moral agent.[92]

In his discussion of Scheler's order of values which is open only to emotion, Quentin Lauer reminds us that "it might not be amiss to re-examine in this light what St. Thomas Aquinas has to say about 'knowledge by connaturality.' It is questionable whether a purely rational logic can ever come to terms with the existential." [93] During the last decades, Neo-Scholastic treatises on ethics—for example, the widely used textbook by Austin Fagothey [94]—have increasingly stressed the importance

[90] *Ibid.*, pp. 98-99.

[91] Abraham H. Maslow, *Religions, Values, and Peak-Experiences* (New York: The Viking Press, 1970). Abraham H. Maslow, *Toward a Psychology of Being* (2nd ed.; New York; Van Nostrand, 1968). Abraham H. Maslow, ed., *New Knowledge in Human Values* (Chicago: Henry Regnery, 1970).

[92] Cf. Max Scheler, VEIM, pp. 83-92; NACH, pp. 345-376; FORM, pp. 260-261; *Liebe und Erkenntnis*, pp. 5-28; 69-72.

[93] Quentin Lauer, S.J., "The Phenomenological Ethics of Max Scheler," *International Philosophical Quarterly*, I (May, 1961), 289.

[94] Austin Fagothey, S.J., *Right and Reason: Ethics in Theory and Practice* (5th ed. rev.; St. Louis: C. V. Mosby Company, 1972), pp. 95-96.

of connatural knowledge. Jacques Maritain, in his interpretation of moral knowledge, exhibits a remarkable similarity to
Scheler's view, although in his terminology it is the intellect
and not the emotions that grasp the moral good.

It is through connaturality that moral consciousness attains a kind of knowing—inexpressible in words and notions—of the deepest dispositions—longings, fears, hopes
or despairs, primeval loves and options—involved in the
night of the subjectivity. When a man makes a free decision,
he takes into account, not only all that he possesses of moral
science and factual information, and which is manifested
to him in concepts and notions, but also all the secret
elements of evaluation which depend on what he is, and
which are known to him through inclination, through his
own actual propensities and his own virtues, if he has
any.[95]

More than any other philosopher Dietrich von Hildebrand
has appropriated and advanced the Schelerian insights concerning the role of affectivity in morality.[96] He insists on the spiritual
character of affective responses such as love, joy, sorrow and
contrition. The duality of intellect and will should, according to

[95] Jacques Maritain, *The Range of Reason* (New York: Charles
Scribner's Sons, 1952), p. 26.

[96] Dietrich von Hildebrand, "The Role of Affectivity in Morality,"
Proceedings of the American Catholic Philosophical Association, Vol.
XXXII (Washington: The Catholic University of America, 1958), pp.
85-95; "Die geistigen Formen der Affektivität," *Philosophisches Jahrbuch*
LXVIII (Summer, 1960), pp. 180-190; *The Sacred Heart: An Analysis
of Human and Divine Affectivity* (Baltimore: Helicon, 1965); *Christian
Ethics* (New York: David McKay Company, 1953); *The Art of Loving*
(Chicago: Henry Regnery, 1967). Dietrich von Hildebrand's most recent
teaching on the role of affectivity in morality can be found in his
monumental study on the essence of love: *Das Wesen der Liebe*
(Regensburg: Verlag Josef Habbel, 1971). This constitutes volume
three of his *Gesammelte Werke* which are now being published in a
ten-volume edition. For a discussion of von Hildebrand's view on
affectivity cf. Otfried Reuter, O.F.M., *'Sittlichkeit und ethische Werterkenntnis' nach Dietrich von Hildebrand im Zusammenhang mit der
Tugend der Klugheit* (Regensburg: Verlag Josef Habbel, 1966), pp.
71-75: "Die affektive Antwort."

42   PROCESS AND PERMANENCE IN ETHICS

von Hildebrand, be replaced by the trilogy of intellect, will
and heart.[97] The heart's conforming to a value in the moral
sphere (*adaequatio cordis an den Wert*)[98] is explained as
quite analogous to the *adaequatio intellectus ad rem* in the cognitive process. The affective response to a moral value adds a
dimension that a mere response of the will does not possess,
namely "affective plenitude." The will has a "one-dimensional, linear character"; the affective response of the heart, on
the other hand, involves and commits the entire person on all
levels of its being. "New dimensions of the person are actualized
in the affective responses; that is, facets and manifestations of
the self more intimate than those to be found in the will."[99]

The widespread philosophical view which denies the character of spirituality to affectivity is based on the erroneous
method of using the lowest type of affective experience as the
pattern for affectivity as such. Von Hildebrand analyzes the
higher types of affective responses—sympathy, hope, veneration,
longing, bliss, love—and concludes that they manifest a spirituality quite equal to that found in the acts of intellect and will.
In the past, an alleged incompatibility between affectivity and
spirituality led to an interpretation of love as a volitional act
to save its spiritual character. Von Hildebrand reminds us that
St. Augustine—one of the few thinkers who understood the true
nature of affectivity—had already distinguished the naked will
from the full, affective value response of love without denying
the character of spirituality to the latter.[100] Augustine wrote:
"Little is it to be drawn by the will, also by delight shalt thou be
drawn."[101]

In establishing the spiritual character of affectivity, Scheler

[97] "The Role of Affectivity in Morality," p. 85.
[98] "Die geistigen Formen der Affektivität," p. 182.
[99] "The Role of Affectivity in Morality," p. 90.
[100] *Ibid.*, p. 95; also *Christian Ethics,* p. 205.
[101] St. Augustine, *Tractatus 26 in Joannem:* "Parum est voluntate,
etiam voluptate traheris." For a fuller discussion of the prominent role
of the "heart" and of affectivity in the philosophy and theology of St.
Augustine see the recent study of Anton Maxsein, *Philosophia Cordis:
Das Wesen der Personalität bei Augustinus* (Salzburg: Otto Müller,
1966).

and von Hildebrand have restored to modern philosophy a basic insight of St. Augustine. They have done this by exposing as erroneous both the theory which reduces emotions to merely corporeal passions, and the other theory which interprets emotions simply in terms of will acts. Both authors analyze extensively the nature of love [102] and use this analysis as the foundation for vindicating the unique nature of affective value-responses and their irreducibility to mere passions or mere acts of the will.

Von Hildebrand discusses another aspect of affectivity in morality which is both of great importance in itself and also of particular interest because it is a point which Scheler failed to clarify satisfactorily. I am referring here to the relationship between freedom and the affective responses to values. Since affective responses are not in our direct and immediate power, that is, since it is impossible to command an affective response, how can these acts still be of moral significance? Von Hildebrand offers an extensive analysis of this basic problem [103] and he comes to the following conclusion. Affective responses, although they are not in our free power as are the acts of the will, are still within the range of our indirect power. We can, through our free will, liberate our heart from those obstacles that prevent us from giving the appropriate affective value-response. Furthermore, "affective value-responses . . . can share in our direct freedom by the fact that we explicitly identify ourselves with them, or . . . sanction them with our free will. It lies within the zone of man's direct power to say 'yes' or 'no' to affective responses." [104] Freedom and the will, therefore, play here a decisive role by means of "sanction" and "disavowal." In sanctioning a certain affective response, "our free spiritual center expressly identifies itself with the response." [105] By disavowal "the person emancipates himself expressly from this affective response and counteracts it with his spiritual center. . . . The free 'no' effects the

[102] Dietrich von Hildebrand, *Das Wesen der Liebe*.
[103] Von Hildebrand, *Christian Ethics*, pp. 316-337 and "The Role of Affectivity in Morality," pp. 92-94.
[104] "The Role of Affectivity in Morality," p. 93.
[105] *Christian Ethics*, p. 323.

response from within and takes from it its character of a valid position toward the object." [106] The freedom which we realize in the sanctioning, or disavowal of our affective responses to values involves the deepest stratum of our free spiritual center and is, therefore, of even greater significance on the moral level than a mere decision of the naked will. For in this act we commit our whole personality to the value to which we respond. The paradigm of such a value-response would be genuine love for another person, a love characterized both by a high degree of freedom and spirituality, and by affective fulfillment.[107]

IV
THE HIERARCHY OF VALUES AND THE LAWS
OF VALUE-PREFERENCE

According to Scheler, there exists an a priori hierarchy of higher and lower values. This hierarchy cannot be empirically deduced, but is revealed in the act of preference (*Vorziehen*), i.e., through an intuitive "preference-evidence" (*Vorzugsevidenz*). Since this hierarchy is absolute and beyond all historical changes, it constitutes an absolute reference system in ethics, according to which the variations of ethos and all moral changes in history are to be measured and evaluated.

. . . the hierarchy of values . . . is not relative. . . . The theory of the dimensions of relativity of value relations (FORM, pp. 300-321) does not only give us the possibility of relating all historical moralities and forms of ethos to a universal system of reference—however only one of the order of value-modalities and qualities, not of goods and norms—but it also gives—although only a negative—domain in which each positive historical age and each

---

[106] *Ibid.*, p. 322.
[107] *Das Wesen der Liebe*. This most recent book of von Hildebrand—with its 532 pages it is also his most extensive published work—contains a perceptive chapter on the difference between love and other value-responses: "Kapitel II: Liebe im Unterschied zu anderen Wertantworten," pp. 65-86.

specific group has to find its own, always only relative system of goods and norms.[108]

The graded hierarchy of values contains the following four classes:

1. Pleasure-values.[109] On this lowest level we find the axiological series of the pleasant and the unpleasant (*die Wertreihe des Angenehmen und Unangenehmen*), or of the agreeable and the disagreeable. This class of values corresponds to the functions of sensorial feelings (*sinnliches Fühlen*) along with their modes of enjoyment and suffering as well as the affective states of sensibility, namely pleasure and pain. The proposition that the pleasant is preferred to the unpleasant is not established through observation or induction, but is a priori contained in the essence of these values. The a priori character of these values is evident from the fact that we cannot conceive of a man who would not prefer the pleasant to the unpleasant. If a traveler should tell us of a man for whom the contrary proposition held true, we would, on a priori grounds, reject his assertion. We would rather think that such a man differs from us in the things he feels to be pleasant and unpleasant.[110]

2. Vital values (*Vitale Werte*).[111] The second axiological modality consists of the values of vital feeling (*Werte des vitalen Fühlens*). They range from the noble (*edel*) to the vulgar or common (*gemein*) and encompass also the "good" in the sense of "excellent, capable" (tüchtig), as opposed to "bad" (*schlecht*) rather than to "evil" (*böse*). Derivative values of this modality are those pertaining to the general well-being (*Wohlfahrt*) of the individual and of the community. In English these may best be described as welfare-values.[112] Corresponding

---

[108] Max Scheler, *Die Wissensformen und die Gessellschaft* (2nd ed. rev.; Bern: Francke Verlag, 1963), p. 154. (Hereinafter referred to as GES.)

[109] FORM, p. 122.

[110] *Ibid.*, pp. 122-123.

[111] *Ibid.*, pp. 123-124.

[112] Werner Stark refers to them as "welfare-values." Cf. Werner Stark, "A General Introduction to Max Scheler's Work," in Max Scheler, *The Nature of Sympathy* (London: Routledge & Kegan Paul, 1970), p. xvi.

states are those of health, vitality, disease, aging, weakness and the feeling of approaching death. The vital values represent a completely independent modality that cannot be reduced either to the higher level of the spiritual values or to the lower level of useful and pleasant values.

It has been said that the establishment of vital values as an independent class "constitutes Scheler's original addition to the traditional list of value qualities." [113] We may also see in this Scheler's attempt to assimilate and integrate the values which Nietzsche had described as all-important.[114] The recognition and proper understanding of the vital values as an independent class depends on the recognition of life as a true essence. Kant tacitly assumed that vital values can be reduced to mere hedonistic ones. A failure to recognize that vital values are autonomous and independent constitutes a basic weakness of traditional ethical teaching.

3. Spiritual values (*geistige Werte*).[115] The third modality consists of spiritual values, which are characterized by their independence from the whole sphere of the body and the environment. The superior status of this class manifests itself in the clear evidence that one is obliged to sacrifice vital values to them. We grasp spiritual values in spiritual feeling (*geistiges Fühlen*) and in spiritual acts of preferring, loving and hating. These spiritual feelings and acts are different from vital functions and cannot be reduced to the biological level.

The main kinds of spiritual values are: (a) the esthetic values of beauty and ugliness; (b) the values of right and wrong or of justice and injustice (*die Werte des Rechten und Unrechten*), which are the ultimate basis for an objective juridical order; (c) the values of pure knowledge for its own sake such as philosophy tries to realize (in contrast to science, which is motivated by the purpose of controlling the appearances).

The correlative feeling states for spiritual values are spiritual joy and sorrow, which differ from the vital states of gladness

[113] Herbert Spiegelberg, *The Phenomenological Movement* (The Hague: Martinus Nijhoff, 1965), Vol. I, p. 254.
[114] *Ibid.*
[115] FORM, pp. 124-125.

and sadness (*Froh- und Unfrohsein*). Since spiritual joy and sorrow are not mediated through the body, they exist independently of any vital states. Their origin and change is directly dependent on the variations of the corresponding spiritual values.[116]

4. The value-modality of the holy and unholy (*Wertmodalität des Heiligen und Unheiligen*).[117] These values appear only in objects which are given intentionally as "absolute objects." The value-modality of the holy is independent of what different times and different peoples have held to be "holy."

The states of feeling corresponding to these values are bliss (*Seligkeit*) and despair (*Verzweiflung*) which must be clearly distinguished from the states of mere happiness and unhappiness (*Glück und Unglück*). Bliss and despair reflect and measure man's experience of nearness to and distance from the holy. Typical responses to this value modality are belief and unbelief, awe, adoration and worship. The act in which we originally grasp the values of the holy is a special kind of love that is essentially directed toward persons. This modality, therefore, consists primarily in personal values. Derivative values are the "value-things" in cults, sacraments and forms of worship.[118]

The hierarchy of the four value modalities that we have sketched above may appear somewhat abstract and in need of further concretization. Scheler was, of course, aware of this and

[116] *Ibid.*, p. 125.

[117] *Ibid.*, pp. 125-126.

[118] *Ibid.*, p. 126. Johannes Hessen, who acknowledges his deep indebtedness to Scheler, has explored in a more systematic fashion the values of the holy. Cf. Johannes Hessen, *Die Werte des Heiligen* (Regensburg: Pustet, 1951). Bernhard Häring has investigated—always in close dialogue with Max Scheler—the relationship between the value of the holy and that of moral goodness: Bernhard Häring, *Das Heilige und das Gute* (Krailling: Ernst Wewel Verlag, 1950). It is interesting to note that Häring, probably the most influential Catholic moral theologian in our century, started his career as a moralist with an investigation into the moral philosophy of Max Scheler. The profound influence of Scheler is manifest in most of his published works. See, for example, Bernhard Häring, *Das Gesetz Christi* (3 vols.; 7th ed rev.; Freiburg: Erich Wewel Verlag, 1963). Häring begins the introduction to his book *Das Heilige und das Gute* with the revealing statement: "Die Abhandlung ist entstanden aus der Begegnung mit Max Scheler."

tried to concretize the hierarchy of values by establishing a corresponding hierarchy of value-person-types (*Vorbilder*) and a
hierarchy of societal forms.[119] The same order that exists
among the four classes of values can also be found among the
four types of ideal model persons and the four forms of society.
In chapter VIII we shall explore in greater detail the four value-
person-types. Here it suffices to correlate briefly the three parallel
hierarchies, that of values, of value-person-types, and of societal
forms.[120]

Values	*Value-person-types* [121]	*Societal Forms*
pleasure-values	the artist of enjoyment or the connoisseur (*Künstler des Genusses*)	atomistic society (*Gesellschaft*)
vital values	the hero, the leading spirit of civilization	the organic community (*Lebensgemeinschaft*)
spiritual values	the genius	the legal and cultural community (*Rechtsgemeinschaft und Kulturgemeinschaft*)
the values of the holy	the saint	community of love, the Church Universal (*Liebesgemeinschaft, Kirche*)

[119] FORM, p. 126. Cf. Kaspar Hürlimann, "Person und Werte. Eine
Untersuchung über den Sinn von Max Schelers Doppeldevise: 'Materiale
Wertethik' und 'Ethischer Personalismus,'" *Divus Thomas*, XXX
(September, 1952), pp. 273-298; XXX (December, 1952), pp. 385-416.
[120] FORM, p. 126.
[121] There is a certain discrepancy between the four value modalities
and the number of value-person-types. In some texts, Scheler speaks of
five models instead of four. In his *Formalismus*, he mentions these five
"pure person-types": "Heiliger, Genius, Held, führender Geist, Künstler
des Genusses" (FORM, p. 126). In the above scheme I have correlated
both "the hero" and "the leading spirit of civilization" to the modality
of vital values.

The four classes of value-modalities which we have delineated above do not, surprisingly, include the moral values
of good and evil. The reason is that for Scheler these are values
that belong to a different level. Moral values are found only in
the realization of non-moral values. They are attached to acts
which realize other values in the right order, and ride, as Scheler
puts it, "on the back" (*auf dem Rücken*) of these acts. For
Scheler, "good" is the will to realize the higher or the supreme
value, and "evil" to choose the lower one. "The morally good
act is the value-realizing act which, with regard to its intended
value-content, is in accord with the 'preferred' value and in opposition to the 'subordinated' value." [122] Similarly, the morally
evil act is the one which rejects a "preferred" (higher) value
and realizes instead a "subordinate" (lower) value.

The phrases "preferred values" and "subordinate values" can
easily be misunderstood and need, therefore, a clarification. "Preferring" (*Vorziehen*) and "subordinating" or "placing-after"
(*Nachsetzen*), according to Scheler's use of the terms, do not
denote acts of the will but rather acts of cognition (*Erkenntnisakte*).[123] Preferring one value to another does not mean
choosing it. Values are comprehended as higher or lower in
the cognitive acts of preferring and subordinating or placing-
after. Choosing a value is an act subsequent to preferring. The
"a priori preferring" which obtains with respect to values must,
therefore, be clearly distinguished from "empirical preferring"
which obtains with respect to goods.[124] That a certain value
is "higher" than another is intuited in the very act of preferring
(*Vorziehen*). Whereas the ordered ranks of values (*Rangord-
nung der Werte*) remain invariable throughout history, the rules
of preferring one value to another vary according to time and
space. As we shall see in greater detail in a later chapter, the
historical variability of rules of preference can reveal itself in a
negative way as a falsification and impoverishment of the moral

[122] FORM, p. 47.
[123] *Ibid.*: "Nicht der Akt des Vorziehens und Nachsetzens is 'gut' oder
'böse'; denn diese Akte sind Erkenntnisakte, nicht Willensakte."
[124] *Ibid*, p. 105.

order. Resentment, for example, can become a major cause of a damaged and poisoned value-consciousness of man. On the other hand, man can also widen his value horizon and discover new values by cultivating and developing the acts of proper "preferring" and "subordinating" of values.[125]

The moral value of "good" must never be the content or material (*Materie*) for a realizing act of the will. If a man chooses "good" as a content of his acts he is a Pharisee, for he only wants to appear good to himself.[126] For example, he who helps his neighbor, but does so in order "to be good himself" or "to do good" instead of being concerned with achieving the neighbor's well-being, does not act in a morally good way, but rather behaves like a Pharisee. Scheler concludes that the value "good" may never be intended as a goal of our moral acts. It appears only "on the back" (*auf dem Rücken*) of another act in which we realize a higher positive value.[127]

The question arises now as to what is the basis for the proper "laws of preference" (*Vorzugsgesetze*) within the hierarchy of values. Scheler establishes the following axioms which provide the criteria for the right preferring (*Vorziehen*), subordinating (*Nachsetzen*), choice and realization of values:

I. 1. The existence of a positive value is itself a positive value.
    2. The non-existence of a positive value is itself a negative value.
    3. The existence of a negative value is itself a negative value.
    4. The non-existence of a negative value is itself a positive value.

II. 1. The good is the value in the domain of the will which attaches to the realization of a positive value.

[125] *Ibid.*, p. 107.
[126] *Ibid.*, p. 48.
[127] *Ibid.*: "Der Wert 'gut' erscheint, indem wir den (im Vorziehen gegebenen) höheren positiven Wert realisieren; er erscheint *an* dem Willensakte. Eben darum kann er nie die Materie dieses Willensaktes

2. Evil is the value in the domain of the will which attaches to the realization of a negative value.

3. Good is the value in the domain of the will which attaches to the realization of a superior (or supreme) value.

III.   The criterion of good (and evil) consists on this level in the accordance (opposition) of the value whose realization is intended with the preferred value, or in its opposition (accordance) to the subordinated value.[128]

These axioms must now be related to the previously mentioned fourfold hierarchy of values, namely the pleasure-values, vital values, spiritual values and the sacred values of the holy. It follows, then, that we ought to sacrifice pleasure and physical enjoyment to our duties toward the value of the noble and the welfare-values. Again, we ought to sacrifice social well-being to the spiritual values, i.e. to truth, justice and beauty. Spiritual and cultural values must finally be subordinated to the supreme values of the holy.

Scheler's theory of the fourfold hierarchy of values and the inherent summons to strive for the "higher" values presents itself as a moving appeal to the moral sense and the idealistic yearnings in every man's heart. It reveals both an attractive and an important dimension of the moral cosmos. However, this theory manifests also a fundamental weakness of Scheler's whole ethical system. Quentin Lauer has put forward an incisive critique of Scheler's theory.[129] He rightly asks, "can a mere comparison of values add an obligation which is not intrinsic to the values themselves?"[130] One cannot say that there is always an

---

sein. Er befindet sich gleichsam 'auf dem Rücken' dieses Aktes, und zwar wesensnotwendig."

[128] *Ibid.*

[129] Quentin Lauer, S.J., "The Phenomenological Ethics of Max Scheler," *International Philosophical Quarterly,* I (May, 1961), pp. 273-300. Cf. also Maurice Dupuy, *La Philosophie de Max Scheler* (Paris: Presses Universitaires de France, 1959), II, pp. 508-513: "Valeur et Obligation."

[130] Quentin Lauer, *op. cit.,* p. 295.

obligation to realize the higher value. Life could, indeed, not be lived in a human way if one were always obliged to do the more perfect deed. The norms of Scheler's ethics do not enable us to make valid preference-judgments in the concrete situations of daily life and they do not give a sufficient answer to the question of obligation, a question that must be of central importance in any scientific ethics.[131]

This basic lacuna in Scheler's ethical system of not providing satisfactory norms for moral decisions and of not coming to grips with the problem of obligation should not blind us to the genuine wealth of insights that Scheler does provide concerning criteria for moral choices. In the *Formalismus* we find some profound observations on how to evaluate the relative "height" of values (*Höher- und Niedrigersein eines Wertes*) which retain their validity even if—as we have seen above—additional categories are required to solve the problems of obligation and norms. We shall now take a closer look at the five characteristics on which the relative "height" of values is said to depend. Scheler reminds us that the relative rank of a value is a matter of intuitive insight. It can never be logically deduced but is comprehended in acts of "preferring" and "subordinating" by means of intuitive "preference-evidence" (*intuitive "Vorzugsevidenz"*).[132]

(1) The more enduring in time the values are (*je dauerhafter sie sind*), the higher they are. (2) The less susceptible the values are to extension and divisibility, the higher they are. (3) The less the values are grounded (*fundiert*) on other values, the higher they are. (4) The deeper the satisfaction (*Befriedigung*) that they yield, the higher they are. (5) Finally, the values are higher to the degree in which the experiencing of them is independent of certain carriers of feeling and preferring (*Träger des "Fühlens" und "Vorziehens"*).[133]

These five criteria for the relative height of values need some further clarification. In describing them more fully we shall also

---

[131] *Ibid.,* pp. 297-298.
[132] FORM, p. 107.
[133] *Ibid.*

provide a deeper justification for the hierarchy of values which we have characterized earlier. Applying these five criteria, we shall understand better why there exists an order of value-ranks beginning with pleasure-values, ascending to vital values and spiritual values, and reaching the apex of the hierarchy in the value-modality of the holy.

Enduringness or duration (Dauer), i.e. the intrinsic tendency to last long, is the first criterion for the height of a value. Endurance with respect to values must not be interpreted as a mere succession in time. Rather, it signifies a qualitative phenomenon of time as distinguished from mere objective time and objective duration which is characteristic of goods *(Güter)*. A value is enduring if it possesses the "ability-to-exist-through-time." [134]

Scheler illustrates the phenomenon of duration by describing the value of love. Of necessity genuine love always implies duration. It would be a contradiction to say to someone: "I love you *now*," or " I love you *for a certain time*." The dimension of *sub specie quadam aeterni* belongs to the very essence of genuine love. Continuous duration *(Fortdauer)* is an essential and necessary aspect of the value of the act of love, and also of the values toward which our love is directed. It does, of course, happen that a person terminates his love for another person. But this would be an indication that no genuine love existed from the beginning, that the alleged love was only a union of convenience and interest *(Interessengemeinschaft)* or that one has deceived oneself regarding the other person and his true value.[135]

In contrast to genuine love, a union of convenience and interest is by its very nature only transitory. Pleasure-values and utility-values are not durable and can be enjoyed only for a limited time. Bliss *(Seligkeit)*, on the other hand, endures throughout all changes of happiness and unhappiness. Happiness, in turn, is more durable than mere pleasure: a man can still experience inner happiness in the midst of suffering. The lowest values and their corresponding emotional states are the

[134] *Ibid.,* p. 109: "Es is dauerhaft ein Wert, der das Phänomen des Durch-die-Zeit-hindruch-Existieren'könnens' an sich hat."
[135] *Ibid.*

most transitory ones; the highest values and their corresponding emotional states (beatitude) are the most durable ones, indeed, they are "eternal." [136]

Indivisibility is the second criterion for the height of values. The less divisible values are—i.e. the less they must be "divided up" if a number of people are to participate in them—the higher they are. People can share in material goods only by dividing them. A loaf of bread, for example, must be cut in pieces and divided if several men want to eat it. A work of art, on the other hand, cannot be divided. A painting, for example, can be shared and yet need not be sliced up in order to be equally enjoyed by many people. Material goods often divide those who strive after them. Higher values, however, by their very nature tend to unite people. The spiritual values of knowledge and beauty and especially the values of the holy can be shared by a multitude. Nothing unites people more than worshipping the holy together. Although in the past religious wars may have divided people in a false understanding of the holy, it is of the very essence of a genuine quest for the holy that it joins and unites people.[137]

Relative independence of one value from other values is the third criterion. A value is higher the less it is dependent on another value. Scheler shows that with the exception of the highest value of an infinite, personal spirit, all values are grounded (*fundiert*)[138] on others, i.e. that they can exist only as contingent to another higher value. Thus, the value of utility depends on the value of the agreeable, since the useful is a means to achieve the agreeable. The value of the agreeable in its turn is grounded on the values of vitality, for example that of health. In a critique of Nietzsche's transvaluation of values and his one-sided emphasis on the values of life, Scheler shows that

[136] *Ibid.*, p. 110.
[137] *Ibid.*, pp. 110-112.
[138] *Ibid.*, p. 112: "Dann ist der jeweilig 'fundierende' Wert . . . auch jeweilig der 'höhere' Wert. So ist der Wert des 'Nützlichen' 'fundiert' in dem Wert des 'Angenehmen' . . . ist der Wert des Angenehmen . . . wesensgesetzlich 'fundiert' in einem vitalen Wert, z.B. der Gesundheit. . . ."

the latter have to be grounded (*fundiert*) on spiritual values. Man can become aware of his own uniqueness and of the fact that he represents the highest form of life only through a spiritual act of knowledge. "It is only to the extent that there are spiritual values and spiritual acts . . . that *life* assumes any value at all."[139] Ultimately, all values have their foundation in the value of an infinite, personal spirit.[140]

Depth of satisfaction (*Tiefe der Befriedigung*) is the fourth criterion for the height of a value.[141] The deeper the satisfaction that it yields, the higher a value is. "Satisfaction," however, does not mean a pleasurable sensation (*Lust*), but rather the experience of inner fulfillment (*Erfüllungserlebnis*). [142] The hierarchization of values and of satisfaction is made manifest in the interesting phenomenon that full satisfaction on the level of lower values (for example, sensory pleasures and external enjoyments) is possible only if we feel also satisfied on the higher levels, i.e. in the more central spheres of our life. If a man is happy deep down in his heart, he can also fully enjoy the external merriments of life. If not, he will be restlessly driven in a perpetual search for ever new pleasure-values and still remain unsatisfied. Practical hedonism is always an indication that a man is not "satisfied" with regard to higher values. The degree of man's craving for pleasure is, in fact, in inverse proportion to the depth of his inner fulfillment.[143]

The fifth criterion for the height of a value—and the most essential one [144]—is *the degree of relativity a value has with regard to an absolute value.*[145] The less relative a value is, the higher is its rank in the hierarchy.

Scheler distinguishes a primary and a secondary relativity. The latter refers to types of goods (*Güterarten*) and their particular psychophysical constitution. An example of this type of

[139] *Ibid.*, p. 113.
[140] *Ibid.*
[141] *Ibid.*, pp. 113-114.
[142] *Ibid.*, p. 113.
[143] *Ibid.*, p. 114.
[144] *Ibid.*, p. 117: "ursprünglichstes . . . Wesensmerkmal . . ."
[145] *Ibid.*, p. 114: "die Stufe der 'Relativität der Werte' oder auch ihr Verhältnis zu den 'absoluten Werten.' "

relativity is the phenomenon that the same thing may be poison to one animal and nourishment for another. This secondary relativity which obtains among goods is known through acts of reason, of thinking, judging and comparing.

The primary relativity which obtains only among values signifies an essential relationship (*Wesenszusammenhang*), a relationship which is intrinsic to the hierarchy of values. This relativity cannot be known through acts of reflection and judgments. Rather, it is given in an immediate intuition in the act of preference-feeling. "There is a depth in us where we always secretly know the truth concerning the relativity of experienced values." [146] Scheler illustrates this point by the following example. In the experience of a pure act of love for a person we immediately intuit that the value of this person and of our pure love are absolute values. It is immediately evident to us that this "felt absoluteness" (*gefühlte Absolutheit*) may never be sacrificed in favor of another value, and that by sacrificing it we would incur guilt. We do not have to wait for the "experience of life," or to use any consequential calculus to find out that the values of love and of the person are not relative but absolute; we grasp this truth in immediate intuition.

Pleasure-values presuppose a being with the capacity of sensible feeling (*sinnlich-fühlendes Wesen*) and are, therefore, "relative" to such sensing beings. Similarly, vital values are "relative" to certain living beings. Absolute values, on the other hand, do not depend on the essence of sensibility (*Wesen der Sinnlichkeit*) and the essence of life. Rather, they exist independently for pure acts of feeling, i.e. for pure acts of preferring and love.[147] Moral values and those of the third and fourth modalities (spiritual values and the values of the holy) are, according to Scheler, such absolute values. They make a definitive

[146] *Ibid.*, p. 116: "Es gibt eine Tiefe in uns, wo wir immer heimlich wissen, was es mit den von uns erlebten Werten hinsichtlish ihrer 'Relativität' für eine Bewandtnis hat."

[147] *Ibid.*, p. 115: "Dagegen sage ich, es seien absolute Werte diejenigen Werte, die für ein 'reines' Fühlen (Vorziehen, Lieben), d.h. für ein von dem Wesen der Sinnlichkeit und dem Wesen des Lebens in seiner Funktionsart und seinen Funktionsgesetzen unabhängiges Fühlen existieren. Solcher Art sind z.B. die sittlichen Werte."

demand on man and may not be sacrificed to "relative" values.

In his theory of absolute values Scheler reaffirms his strong conviction that values are not subjective but rather are of an objective nature. Values and their hierarchical order are not created by man but are an objective datum. Man must attune his heart to this objective order of "higher" and "lower" values. To the extent that he transcends the "relative" values and chooses and loves those values that are "absolute" he will grow as a moral agent and as a human being.

The basic insight of Scheler concerning the existence of a hierarchy of higher and lower values and of corresponding laws of preference (*Vorzugsgesetze*) is, no doubt, of immense significance for moral philosophy. Ethicians have greatly profited by Scheler's theories and have found the laws of preference to be valuable guidelines for determining moral choices. However, valuable as the laws of preference may be, they remain seriously deficient, for they are too narrow in scope and consequently cannot provide sufficiently workable norms for the concrete moral life.

In a critique of Scheler, Nicolai Hartmann has pointed out that it is inadequate to make the height of values the sole principle for value-preference.[148] He says that "the graded order of values is not determined exclusively by the principle of valuational height (*Werthöhe*) but involves also a second determining factor: valuational strength (*Wertstärke*), or weight (*Wertgewicht*)."[149] The lower values are, according to Hartmann, the "stronger" ones because they are more fundamental and elementary.

> The higher value is always the more conditioned, the more dependent and in this sense the weaker; its fulfillment is conceivable only in so far as it is raised upon the fulfill-

---

[148] Nicolai Hartmann, *Ethik* (4th ed.; Berlin: Walter de Gruyter, 1962), pp. 595-613. English translation: *Ethics* (3 vols.; 3rd ed.; New York: The Macmillan Company, 1958-1963), II, pp. 444-463. Meta Hübler, "Werthöhe und Wertstärke in der Ethik von Nicolai Hartmann," *Philosophische Studien*, II (Spring, 1950), 117-125.

[149] *Ethik*, p. 597; *Ethics*, II, p. 446.

ment of the lower values. But the more unconditioned, the more elementary, and in this sense the stronger value is always the lower; it is only a base for the moral life, not a fulfillment of its meaning. This is equivalent to saying: the most grievous transgressions are those against the lowest values, but the greatest moral desert attaches to the highest values.[150]

The realization of higher values presupposes the realization of lower ones. The man who is hungry must first satisfy his hunger and secure his very survival and physical existence before he can concern himself with the ontologically higher intellectual and artistic values. Again, the value of justice is lower than that of personal love, yet it is more fundamental and therefore "stronger." Man ought first to fulfill the requirements of justice before he can realize the higher values of love. He would, indeed, jeopardize his "higher morality" if he were to neglect the lower values which are the necessary foundation and presupposition for any higher moral life. At the same time, a man's moral life would remain impoverished if it were consumed in an exclusive quest for the "stronger" yet ontologically lower values without aspiring to a higher morality. Ultimately, Hartmann envisages a synthesis between Scheler's laws of preference which are based on the height of values (*Werthöhe*) and his own which give priority to valuational strength (*Wertstärke*).[151]

With his principle of valuational strength, Hartmann has provided an important complementary principle to Scheler's theory of value-preference. Yet, even a synthesis of both theories fails to furnish satisfactory norms for concrete moral decisions. Hans Reiner, one of the leading moral philosophers in the phenomenological tradition,[152] has taken up this question and signifi-

---

[150] *Ethik,* p. 602; *Ethics,* II, pp. 451-452.

[151] *Ethik,* pp. 605-613; *Ethics,* II, pp. 455-463.

[152] Hans Reiner wrote his doctoral dissertation under Husserl and was profoundly influenced by the value ethics of Scheler. Cf. Jean Hering, "De Max Scheler à Hans Reiner," *Revue D'Histoire et de Philosophie Religieuses,* XL (Summer, 1960), pp. 152-164.

cantly advanced the discussion of the laws of value-preference, or as he calls them, "principles of value-preference" (*Wertvorzugsprinzipien*).[153] Reiner accepts the theories of both Scheler and Hartmann but with an important qualification. Value-height (*Werthöhe*) and value-strength (*Wertstärke*) are, in Reiner's opinion, two important principles of value-preference but they are as such insufficient and must be complemented by several other principles in order to achieve a workable set of moral norms. Reiner develops a series of eleven principles of value-preference—the first two are those of Scheler and Hartmann—which have to be applied to determine what a person ought to do here and now in a concrete situation.[154]

Hans Reiner's principles of value-preference are based on the following characteristics: [155]

1. Value-height (*Werthöhe*) as developed in the theory of Max Scheler.

2. Value-strength (*Wertstärke*) as developed in the theory of Nicolai Hartmann. Reiner reformulates this as "principle of value-urgency" (*Prinzip der Wertdringlichkeit*). When Hartmann says that we ought to prefer those values which are the "stronger" ones he means basically, in Reiner's interpretation, that we must realize first the values which are of greater ontic "urgency" (*Dringlichkeit*). For example, securing one's physical survival is more basic and more urgent than realizing higher values and may take priority therefore in certain circumstances.

3. Temporal urgency (*zeitliche Dringlichkeit*) is a third principle of value-preference. A drowning person has to be helped immediately, or an artistic edifice in danger of collapse must be preserved without delay. In such situations the realization of other values, even higher ones, may have to be postponed.

4. Quantity of value-realization is the fourth principle. Other things being equal, one ought to aim at the realization of the

---

153 Hans Reiner, *Pflicht und Neigung* (Meisenheim/Glan: Westkulturverlag Anton Hain, 1951). Hans Reiner, *Die Philosophische Ethik* (Heidelberg: Quelle & Meyer, 1964).
154 *Pflicht und Neigung*, pp. 168-178.
155 *Ibid.*, pp. 168-178.

greatest quantity of values. Reiner tries here to incorporate a valid insight of utilitarianism, albeit as a principle which remains subordinate to other more important ones.

5. The greater chance of success is a fifth principle which has, however, to be applied only in certain circumstances. If, for example, all other principles have been taken into consideration and one is still faced with two possible choices which are backed by equally cogent reasons, one ought to choose that course of action which promises the greater chance of success.

6. The greater or more pressing need is a sixth principle.

7. The seventh principle says that the negative demand of not violating already existing values usually has priority over the positive demand of realizing new values. There are, however, exceptions to this rule as in the case where one must damage another person's property in order to save a human life.

8. A person can be obliged to perform one task rather than another if there is a scarcity of people who can do the job equally well.

9. Special abilities and the possession of particular means for performing certain tasks can present a personal call and impose a unique obligation on an individual.

10. If a person is more gifted for one task rather than for another he may have a special calling to choose that undertaking which he can do best and in which he will perform best.

11. The eleventh principle is called "the principle of the daimonion" (*das Prinzip des Daimonion*). It is the voice of conscience which can call a person to a unique task. Joan of Arc as well as Socrates are examples of people for whom this principle was of decisive importance in making certain choices. There are situations, according to Reiner, where all the above-mentioned ten principles of value-preference may prove to be insufficient to reach a clear moral decision. It is particularly in such a situation that the voice of conscience, or the "principle of the daimonion" may have to function as the decisive moral principle.[156]

[156] *Ibid.,* pp. 173-174.

II
The Historical Character
of Value Comprehension

There exist some interesting parallels between Scheler's approach to ethics and his approach to philosophy of religion. It seems that Scheler, at times, applied the same basic insight to both areas. The way he treats a question in his philosophy of religion can, therefore, shed important light on the respective area in ethics and vice versa. A case in point is the historicity of man's gradual growth in the knowledge of God. This shows a considerable similarity to the historic character of man's value comprehension, and can, therefore, serve to illustrate and to bring into sharper focus the ethical issue under consideration.

I
THE HISTORICAL CHARACTER OF THE KNOWLEDGE
OF GOD—A PARALLEL TO THE HISTORICITY
OF VALUE COMPREHENSION

We will briefly sketch the historical dimension of man's knowledge of God. Scheler approaches this question from two directions, from the finite nature of the historically developing human reason and mind and from the infinite nature of the fullness and richness of God.[1]

Reason itself evolves and develops in history.[2] Not only is the

[1] VEIM, pp. 195-210; *Eternal,* pp. 198-213.
[2] VEIM, p. 198; *Eternal,* p. 202.

61

whole domain of contingent experience in a process of continuous growth—which explains that the insights enjoyed by different peoples may also differ one from another—but the rational
human mind itself constantly grows and develops.[3]

> Since the human mind, both in the individual and in the
> species, thus grows not only in its knowledge but also in its
> functions and its powers of gathering knowledge, not only
> in its works and achievements (e.g. art and moral life) but
> also in its artistic and moral capabilities, the rational hu-
> man mind cannot at any point in history be completely
> defined; philosophically—in all noetic fields—its defini-
> tion is always markedly incomplete.[4]

Scheler then considers the same question from the aspect of
God's nature. The inexpressible richness and plenitude of the
divine spirit and its infinite perfection make it impossible for
any individual person or any historical epoch to fully exhaust the
knowledge of God.[5] Only part of the fullness of God is accessible to any one man, to one group or to one people at any given
epoch in history.[6] Thus, it is both the infinite richness of God
and the finiteness of human reason that together condition the
historicity of man's gradual growth in the cognition of God.

Scheler then draws some important conclusions from these
presuppositions. First he develops the theory of a socio-historical division of functions of the human cognitive mind.[7] Distinct
noetic-cognitive organs and functions are aligned with different
spheres of possible reality. These organs and functions are irreducible in terms of one another and they are distributed un-
evenly and in differing intensities among mankind, i.e. among
different races, cultures and phases of civilization.[8]

There could be such a distribution of cognitive powers that

[3] VEIM, p. 199; *Eternal*, p. 202.
[4] VEIM, p. 200; *Eternal*, p. 203.
[5] VEIM, p. 205; *Eternal*, p. 209.
[6] *Ibid.*
[7] VEIM, pp. 345-346; *Eternal*, pp. 348-349.
[8] VEIM, p. 346; *Eternal*, 349.

each race, culture and historical phase would have some specific, distinctive contribution to make toward the total knowledge of reality—a contribution which no other group and epoch of history could supply.[9]

Since only mankind in its entirety through the entire course of history is sufficient for the complete development of man's full, exhaustive capacity for knowing the whole of reality, no single socio-historical part should set itself up as the decisive judge of the whole.[10] It follows that any future epistemology must include both a theory of development and a sociological doctrine of structures of the human mind.[11] Scheler is, in this particular context, primarily concerned with growth in the cognition of God, but he reminds us that the historical division of functions between the earlier and later stages of mankind is not only valid with regard to man's cognition, but equally in respect to his volition and discovery of values.[12]

Concerning the nature of this progress in the cognition of God, Scheler makes two important observations. First, he emphasizes that progress in the knowledge of God is inseparable from moral progress. Secondly, he points out that theoretical knowledge cannot be acquired prior to religious practice; rather, religious knowledge evolves only in the process of religious practice.[13] The apprehension and realization of moral values enter into every religious act and determine the degree of progress in religious knowledge.

Morally good volition and conduct, conforming to whatever image of divinity hovers before the mind, necessarily govern as a *conditio sine qua non* the possibility of cognitive advance into the full breadth and depth of the deity. For, of all kinds of cognition, knowledge of God is the most inseparable from moral progress.[14]

[9] *Ibid.*
[10] *Ibid.*
[11] *Ibid.*
[12] VEIM, p. 349; *Eternal*, p. 351.
[13] VEIM, pp. 259-260; *Eternal*, pp. 265-266.
[14] VEIM, p. 259; *Eternal*, p. 265.

Scheler strongly rejects the Lutheran position that moral volition and conduct are mere consequences of religious faith. Rather, good will and conduct widen and deepen at every step one's concrete knowledge of God.

This leads to his second observation, namely that religious knowledge evolves only in the process of religious practice. According to Scheler, religious cognition is far closer to the artistic apprehension of the world than to the cognition of science and metaphysics. The artist does not know before the process of artistic representation but only *in* the very course of it. Similarly religious knowledge only evolves out of religious experience in worship and cultic representation. Scheler here points to the data of the history of religion which show that ritual and the concrete idea of the religious object are mutually interdependent variables. A painter gradually learns to see the landscape in the process of painting it. Similarly, it is with religious knowledge, and Scheler quotes here approvingly Pascal's word, "Do thou but kneel, and faith will come." Scheler summarizes his own position in these words: "Try to perform the moral acts and ritual which this religion lays down, then see whether and how far you have grown in religious understanding." [15]

A further conclusion from the historical character of the cognition of God is the need for cooperation of different peoples and of succeeding epochs to achieve an ever fuller understanding of God.[16] As we shall see later, a similar cooperation is required for an ever fuller comprehension and realization of the whole realm of values.

Scheler approaches the question both from a horizontal and from a vertical perspective. Different peoples and individuals within the same historical period, as well as succeeding peoples of different historical epochs, each have to make their own unique contribution to a deeper understanding of the inexhaustible richness of God. None of them can be substituted for the other.[17] One period of mankind, or one part of humanity,

[15] VEIM, p. 260; *Eternal,* p. 266.
[16] VEIM, pp. 203-207; *Eternal,* pp. 206-211.
[17] VEIM, p. 203; *Eternal,* p. 206.

may penetrate into the realm of being in a way which no other age or group is able to achieve. Succeeding ages are obliged to preserve, as an eternally valid store of knowledge, the insights of their predecessors. Cooperation among the successive ages of mankind is thus an essential requirement for an adequate understanding of God.

> The philosophers must all, in cooperation . . . add their
> brick to the edifice of the one *philosophia perennis*—always bearing in mind the rules of the historical distribution
> of the cognitive powers themselves; to discover these rules
> is itself a highly important task for any epistemology wishing to treat exhaustively the cognitive powers of man.[18]

The more perfect the essence of an object is, the more urgent is the collaboration in inquiry if that essence is to be known in the most adequate way possible. Since God is the essence of all essences, the highest degree of collaboration of peoples and of historical epochs is required for an understanding of his divine essence.[19]

II
The Historicity of Value Comprehension—
Praxis and Knowledge

Scheler approaches the question of the historicity of value comprehension in a manner similar to that of the historical character of the knowledge of God. The richness and plenitude of the value-cosmos make it impossible for any individual person, historical period or culture, to comprehend its total content. The task of realizing values is, indeed, beyond the capacity of any one generation of mankind. Thus, there is a historical division of labor with regard to the knowledge and realization of values. Mankind is divided into different races and cultures, and the

[18] VEIM, p. 204; *Eternal,* p. 208.
[19] VEIM, pp. 205-207; *Eternal,* pp. 209-211.

lifespan of civilization is divided again into various developmental phases. Corresponding to these various divisions there are different noetic-cognitive organs and functions which are unique, irreducible in terms of one another and aligned with the different spheres of spacio-historical reality.

All groups and historical phases have to make their unique contribution to the knowledge and realization of values. They are also obliged to adopt and preserve what other cultures and eras have discovered. Only the whole of mankind in the total course of history suffices to develop mankind's full, exhaustive capacity for the realization of values. By means of this broad conception of mankind's historical evolution in knowledge and value realization, Scheler hopes to overcome the narrow reductionist and positivist trends of his time, and to expand the horizon to include the total treasure of values in both space and time.

In an important passage of his *Formalismus,* Scheler offers a brief summary of his view. He rejects any moral relativism and affirms the absoluteness of moral values. But at the same time he emphasizes the historicity and relativity of our comprehension and realization of values:

> Although the moral values could not be abstracted from the positive history and its worlds of goods, nevertheless, the historicity of their comprehension . . . is as essential to them as the historicity of their realization in one possible "history." As erroneous as relativism, which lets values originate from historical goods, and conceives them as being made within the history, is also the idea according to which the whole fullness of the realm of values and their ordered rank could ever be given to one individual, one people, one nation, or finally within one period of history.[20]

In his book *Wesen und Formen der Sympathie,* Scheler discusses again the historical character of value comprehension.

[20] FORM, p. 485.

Here, his key insight is that human cognition grows and matures in the process of acting and that values are apprehended only in the course of our actions. To explain this, Scheler uses the example of artistic representation. The artist does not possess a complete vision of what he is creating prior to his creative expression. Rather, the artistic idea matures and attains a definite shape only in the process of the creative representation.[21] A painter, for example, does not first see and then depict; he penetrates the full color and chiaroscuro of his subject only in the process of painting it.[22] In a similar way, we broaden and deepen our grasp of moral values in the process of acting morally. "We apprehend the nature of our moral character not by means of some pure antecedent self-intuition, completely divorced from the sphere of action, but only in the course of our actions themselves."[23]

In this connection, Scheler offers a valuable observation on the relationship between experience and language, and on the role of the poet to extend the scope of experience and of self-awareness. In order to appropriate fully his own experience, man must be able to express it in language. Poets and others who are creative in language are fulfilling the important function of expanding the scope of possible self-awareness by creating new forms of language in and through which others can, for the first time, grasp fully what they have encountered in their own experiences.[24] Poets thus enlarge the kingdom of the mind and discover new aspects of reality and new values. It is not the mission of art to reproduce what is already given but to penetrate more deeply the whole of the external world and of the soul, and to make it possible to see and to experience aspects of reality which were hitherto hidden.[25]

In his theory of love, Scheler emphasizes once again his basic point: it is in the process and practice of loving that man discovers and comprehends values. Man does not first have a com-

[21] SYM, p. 272; *Sympathy,* pp. 251-252.
[22] *Ibid.*
[23] SYM, p. 272; *Sympathy,* p. 252.
[24] SYM, p. 273; *Sympathy,* pp. 252-253.
[25] *Ibid.*

plete theoretical knowledge of values which he then realizes through loving deeds. Rather, it is the very experience or exercise of love which discloses these values. "It is *in* the exercise of love that goodness shines forth in the lover in the most original way."[26] Love is here seen as a continuous dynamic movement which leads man to ever higher values and enables him to attain the ideal state of value intrinsic to his nature.

What has been said about the comprehension of values in general as a dynamic historical process applies even more so to knowledge of the value of other persons. Human beings as well as God can never be disclosed to us as objects. Persons cannot be objectivized. It is only in the process of our loving participation in the acts of the other that we can gain an understanding and knowledge of him. "The person of another can only be disclosed to me by my joining in the performance of his acts, either cognitively, by understanding and vicarious re-living, or morally, by following in his footsteps." [27] The love of God in its highest form is, according to Scheler, not to have love "for" God; rather, it is to participate in his love for the world (*amare mundum in Deo*) and for himself (*amare Deum in Deo*).[28]

Since for Scheler the value of a person is the highest value, the way of understanding and knowing another person is not only a revealing paradigm for all value-comprehension but also the supreme model for man's continuous quest in attempting to penetrate the infinite realm of values.

III

THE PHENOMENON OF THE TRAGIC AND THE
HISTORICITY OF VALUE COMPREHENSION

The phenomenon of the tragic is, for Scheler, a moral category. In his essay "On the Phenomenon of the Tragic" [29] and

---

[26] SYM, p. 176; *Sympathy*, p. 164.

[27] SYM, p. 180: "Die Person kann mir nur gegeben sein, indem ich ihre Akte 'mitvollziehe'—erkenntnismässig im 'Verstehen' und 'Nachleben,' sittlich aber in der 'Gefolgschaft.' " *Sympathy*, p. 167.

[28] SYM, p. 177; *Sympathy*, p. 164.

[29] "Zum Phänomen des Tragischen," in *Vom Umsturz der Werte*, pp. 149-169.

again on the last pages of his *Formalismus*,[30] he shows the significance of the tragic in the area of ethics. It is in this context that he also developed some important ideas on the historicity of value comprehension.

For Scheler, the phenomenon of the tragic occurs essentially within the realm of values and their relationships.[31] In a value-free universe such as that constructed by mechanical physics, there are no tragedies,[32] for the tragic consists primarily in a conflict between two positive values.[33] Man is often confronted with a situation where two positive values make their demands on him. But because he is essentially finite he is at times incapable of realizing both values. In the concrete situation one value may exclude the other and man may be forced to reject one of them.[34] It is this type of situation which is tragic.

An even more concrete illustration of the tragic is found in the consideration of the value-person-types. As we will show at greater length in a later chapter, Scheler distinguishes five models of person or value-person-types: the saint, the genius, the hero, the leading spirit of civilization and the artist of enjoyment. These models attract man to realize in his own humanity the values he sees characterized in the value-person-types. But because man is essentially limited, no one person can become an equally perfect example of all five models, i.e. a saint, a genius, a hero, a leading spirit of civilization and an artist of enjoyment. This is what Scheler calls the "essential tragedy of being a finite person and the essential moral imperfection of being a man." [35] Manfred Frings [36] suggests that although the term does not occur in Scheler's published works, *Seinsschuld* (guilt resulting

---

[30] FORM, pp. 575-579.
[31] "Zum Phänomen des Tragischen," p. 153.
[32] *Ibid.*
[33] *Ibid.*, p. 155.
[34] *Ibid.*, p. 154.
[35] FORM, p. 575.
[36] Manfred Frings, *Person und Dasein. Zur Frage der Ontologie des Wertseins* (Den Haag: Martinus Nijhoff, 1969), p. 87. After the death of Maria Scheler, Manfred Frings took over the editorship of the *Gesammelte Werke* of Scheler. Since Frings is one of the best Scheler experts, his judgment would seem to carry particular weight.

from being) [37] would most appropriately express what Scheler has in mind. In the perspective of value ethics, the *Seinsschuld* of the person is the essential tragedy of being a finite person. Frings interprets Scheler's *Seinsschuld* as the "incompleteness and the necessarily finite exemplarity of the individual person as compared to the ideal persons typified by the models." [38]

Scheler distinguishes between a macrocosm of values which contains all possible good and evil, and various microcosms of moral values which differ in individual men according to the extent of their moral awareness.[39] The individual man's moral duties are to be measured on the basis of his own microcosm of values, or according to how deeply his gaze penetrates into the macrocosm of moral values. Consequently, it is possible that certain actions become a duty for one person who has gained insight into higher values but are not expected from another person who has not yet grasped these same values. In this way, the noble individual can more easily become guilty than the ignoble, since he is called to a higher standard.

Scheler emphasizes in this context the fact that value comprehension is bound to history. Not all epochs and not all individuals of the same epoch have an equal breadth and depth of value comprehension. As there is a Prometheus of technology who steals fire from Zeus, there are also "moral Prometheuses in whose vision a moral value suddenly appears which has never been known before." [40] The noble men in history penetrate more deeply into the moral value-cosmos, perceiving values which are higher than those seen by the average persons of that particular historical period. Thus, the noble man or moral hero will often find himself in conflict with the ruling morality of his time. He has to follow the call of the newly experienced values, yet in so doing he frequently suffers the condemnation of his contemporaries who judge according to the accepted norms of

[37] The opposite would be *Tatschuld*, or guilt resulting from a certain deed. Frings points out that in his treatment of repentance Scheler speaks in a parallel way of *Seinsreue* and *Tatreue*. Cf. *Ibid.*

[38] *Ibid.*, p. 87.

[39] "Zum Phänomen des Tragischen," p. 165.

[40] *Ibid.*, p. 166.

their era. The moral Prometheus is a tragic figure. He must necessarily appear guilty before the moral judges of his time when, in fact, he is guiltless. Scheler speaks here of a "guiltless guilt" (*schuldlose Schuld*) [41] which belongs to the very essence of all moral development. The tragic hero of moral awareness appears to his contemporaries like a criminal. Only after his newly experienced values have become the prevailing morality can he, in historical retrospect, be seen and acknowledged as a moral hero.[42]

The tragic fate of the moral genius reveals in a unique way how unpredictable are the steps of man's fated moral progress. Scheler considers Jesus in the experience in Gethsemane as an example of the tragic hero of moral awareness. The moral genius stands in absolute loneliness, and yet the total fate of the world appears compressed into the experience of this one man. He is standing alone and yet is at the center of the universe. Whole epochs of history are decided in him and through him without his contemporaries being aware of the momentous step being taken here and now in the moral development of mankind.[43]

IV

PERSPECTIVISM OF VALUES

As we have pointed out earlier, there exists a considerable similarity between Scheler's approach to ethics and his approach to philosophy of religion. The way in which he deals with one particular question or problem in his philosophy of religion sheds important light on the respective area of ethics and vice versa. Scheler's doctrine of perspectivism also fits this pattern. We will first briefly present the question of perspectivism as applied to religion and then examine the same issue within the framework of value-cognition.

In his sociology of knowledge, Scheler addresses himself to

[41] *Ibid.*, p. 167.
[42] *Ibid.*
[43] *Ibid.*, p. 168.

an extreme position of Durckheim, which he calls sociologism (*Soziologismus*). This sociologism holds that the social group determines essentially the thought forms and the religion of a given people.[44] In a similar fashion, the Marxist theory claims that it is the economic interest-groups that determine the content of a religion. Scheler rejects both sociologism and Marxism on this particular point and corrects their views by showing that it is not religion itself nor its essential content that is determined by social or economic groups but only the selection of particular aspects of religion.[45]

There exist both a sociological and an historical perspective of interest with regard to the world of meanings. According to different perspectives which originate in different social groupings at different times in history, men select certain ideas, values and aspects of religion and make of them the prevailing outlook of that time. The intellect can explicate itself only in a temporal form of gradual becoming. Thus, the limited intellect is capable of grasping only limited perspectives of reality. A changing historical perspectivism does not, however, imply a relativism with regard to truth, values and religion. Scheler holds on to an absolute sphere of values and of truth above and beyond the changes of historical perspectives.

Scheler chooses as a concrete example of perspectivism in religion the varying conceptions of God among different peoples and epochs.[46] The idea of God as such is so rich that no single nation or period can exhaust it. Depending on their own experiences as tribes or nations peoples of the past have considered God from different perspectives and have attributed the characteristics of their own national spirit to the varying images of God. The God of the Jews, for example, was consecutively considered as the God of the mountains, the God of the herds and the God of battles. Later, when the prophets were defending the rights of the down-trodden against the power of the kings, God was presented as the God of justice and redemption.

[44] GES, pp. 423-429.
[45] *Ibid.,* pp. 426-428.
[46] *Ibid.,* pp. 428-429.

The Greeks stressed a different dimension of God; they saw him as the God of wisdom. So too, the God of Mohammed resembles an Arab sheik.

From the plethora of data of sociology and of the history of religions, Scheler comes to the conclusion

> that in every sphere of being which man explores (be it nature, soul, history, or be it the realms of esthetic and ethical values, of figures and forms) there exists a sociologically conditioned perspective of interests which selects the concepts, meanings and eidetic images—and this is true also with regard to "heaven." [47]

As peoples and historical epochs can know God only from a limited perspective and can grasp only certain aspects of the richness of his divinity, so it is with man's approach to the realm of values. The relativity of perspective in ethics presupposes an absolute realm of values which exists above and beyond all changes of history. The perspective-slanted selections from the absolute realm of values differ from epoch to epoch. In the course of history various cultures endeavor to approximate the absolute, but each people and period achieve only a partial participation in the totality of values. Scheler relates here his ideas on perspectivism to his teaching on the history of ethos forms and on the cooperation of peoples and epochs:

> The historical mode of penetration into the metaphysical-absolute realm of values is through the sequence of various epochs and groupings, each with its own distinctive ethos. This successive historical penetration is integrally bound up with the essence of the realm of values and with its timeless coming into being. (The value-hierarchy provides only the most formal, general, a priori makeup of the realm of values.) Hence only the universal and solidary cooperation of all eras and peoples (including every future development) can fully exhaust the realm of values and co-

[47] *Ibid.*, p. 429.

realize it in the "original being," in so far as it is given to man to achieve its realization at all.[48]

The realm of eternal and immutable values discloses itself to each historical epoch and to each social group only in time-bound limited perspective. Any people and any historical period approaches reality and values from a particular vantage point and consequently attains a view which is unique—true yet always socially and historically limited. In its universal striving for values, mankind throws an infinity of searchlights upon the grandiose kingdom of values, lighting up and discovering an unlimited variety of perspectives of different values. Or to use another image, Scheler

compares the eternal and immutable values to a mountain-range which towers high above the valleys in which we humans live. To every age and to every people they reveal, according to their respective points of view a different aspect of themselves; each one is true, and yet each one is unacceptable to all the others. We must not speak of a relativism of values then, but rather of a perspectivism—an altogether different proposition. Only He who is exalted above the highest peak and who surveys the scene from the farthest heaven—only Almighty God, Himself the Value of Values, can know the truth in its entirety.[49]

In his essay "On the Rehabilitation of Virtue," Scheler offers a revealing insight into the intimate tie between the virtue of *Ehrfurcht* (reverence, respect, awe) and the awareness of perspectivism in value perception.[50] Reverence is "the attitude through which one perceives a further dimension which the man without reverence does not see, for which he is blind: the mys-

[48] GES, p. 154.
[49] Werner Stark, "A General Introduction to Max Scheler's Work," in Max Scheler, *The Nature of Sympathy* (London: Routledge & Kegan Paul, 1954), p. xvii.
[50] "Zur Rehabilitierung der Tugend," in UMST, pp. 26-27.

tery of things and the value-depth of their existence." [51] If man approaches reality with an attitude of reverence, reality opens itself on a deeper level and reveals layers which an irreverent observer could never discover. The phenomena of "horizon" and "perspective," with which we are familiar in the optical and visual sphere, exist also in the realm of our intellectual imagination, in our concepts, our interests and in our love. "Horizon" and "perspective" are, in fact, essential laws of functioning of every finite intellect. And it is the virtue of reverence "which sustains in the realm of values this dimension of horizon and the perspectivism of our intellectual nature and world." [52] If man approaches the world of values without reverence, everything will appear to him flat and one-dimensional, for he cannot penetrate into the deeper layers. An attitude of reverence, on the other hand, creates an awareness of both the depth and the inexhaustible super-abundance of values. God, world, the realm of values and man's own self, all reveal their dimension of depth only to the reverent person. And since the reverent man never reaches an end in his discoveries of reality, since he is every day surprised by new and fresh insights into the boundless exuberance of the realm of values, he knows that there is ever more to be explored beyond the present horizon and the present perspective. He becomes aware that whatever he discovers and sees is but one limited horizon, one restricted perspective of the richness of total reality into which he continues to penetrate in a life-long unending quest.

Scheler does not offer a systematic treatment of the causes and the genesis of different perspectives. He mentions, however, various types of perspectives and one of them he characterizes as "the prevailing perspective of social interest" (*die herrschende soziale Interessenperspektive*).[53] In his essay on the sociology

---

[51] *Ibid.*, p. 26: " . . . Ehrfurcht . . . ist die Haltung, in der man noch etwas hinzu wahrnimmt, das der Ehrfurchtslose nicht sieht und für das gerade er blind ist: das Geheimnis der Dinge und die Werttiefe ihrer Existenz."

[52] *Ibid.*, p. 27.

[53] GES, p. 58.

of knowledge, Scheler is dealing with the problem of how far human knowledge is socially determined. He acknowledges his agreement with Karl Marx and Emile Durkheim that knowledge is a social product. However, in some fundamental points his view differs, and in explaining his position he speaks also of the "perspective of social interest":

> It follows, that the sociological character of all knowledge, of all forms of thought, perception, and cognition, is unquestionable. However, this (sociological determination) refers only to the selection of objects of knowledge, which is determined by the prevailing perspective of social interests (*nach der herrschenden sozialen Interessenperspektive*). Neither the content nor the validity of knowledge is sociologically determined, but the forms of the mental acts by means of which knowledge is acquired are always and necessarily codetermined sociologically, i.e. by the social structure of society.[54]

To avoid a misunderstanding or misinterpretation, Scheler hastens to add in a footnote that he is speaking only of a sociological *co*determination. A sociologism (*Soziologismus*) as expounded by Durkheim, is not acceptable. For Scheler, both content and validity of thought are ultimately based in the supra-temporal metaphysical sphere of truth, the participation in which validates all limited human truth. But since no individual, no epoch and no society can exhaust the richness of the eternal realm of truth, a limited perspective of social interest can and must select a certain sector out of the infinite realm of possibilities.

Scheler offers many concrete examples of value perspectivism, although in his descriptions he does not always use the term perspective. Let us here delineate briefly one such instance, namely the perspective of values that originated the modern world-view. In his essay "Knowledge and Work," [55] Scheler

[54] *Ibid.*
[55] GES, pp. 197-198.

describes how from the 17th century on the ideas of power and domination became in Europe a predominant axiological perspective or a central value-attitude which decisively determined both the selection of objects of knowledge and the very aims of knowledge. Francis Bacon, for example, "wants to 'see, only in order to foresee,' and he wants to 'foresee' only because, and insofar as, this promotes man's power over nature." [56]

The new "will to power" over nature presents a value-structure which carves out of various possible modes of experiencing the world this one particular approach of allowing oneself to be directed and controlled by the specific value of power and domination. Scheler introduces here the important concept of "anticipatory schemes" (*antizipatorische Schemata*) [57]—conceptual frameworks in and through which images of reality are captured and arranged in different societies according to the social circumstances and historical situations, the direction of interests and the preference of values. Each "anticipatory scheme" originates from a functionalization of a certain sector of essence-perception and from a certain form of ethos, i.e. a living system of positive and negative ranking of values.

This complex process of new functionalizations, of changing the anticipatory schemes and of shifting the forms of ethos, resulted in the post-Renaissance, modern world-view. In the middle ages, a society of priests and monks had followed a contemplative quest for knowledge which desired to perceive, and mentally to mirror, the essences and forms of reality. The modern world-view ousted this mode of knowledge and replaced it with a knowledge that seeks power and domination over nature. Thus, the man of the Middle Ages and modern man looked at reality and at the realm of values from different perspectives, and they opted for different sets of values as a result of a divergent direction of interests.

Scheler addresses himself repeatedly to the problem of relativism. He is aware that his own ideas on ethos and perspectivism may be misinterpreted in a relativistic fashion. Consequently,

[56] *Ibid.*, p. 197.
[57] *Ibid.*, p. 198.

he never tires of pointing out that, far from being a relativist, he is in fact offering a solution to the problem of relativism.

In his essay "Problems of a Sociology of Knowledge" [58] he explains why and how his theories avoid relativism.[59] First, he acknowledges a pluralism of cultural forms and a multiplicity of ethos forms. The contents of the human mind and even the very categories and forms under which the contents are ordered, differ from society to society, and from age to age. Different societies and different periods of history experience in different ways the objective world. One society is fascinated by one particular aspect of the world, another is struck by a different dimension. These various basic experiences of mankind affect, and eventually dominate, the functioning of the mental structures of a people. Scheler calls this "functionalization" (*Funktionalisierung*), a process whereby the one truth becomes splintered into many.

Scheler agrees, then, with the assertion of relativists that the human mind is not only preoccupied with different ideas in different periods of history, but is even differently constituted. Consequently, there are different truths in different societies and epochs. But Scheler disagrees strongly with the metaphysical basis of relativism. For him, the multiplicity and diversity of truths "all spring from the perception of the one ontic realm of ideas and value orderings." [60] All truths and values perceived by different societies and ages are limited aspects, reflections and manifestations of the one inexhaustible ontological realm of truth and reality that lies outside and beyond the frame of space and time. This ontological realm imparts validity and unity to all differing human truths and values.

> Thus we escape a philosophical relativism . . . in a manner
> similar to that used by the Einsteinian theory in its own
> field—by lifting up the absolute realm of ideas and values
> corresponding to the essential idea of man far above all

[58] Max Scheler, "Probleme einer Soziologie des Wissens," in *Die Wissensformen und die Gesellschaft,* pp. 15-190.
[59] *Ibid.,* pp. 26-27.
[60] *Ibid.,* p. 26.

factual historical value systems; for example, by viewing all orders of goods, ends, and norms of human society in ethics, religion, law, art, as simply relative and as conditioned by a historical and sociological standpoint, preserving nothing but the idea of the eternal objective Logos. To penetrate the mystery of that Logos is the prerogative not of one nation, one cultural unit, one or even all past ages of culture, but it is the prerogative only of all of them together, including those of the future, in the solidarity of spatial and temporal cooperation among the particular subjects of culture, which are irreplaceable because of their individual and unique character in each and every case.[61]

For Scheler, the peculiar perspective of any society or age and its angle of approach to the absolute are relative. Because of their inherent finitude, no people or epoch can exhaust the infinite realm of truths and values. But all apparent relativism is ultimately transcended by the existence of a reality that unifies the partial truths and values of human history, namely, "the idea of the eternal objective Logos." [62] This eternal Logos is for Scheler the Archimedean point beyond time and space in which he could anchor his theory of absolute values and which was the ultimate refutation of any relativism. It is by participating in this "eternal objective Logos" that all particular cultural values and norms gain their validity.

V

THE MUTABLE DIMENSIONS IN ETHICS—
ELABORATION OF SCHELER'S INSIGHTS
BY J. GRÜNDEL

Max Scheler was always acutely aware that his own philosophical reflections on the historical dimensions of ethics were only fragments which were in need of further development, refinement and systematization. He encouraged others to ad-

[61] *Ibid.*, p. 27.
[62] *Ibid.*

vance his own fragmentary insights,[63] and many philosophers and theologians since have taken up the challenge. It would seem appropriate at this point to briefly delineate one recent attempt at explaining the historical character of value comprehension.

Johannes Gründel, in his book on the mutable and immutable elements in morals,[64] offers some valuable philosophical insights on change and progress in ethics. He tries to justify change in morals by applying the ancient axiom *agere sequitur esse*. His basic assertion is: since oughtness or the moral demands are based on being, a change in being rightly brings about also a modification in oughtness. Hominisation or man's "becoming man" (*Menschwerdung*) is a continuous evolutionary process. Man experiences himself as a "becoming being" (*als ein Werdender*) who has to continuously realize his own self.[65] The demands of the natural law and ethics in general at any given time can be discovered only by taking into account both the immutable dimensions of man's nature and the three dimensions of man which are undergoing continuous change. The three basic dimensions of change are based (1) on an expansion and deepening of human knowledge, (2) on a mutation of life-situations, and (3) on a mutation of man himself.[66]

Let us now consider each of these dimensions in turn. The first dimension of change in man is based on an expansion and deepening of human knowledge. A deepening of human knowledge leads to a greater precision in moral questions and frequently to certain modifications of traditional ethical positions. Such changes, however, need not always imply a relaxation of ethical demands. The Church's teaching on abortion, for example, shows that in this case the opposite took place. In 1872 the Holy Office, being asked about the morality of craniotomy, recommended the consultation of approved authors and prudent

[63] For example, FORM, p. 22.
[64] Johannes Gründel, *Wandelbares und Unwandelbares in der Moraltheologie: Erwägungen zur Moraltheologie an Hand des Axioms "agere sequitur esse."* (Düsseldorf: Patmos-Verlag, 1967).
[65] *Ibid.*, p. 37.
[66] *Ibid.*, pp. 46-73.

action.[67] However, the Church took a much firmer stand as she gradually gained deeper insight into human life and personhood. By 1889 the Church's attitude concerning the morality of craniotomy was still a mere *tuto doceri non posse;* only in 1895 was craniotomy clearly condemned.

During the past decade significant insights have been gained regarding human personhood. On the basis of this new knowledge man feels, for example, morally justified while intervening in physiological processes which may harm the bodily integrity but which are for the good of the person.

The "dialogic character" of man, as developed by Ferdinand Ebner and Martin Buber, and the personalism of Theodor Steinbüchel, Romano Guardini, Emil Brunner and Karl Rahner, revealed new insights into the moral significance of interpersonal relationships. These relationships had not previously been adequately taken into account by moral philosophers. Sin, for example, is no longer considered primarily a transgression of a law, but is considered in four dimensions as a wrong against society, a personal offense against God, an offense against one's fellow men, and a failure in the self-realization of one's own personhood.[68]

The more man gets to know himself, the more he discovers the incomprehensible and mysterious character of the human person (the *ineffabile*). As God is ultimately a *Mysterium,* so man, his image, is something of a mystery. In an analogy to a *theologia negativa* one could speak also of an *anthropologia negativa.* To the extent man deepens his knowledge, he will become more aware of his ignorance; and, penetrating more deeply into the growing complexities of life, he will begin to see ethics no longer as a static set of rules, but as a continuous quest that at any given time has to start anew searching and groping for the true and the good.[69]

---

[67] *Acta Apostolica Sedis* 7 (1872), pp. 285ff.; 460ff.; 516ff.: Consulat probatos auctores sive veteres sive recentiores et prudenter agat.

[68] Gründel, pp. 50-51. Cf. also Karl Rahner, "Vergessene Wahrheiten über das Bussakrament," in *Schriften zur Theologie,* II (Einsiedeln: Benziger Verlag, 1957), pp. 144-148.

[69] *Ibid.,* pp. 47-59.

The second dimension of change in man is based on a mutation of life-situations.[70] The conditions of modern life have undergone extensive modifications, and consequently, numerous moral evaluations will differ from those of former times. Historical studies show that changes of this kind have taken place, for example, in the appraisal of sexuality and marriage, in the doctrine on property and interest, on the just war, and in the whole realm of social ethics.

A presently much discussed question is the morality of atomic warfare. It is felt that one cannot simply apply the old norms for a just war in a situation where the total destruction of mankind becomes a real possibility.

A classical instance in which change of the situation has resulted in a change of moral teaching is lending money for interest. The medieval Church, condemning lending money for interest, intended to protect the poor from exploitation by rich money-lenders. When economic conditions changed and money changed its nature and became productive as "capital," the morality of money-lending and interest was modified, too.

During the past centuries, individualism has been predominant both in society and in moral philosophy. As mankind emerges now from an individualistic age and realizes the need of developing into a community-oriented universal family of men, moral awareness is also shifting from an individualistic morality to a community-conscious moral philosophy and theology.[71]

The third dimension of change in man is based on a mutation

[70] *Ibid.*, pp. 59-65.

[71] The shift in moral teaching is reflected in the documents of Vatican II. The following text is an informative example: "Profound and rapid changes make it particularly urgent that no one, ignoring the trend of events or drugged by laziness, content himself with a merely individualistic morality. It grows increasingly true that the obligations of justice and love are fulfilled only if each person, contributing to the common good, according to his own abilities and the needs of others, also promotes and assists the public and private institutions dedicated to bettering the conditions of human life." Walter Abbot, S.J., ed., *The Documents of Vatican II* (New York: Guild Press, 1966), p. 228 (=*Pastoral Constitution on the Church in the Modern World*, no. 30).

of man himself.[72] A simple example of "change of being" (*Seinsänderung*) in the life of an individual and a consequent change of moral obligation can be seen in the relationship between children and parents. A young child has a true obligation to obey his parents. But to the extent he grows up and reaches maturity this obligation decreases and eventually terminates completely. Of course, there always remain certain obligations of a child toward his parents, but the obedience that is characteristic of a minor (*Führungsgehorsam*) will and must come to an end. This example shows that to the extent that the being of man changes, i.e. as a man matures, the corresponding oughtness undergoes a transformation too.

The same principle not only holds true with regard to an individual human being, but it also applies to a whole community. A good example would be the attitude of citizens toward their civil and ecclesiastical authorities. If the obedience demanded by these authorities were based on the immaturity of the citizens (*Führungsgehorsam*)rather than on the necessity of securing order in the community (*Gemeinschafts- oder Ordnungsgehorsam*), these demands would oblige only as long as the immaturity in the individual persisted.

In the past, Christian thought has been strongly influenced by a static conception of the world and of man, a view which was taken over from the Greeks. It was not sufficiently realized that man's nature is not a fixed entity but it is in the process of constant evolution. An important aspect of human historicity is the truth that man is not simply subject to an historical process that affects him from the outside; he himself is also a maker of history and in this process can change his own being to a certain extent. As Karl Rahner has pointed out, it may well be in the plan of the *creatio continua* that man should, through self-manipulation and active hominisation, transform his own being and develop new human dimensions the exact forms of which only the future will disclose.[73]

[72] *Gründel*, pp. 66-73.
[73] Karl Rahner, "Experiment Mensch. Theologisches über die

Gründel concludes that, besides the principles of natural law, we must accept another source of moral oughtness.[74] This one would be based on the mutable layers of man's being. Man evolves in history and in this historical process only gradually becomes himself (*geshichtliche Selbstwerdung des Menschen*). It follows that certain moral obligations of yesterday no longer apply, and that new moral obligations might emerge today which did not possess the same urgency in former times. Applying the principle *agere sequitur esse,* one may infer that, as a man's being changes, so will the demands of moral oughtness.

Selbstmanipulation des Menschen," in *Die Frage nach dem Menschen. Aufriss einer philosophischen Anthropologie. Festschrift für Max Müller zum 60 Geburtstag,* ed. H. Rombach (Freiburg: Alber, 1966), pp. 45-69. Karl Rahner, "Experiment Man," *Theology Digest* (February, 1968), 57-69.

[74] Gründel, p. 73.

III
Ethos and the Historicity of Ethics

Scheler understands by ethos the structure of value experience, of the rules of preference of values, and of the forms of love and hate that are prevalent among a specific group of people at a given historical period.[1] In further clarifying the concept of ethos, Scheler states that ethos corresponds to the concept of *Weltanschauung* in the intellectual sphere and to the "structure of living faith" in the religious sphere.[2] As *Weltanschauung* is the basic structure of looking at the world in general, so ethos signifies man's basic approach to the realm of moral values. Or as "living faith" concerns the actual religious experience and practice of man in contrast to the theoretical sphere of theological reflection, so ethos is concerned with the actual moral experience and practice of man as distinguished from the intellectual reflections on morals which are the field of ethics.

I
ETHOS

Ethics, according to Scheler, is the philosophical systematization, carried out in judgments, of the values and hierarchical value relations which are given in the acts and functions of feeling, preferring and loving.[3] Scheler also defines ethics as "the

[1] FORM, pp. 303, 306.
[2] FORM, p. 303.
[3] UMST, p. 410.

85

judgmental and conceptual formulations of values and of the hierarchical relations between them given in emotional intentions, and of the principles of valuation and the establishing of norms based on these values and relations." [4]

The ethos is a social and historical reality, always subject to historical change and further development. The full experience of the cosmos of values is dependent on the historically evolving forms of ethos.[5] We are touching here the very nerve center of Scheler's understanding of historicity: "The inner history of ethos itself [is the] most central history of all history." [6]

By rendering explicit the central role of ethos and ethos forms within moral philosophy, Scheler championed in pioneer fashion an important dimension in the realm of ethical thought.

II

ETHOS AND THE REALM OF VALUES

The realm of values is beyond time and history, absolute and eternally valid. The eternal values possess, however, an inner dynamism toward actualization in history and are thus in need of a finite historical concretization and incarnation in the medium of lived and experienced forms of ethos. A concrete ethos is a finite, selective participation in the infinite sphere of values. The totality of the realm of values remains always beyond the limited horizon of human knowledge and experience. But through the lived experience of types of ethos, which vary in history and yet make their definite demands on people of a given period, man can share in a limited way in the absolute sphere of values.

This theory of participation is Scheler's attempt at overcoming moral relativism. Scheler extols the importance of the variable dimension of historically changing forms of ethos. At the same time he tries to safeguard the absoluteness of the infinite sphere of values.

[4] FORM, p. 311.
[5] *Ibid.*, p. 308.
[6] *Ibid.*, p. 309.

Lewis A. Coser has described Scheler's theory of the relationship between the varying forms of ethos and the absolute sphere of values this way:

Different value systems and different forms of knowledge testify to the universal striving to reach a world of pure essences through a plurality of avenues. We can attain a view of this world only through glasses ground by the temporal, historical, social conditions in which we have been placed, but this does not deny the reality of this world. The unlimited variety of perspectives is like an infinity of searchlights which human beings throw upon the hidden grandeur of the world of essences.[7]

Johannes Messner, whose ethical thinking is profoundly influenced by Scheler,[8] has reformulated in a felicitous manner some of Scheler's basic insights. For example, he applies the relationship between the immutable realm of values and the mutable forms of ethos to the problem of the invariability and variability of the natural law:

For nations also there is but one natural law—the same for all—with which, however, the diversity of their individual ethos forms can harmonize well. Because of their distinctive gifts and the state of their cultural development, individual nations display a variety of special moral faculties and special moral values, for example, courage, purity, loyalty, sobriety, industry, thrift. Just as some nations are extolled for their outstanding achievements in various fields of cultural life, such as statecraft, philosophy, poetry, and music, so also the moral order common to all mankind

---

[7] Lewis A. Coser, "Max Scheler: An Introduction," in Max Scheler, *Ressentiment,* trans. by William W. Holdheim, and ed. with an introduction by Lewis A. Coser (New York: The Free Press of Glencoe, 1961), p. 18.

[8] Johannes Messner, *Das Naturrecht* (5th ed. rev.; Innsbruck: Tyrolia-Verlag, 1966), p. 246: "Dies ist eine Gelegenheit wieder daran zu erinnern, wie sehr wir uns (unser 'Naturrecht' and unsere 'Kulturethik' zeigen es) dem Werk Schelers verpflichtet wissen."

shines forth in a colorful spectrum of moral traits distinctive of the various nations. Again, however, it is clear that in the very diversity in the functioning of natural law there is evident testimony of its invariability with regard to its fundamental principles and of the sameness of the elementary moral consciousness of mankind.[9]

Scheler's view of the relationship between ethos and the total realm of values could be described as a value-perspectivism of historical and sociological units. There is no relativism of moral values themselves and of their essential hierarchy. Rather, depending upon the perspectives from distinct socio-historical vantage points, various people grasp and actualize, through the medium of different forms of ethos, particular dimensions of the cosmos of values.[10]

III

THE VARIATIONS OF ETHOS

In an important chapter of his *Formalismus,* Scheler addresses himself to the problem of ethical absolutism and the different types of relativity in morals.[11] His major concern is to show that changes and transformations in ethics can be explained in a manner which does not necessitate that one embrace the position of ethical relativism. Scheler achieves his objective by analyzing different types of relativity and by establishing that these types of variations do not affect the objectivity of the values themselves. By admitting and, in fact, emphasizing various historical changes in ethics, Scheler acknowledges the validity of most data proffered by ethical relativists. But by interpreting these facts in the light of his theory of multiple "variations" and

[9] *Ibid.,* p. 117. Cf. Johannes Messner, *Social Ethics. Natural Law in the Western World,* trans. by J. J. Doherty (3rd ed. rev.; St. Louis: B. Herder, 1965), p. 74.

[10] GES, p. 27; FORM, pp. 530-531.

[11] FORM, pp. 300-321: "Historische Relativität der ethischen Wertschätzungen und ihre Dimensionen."

of the underlying value philosophy, Scheler disproves the theory of relativism and replaces it with an explanation that can account for changes and yet maintain an ethical absolutism.

> There does exist an *ordre du coeur* and a *logique du coeur* —as Pascal says—which the moral genius gradually uncovers in history, and it is eternal—only its apprehension and acquisition is "historical." [12]

Scheler claims that an ethical absolutism which holds that there are eternal evident laws of preference and a corresponding eternal hierarchy of values can afford to acknowledge a far-reaching relativity of value-judgments. He compares the relation between the various moralities and the eternally valid sphere of values to that existing between different astronomical systems (for example, the Ptolemaic and the Copernican system) and the ideal system sought by astronomy. "That intrinsically valid system is represented more or less adequately in the different moralities." [13]

Thus, one can fully account for the cultural variables without sacrificing the transcultural constants.

> We avoid philosophical relativism . . . by lifting up the absolute realm of ideas and values corresponding to the essential idea of man far above factual historical value systems; for example, by viewing all orders of goods, ends, and norms of human society in ethics, religion, law, art, as something relative and as conditioned by a historical and sociological standpoint, preserving nothing but the idea of the eternal objective Logos.[14]

In his analysis of historical relativities which coexist with an authentic objectivism of values, Scheler distinguishes five main types of variations or dimensions of relativity. We will briefly

[12] UMST, p. 63.
[13] UMST, p. 69.
[14] GES, pp. 26-27.

present these five variations and then discuss in somewhat greater detail the first type, namely the variations of ethos.[15]

1. Variations of ethos. These refer to variations in value feeling and value knowledge as well as variations in the structure of value preference and of love and hatred.

2. Variations of ethics, that is, variations on the level of judgments concerning values, their mutual relations and their hierarchical order of rank.

3. Variations of morals. These are variations of the types of institutions, goods and actions which function as units because they are founded upon particular units of values. Marriage, monogamy, murder, theft and lying are examples of such units which presuppose certain values. Not all forms of killing are murder, for murder presupposes the conscious destruction of a person as the carrier of personal values. Similarly, there would be no adultery or theft without specific organizations regarding sex or property.

4. Variations of practical morality. These are variations in the evaluation of practical conduct based on norms which are derived from values recognized in the ethos of a given time. The value of practical conduct depends upon the prevailing ethos and may not be appraised according to the ethos of another historical period or of a different people.

5. Variations of mores (*Sitten*) and customs (*Bräuche*). Mores and customs are forms of action and expression rooted in tradition. The tradition is of moral relevancy since it originates from and is shaped by an underlying ethos which is the norm of practical morality as well as of mores and customs.

Of the five types of variations sketched above, the first one, that is the variation of ethos, is dealt with at greater length in Scheler's writings. The main point Scheler wants to establish is that the alleged relativity of values is in reality a relativity of valuations. Ethical relativism falsely concludes from a historically evolving experience of values that the values themselves are changing.[16] Such value relativism results from absolutizing the

15 FORM, pp. 300-321.
16 *Ibid.*, pp. 307-308.

value perception of one's own time and culture and from a lack of reverence for the richness of the realm of values that far transcends the limited perception of any particular historical period.

Scheler sees the most radical form of a change and growth of ethos in the discovery of higher values which takes place in and through the dynamism of love. It is the "moral-religious genius" to whom the kingdom of values discloses itself and reveals values formerly not intuited and experienced.[17]

The most impressive example of such a discovery of new dimensions of values can be seen in the Sermon on the Mount. The perception of new and higher values goes hand in hand with a certain relativization of the old values as is evident in the reappraisal of the "law-values" in view of the "But I say to you" (Mt 5:22).[18]

Besides discovering new areas in the realm of values there can be variations in the experience of values already known. Since these are always intuited as a hierarchical order of higher and lower values, in the course of history some values may be experienced as being higher than was previously realized.

We might concretize this insight of Scheler by offering one example. During the cosmological age man considered himself as part of a sacred cosmos and he patterned his moral life largely in terms of a legal order which was similar to the general natural law and order he observed around him in nature. When the cosmological age was superseded by the anthropological age, man freed himself more and more from nature, defining himself no longer in terms of cosmos or nature, but rather as a unique human person. A new personalistic and anthropologically-oriented ethics resulted from this evolution of man's self-understanding. The transition from a nature-oriented to a man-centered outlook brought about a profound reappraisal of the relative importance of different moral values, imparting a high priority on those values that are person-oriented.[19]

[17] *Ibid.*, p. 309.
[18] *Ibid.*
[19] Cf. Hans Urs von Balthasar, *The God Question and Modern Man* (New York: The Seabury Press, 1967).

As the above example shows, the ethos is capable of progress and growth. It is, however, also capable of decline and falsification. In chapter V we will investigate this point in greater detail. Scheler studies especially one factor as being responsible for the decline of an ethos, namely resentment. Resentment is characterized as "the feeling of revengeful impotence which substitutes pseudo-values of its own making for the genuine values which it is unable to reach." [20]

We mentioned earlier that in developing his ideas on the variations of ethos Scheler was primarily concerned with a refutation of ethical relativism. He wanted to show that we can acknowledge multiple variations in the ethical sphere and yet maintain a realm of absolute values beyond all historical changes. Scheler had, however, one more objective in mind. He wanted to counteract the tendencies prevalent in his time which narrowed the plenitude of the moral realm and excluded those dimensions that would not fit into the neat but inadequate categories of a rationalist mind. The theory of multiple types of ethos provides an antidote to the temptations of reductionism, i.e. to the temptations of reducing the abounding plenitude of moral values to some selected ones in accordance with the limited axiological horizon of a given historical period. The theory of varying types of ethos takes into full account all aspects of axiological experience, including those of the past and of the future. It remains always open for new ethical experiences. Future generations may, indeed, penetrate more deeply into the realm of values and discover dimensions not yet disclosed to the present period of history.[21] Narrowness in the ethical realm and value-

[20] Herbert Spiegelberg, *The Phenomenological Movement* (2 vols.; The Hague: Martinus Nijhoff, 1965), I, 258.

[21] Henri Bergson would later take up this question and reemphasize the importance of an open morality as a complimentary dimension to a closed morality. Bergson does not use the term "ethos" but his ideas show a remarkable affinity to Scheler's when he speaks of an open, creative and dynamic morality which looks to the future and represents a forward thrust of the *élan vital*. The role that Bergson, in his open morality, accords to leaders, saints and mystics bears considerable semblance to the ideas on the function of models (*Vorbilder*) for the growth of ethos forms which Scheler had developed twenty years earlier. Cf. Henri Bergson, *The Two Sources of Morality and*

blindness are among the major shortcomings of modern society. The doctrine on ethos provides a cure by widening man's vision toward the inexhaustible richness, the variety and multiplicity of the axiological horizon and toward the total breadth and depth of man's potential axiological experience.

IV
ETHOS AND MODELS (VORBILDER)

Regarding the origin and change of different types of ethos Scheler attaches particular significance to the role of the models (*Vorbilder*) or the value-person-types (*Wertpersontypen*).[22] Each period in history has its own special models or exemplary persons, and these personal models ultimately determine the predominant ethos of an age.[23] Changes and transformations in types of ethos occur through the emergence of new value-person-types.

With his doctrine on value-person-types, Scheler intended to give a concrete status to the otherwise abstract values.[24] The eternal values need to be embodied in social models or value-person-types of a specific historical epoch. Only through the medium of such exemplary persons do the values inspire people and attract them to actualize these values in their own lives.

The different value-person-types represent a hierarchy which corresponds to the hierarchy of values. Scheler delineates the following basic types: saint, genius, hero, leading spirit of civ-

---

Religion, trans. by R. Ashley Audra and Cloudsley Brereton (Garden City, N.Y.: Doubleday, 1954). The French edition of the book was first published in 1932.

[22] Since we shall discuss systematically the question of "Value-Person-Types" in chapter VIII, we shall restrict ourselves here to a brief description of the function of models (*Vorbilder*) in the origin of new forms of ethos.

[23] Max Scheler, *Philosophische Weltanschauung,* pp. 33-35; FORM, pp. 558-568.

[24] Kaspar Hürlimann, "Person und Werte. Eine Untersuchung über den Sinn von Max Schelers Doppeldevise: 'Materiale Wertethik' und 'Ethischer Personalismus,'" *Divus Thomas,* XXX (September, 1952), 273-298; (December, 1952), 385-416.

ilization and "artist of enjoyment" (*Künstler des Genusses*).[25] In real life, these basic types usually occur in various combinations. A saint, for example, may also be a hero or a genius.

To understand the ethos of a certain period, one must explore the value-person-types who ultimately originated and shaped this ethos.[26] Scheler has investigated in greater detail the mutual relationship between models and ethos with regard to one historical period, the epoch of modern capitalism.[27] He concludes that it was the model of the *bourgeois* which brought about the new ethos of modern capitalism.

In his reflections on the philosophy of history, Scheler emphasizes again the extraordinary function of models (*Vorbilder*) in the history of ethos forms. He distinguishes three layers in history: first, what actually happened (*das wirkliche Geschehen*); second, the types of ethos, the ideals, systems of values and norms which precede and underlie the factual events and which are the "soul of all history" (*Seele aller Geschichte*); third, the models (*Vorbilder*). The history of these models, of their origin and transformation, is "the innermost core of the soul of history" (*der eigentliche Kern dieser Seele der Geschichte*).[28]

V

ETHOS AND SOCIAL CLASSES

Scheler does not offer a systematic study on the origin of different ethos forms in history, but scattered throughout his work are examples explaining the genesis of specific ethos forms and the causal factors that helped a certain ethos to become dominant in a particular people at a particular time.

One interesting paradigm for the origin of an ethos form can

[25] FORM, p. 570; NACH, pp. 257-344.
[26] FORM, p. 565.
[27] Max Scheler, "Der Bourgeois—Der Bourgeois und die religiösen Mächte—Die Zukunft des Kapitalismus. Drei Aufsätze zum Problem des kapitalistischen Geistes," *Vom Umsturz der Werte*, pp. 341-395. Cf. FORM, p. 565: "Vgl. dazu meinen Aufsatz über den 'Bourgeois.' "
[28] Max Scheler, "Vorbilder und Führer," *Schriften aus dem Nachlass*, Band I, p. 268.

be found in the essay "Problems of a Sociology of Knowledge." [29] Scheler states here that social classes "determine largely not only the object and content of thinking and knowing but also the ethos and the thought pattern." [30] Even the formal types of thinking and of value-perception (*Wertnehmung*) differ according to social classes. Scheler refers here to living thought patterns, or "class-conditioned tendencies of a subconscious nature," [31] not to a reflective knowing of these forms of perception. Setting his own position clearly apart from the Marxist view, Scheler states that social classes cannot impart objective validity to systems of thinking and of valuating, they can only select and choose from among possible systems. Besides, no member of a social class is determined by the type of thinking and value-perception (*Wertnehmung*) of his class; everyone has the freedom to break out of the bonds and ties that are operative in a social class. The following sketch of typical class-conditioned modes of thinking should, therefore, be understood as presenting general tendencies or trends, not as a social determination of every member of the lower or upper class. These modes of thinking influence the ethos of a certain period and people; they are, however, not exclusive determinants, since other factors, too, enter into the genesis of a certain form of ethos.

Lower class tendencies: [32]	Higher class tendencies:
1. Prospective time consciousness	Retrospective time consciousness
2. Emphasis on becoming	Emphasis on being
3. Mechanistic conception of the world	Teleogical conception of the world

[29] "Probleme einer Soziologie des Wissens," in *Die Wissensformen und die Gesellschaft,* pp. 170-175.

[30] *Ibid.,* p. 171.

[31] *Ibid.,* p. 172.

[32] *Ibid.,* pp. 171-172. What follows is partly a paraphrase of Scheler's table by Werner Stark in *The Sociology of Knowledge* (Glencoe, Ill.: The Free Press, 1958), pp. 77-78.

4. Realism in philosophy; the world as "resistance"	Idealism in philosophy; the world as a "realm of ideas"
5. Materialism	Spiritualism
6. Induction, empiricism	A priori knowledge, rationalism
7. Pragmatism	Intellectualism
8. Optimism with regard to the future; the past as the "bad old days"	Pessimism with regard to the future; the past as the "good old days"
9. A dialectical mode of thinking; search for contradictions	Search for identities and harmonies
10. Emphasis on environmental influences	Emphasis on heredity and tradition

VI
ETHOS AND HISTORY

The idea that history reveals a multiplicity of ethos structures has been developed by several philosophers and historians. The conceptual formulations and the particular aspects under which they approach the subject differ, but basically there is an underlying similarity of insight. Friedrich Nietzsche spoke of "tablets of values" (*Tafeln der Güter*).[33] Wilhelm Dilthey wrote of different types of "world views" (*Weltanschauungen*),[34] each of which is historically conditioned by space and time.

[33] Friedrich Nietzsche, *Also sprach Zarathustra* (München: Goldmann-Verlag, 1966), pp. 46-47.
[34] Wilhelm Dilthey, *Gesammelte Schriften* (12 vols.; Leipzig: Teubner, 1940), VIII, 222: "Dieses unermessliche, unfassliche, unergründliche Universum spiegelt sich mannigfach in religiösen Sehern, in Dichtern und Philosophen. Sie stehen alle unter der Macht des Ortes und der Stunde. Jede Weltanschauung ist historisch bedingt, sonach beschränkt, relativ."

Eduard Spranger called it "life-forms" (*Lebensformen*).[35] Erich Rothacker, who is strongly influenced by Scheler, developed the idea of "life-styles" (*Lebensstile*);[36] Otto Friedrich Bollnow distinguished different "forms of high ethos" (*Formen des hohen Ethos*).[37] Finally, Tetsuro Watsuji proposed a theory of different ethos structures evolving out of and conditioned by the climatic features of various geographic regions (*fuudo*).[38]

Nicolai Hartmann who acknowledges his inspiration from, and indebtedness to Scheler's ethics, offers a theory on the "revolution of ethos" which illustrates and further develops Scheler's ideas on this subject.[39] According to Hartmann, we can observe an historical development in the perception of values by mankind as a whole, in an analogous fashion to the growth of value perception in an individual. This maturing is, however, not necessarily a true progress. For, due to the essential limitations of man's value consciousness, the discovery or unveiling of new values brings with it a forgetting or vanishing of values which were prevalent during previous periods of human history.[40] In any given period, mankind can perceive and actualize only a limited sector of the total realm of values. But the selected sets of values which constitute the ethos of a time are frequently changing. Hartmann illustrates the change of ethos with the image of a circle of light (M_1 to M_4 in the drawing) which is shifting and, at any given period of history, illuminates one particular sector of the realm of values.[41]

[35] Eduard Spranger, *Lebensformen: Geisteswissenschaftliche Psychologie und Ethik der Persönlichkeit* (Hamburg: Siebenstern Taschenbuchverlag, 1965). English translation: *Types of Men. The Psychology and Ethics of Personality* (Halle: Niemeyer Verlag, 1928).

[36] Erich Rothacker, *Geschichtsphilosophie* (Munich: R. Oldenbourg Verlag, 1934).

[37] Otto Friedrich Bollnow, *Einfache Sittlichkeit* (3rd ed. rev.; Göttingen: Vandenhoeck & Ruprecht, 1962), pp. 20-30.

[38] Tetsuro Watsuji, *Fuudo* (Tokyo: Iwanami, 1963). English translation: *A Climate* (Tokyo: Japanese National Commission for UNESCO, 1961).

[39] Nicolai Hartmann, *Einführung in die Philosophie* (Hannover: Luise Hanckel Verlag, 1952), pp. 175-177. Nicolai Hartmann, *Ethik* (Berlin: Walter de Gruyter, 1962), pp. 47-63.

[40] *Einführung in die Philosophie*, p. 175.

[41] *Ibid.*, p. 176.

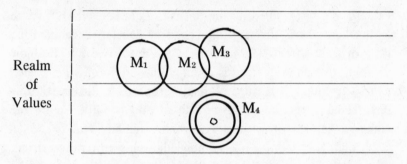

This, however, does not result in an ethical relativism. In the change of ethos, the values themselves do not shift. Their nature is beyond time and history. It is only the consciousness of values that shifts and changes in history. At any given period in history, this consciousness cuts out from the whole a small circle of perceived values. As the drawing shows, the small circle wanders on the ideal plane of values.

It is not necessarily a desirable goal to develop the broadest possible value consciousness. For, if the value content broadens, the intensity and immediateness of the sense of values decrease. A limited, distinct ethos may be one-sided, but it is precisely this one-sidedness that gives man's moral life a characteristic acuteness, a passionate devotion and a creative dynamism.[42]

With regard to the historical changes of ethos forms, Hartmann offers an interesting distinction between a new ethos as a lived experience and as a reflective intellectual appropriation and explicit formulation by the men of ideas.[43] Men of ideas do not have the power to create a new ethos; they play the role of secondary discoverers and systematizers. First there has to be the lived experience of the masses:

> Only that for which the times are ripe, only that which has matured in the living ethos of man, only that which through moral suffering and yearning has become ripe for utterance, has effective power.[44]

[42] Nicolai Hartmann, *Ethik* (Berlin: Walter de Gruyter, 1962), p. 49.
[43] *Ibid.*, pp. 49-54.
[44] *Ibid.*, p. 50.

A man of ideas can live before the ground is ready for the new ethos. This man will die in solitude without seeing his ideas become alive in his time. The man of ideas has to be present when in the lived experience of the masses the new ethos is arising. Then, he is the "midwife of the crowd, and compels it at the fateful hour of its ethos to bring forth that which is most alive in it." [45]

Otto Friedrich Bollnow, who shows a remarkable affinity to the ethical insights of Max Scheler, in his moral teaching takes up the idea of ethos and develops it a step further. Faced with the chaotic situation of post-war Europe and groping for a new ethos as a basis for spiritual renewal, in 1945 Bollnow wrote his *Einfache Sittlichkeit*.[46] According to Bollnow, we must distinguish between forms of high ethos which are changing in history, and an underlying simple morality (the *einfache Sittlichkeit* of the title) which remains the same in history. Forms of high ethos are, for example, the ascetical ideal of early Christianity, the knighthood ideal of the Middle Ages, the humanistic ideal of German classicism and the Kantian ethics of duty. Such ideals arise at a given point in history and then decline. Underlying these changing forms of high ethos, is a simple morality which lacks the greatness and heroic dimension of the forms of high ethos but which presents instead in its commonness and simplicity, a permanent element in ethics. This simple morality is characterized by virtues like honesty, veracity, reliability, openness, natural goodness, compassion for the sufferings of one's fellow men and a readiness to help them. This simple morality offers a solid foundation for man's moral life. It is by itself, however, not sufficient and needs the complementary dimension of high ethos. Each dimension needs the other, and both complement one another.

An interesting, although limited, parallel to Scheler's view regarding the changing types of ethos in history can be found in

[45] *Ibid.*, p. 51.
[46] Otto Friedrich Bollnow, *Einfache Sittlichkeit* (3rd ed. rev.; Göttingen: Vandenhoeck & Ruprecht, 1962).

the philosophy of history of Japanese Buddhism.[47] Mahayana Buddhism divides history after Buddha's death into three periods. The first thousand years is called the Period of the Perfect Law (*Shoo-boo*). It was the time when the religious discipline was genuinely and perfectly observed. The second thousand years was the Period of the Copied Law (*Zoo-boo*). During this time true faith declined and the religion of Buddha was practiced only by imitating the religious personalities of the past. The third and last phase of history is called the Period of the Latter Law (*Map-poo*). This is the age of open degeneration, of corruption, of vice and violence. Assuming the year 949 B.C. as the date of Buddha's death, Buddhists widely held that the Period of the Latter Law was to start in the year A.D. 1052.

The parallel to Scheler's view lies in the emphasis Japanese Buddhists put on the fact that "man is an existence in history" [48] and in the close relationship they posit between the three periods of history and the religious-moral life corresponding to each of these periods. With the beginning of the third period, most Buddhist sects in Japan taught that doctrine and morality should be adapted and accommodated to the present time. Realizing that they were living in the age of degeneration, Buddhist leaders did not exhort their followers to return to the Perfect or even to the Copied Law. Instead "they claimed that the exigencies of the time should be considered and religious doctrines made suitable to them." [49] Nichiren, the founder of the Nichiren sect, welcomed the processes of time and history, even if they brought corruption. Both Nichiren and Saichoo regarded time and space as important factors for evaluating religious truth, and moral imperatives. The emphasis on the time element stands out in the following passage from Nichiren:

[47] Hajime Nakamura, *A History of the Development of Japanese Thought* (2 vols.; Tokyo: Kokusai Bunka Shinkokai, 1967), I, pp. 100-104. Ryusaku Tsunoda, Wm. Theodore de Bary, and Donald Keene, *Sources of Japanese Tradition* (2 vols.; New York: Columbia University Press, 1964), I, pp. 203-224. Masaharu Anesaki, *History of Japanese Religion* (Tokyo: Charles E. Tuttle, 1968), pp. 149-151.

[48] Nakamura, *op. cit.*, p. 102.

[49] *Ibid.*, p. 100.

The learning of just one word or one phrase of the Right
Law, if only it accords with the time and the propensity of
the learner, would lead him to the attainment of the Way.
The mastery of a thousand scriptures and ten thousand
theories, if they should not accord with the time and the
propensity of the one who masters them, would lead him
nowhere.[50]

Japanese Buddhists display a remarkable awareness of historicity in both religion and morals. However, this historical
consciousness is tainted by a major deficiency. Unlike Scheler's
value philosophy, the Buddhist philosophy of history lacks a
clear sense of an unchangeable, absolute realm of values; and,
consequently, it leads to relativism and develops an attitude of
easy compromise.[51] Furthermore, one cannot help detecting
a certain tone of fatalism, of simply yielding as to an inescapable
destiny. Scheler's awareness of historicity stands out more clearly
when contrasted to this Buddhist position. In Scheler's philosophy, man, in his thinking and in his ethos, is profoundly influenced by the process of history. But ultimately it is the free
decision of man that creates and shapes the ethos of any given
historical period. Man in his freedom is the subject and maker
of history.

VII

SOME CONCRETE FORMS OF ETHOS

So far, we have discussed the problem of ethos in a rather
general way. Scheler concretizes his general ideas by delineating
some concrete forms of ethos. The descriptions of these different types can help to illuminate and clarify points that have
remained somewhat vague in the preceding theoretical discus-

[50] *Shoowa Shinshuu Nichiren Shoonin Imon Zenshuu* (Kyoto:
Heirakuji Shoten, 1934), vol. I, p. 842. Quoted in Nakamura, *op. cit.*,
p. 101.
[51] Shoko Watanabe, *Japanese Buddhism: A Critical Appraisal* (Tokyo:
Kokusai Bunka Shinkokai, 1968), pp. 58-59.

sion. We will now take a closer look at four concrete forms, (a) the Prussian ethos, (b) the Franciscan ethos, (c) the ethos of modern industrialism, and (d) the esthetic ethos of Japan.

The Prussian Ethos

In his essay "On the Betrayal of Joy" (*Vom Verrat der Freude*),[52] Scheler describes an important aspect of the Prussian ethos. As the title indicates, the ethos of Prussia has betrayed the Christian spirit of joy, opting instead for a spirit of false heroism and inhuman duty. The betrayal of joy began with Kant who, in his battle against eudaimonism in ethics, threw the baby out with the bathwater. Kant did not comprehend the genuine significance of joy in the moral life of man. His was a truncated view which failed to appreciate the deeper dimensions of joy. His was unlike the intellectual joy of activity included in Aristotle's concept of *eudaimonia,* the *hilaritas et serenitas* of the Romans, and the Christian beatitude which could fill the hearts of martyrs even amid the agony of burning flames.[53] Kant, whose thinking proved to be decisive in the formation of the Prussian ethos, reduced the concepts of happiness and joy to sensual feelings. According to Scheler, the heroic anti-eudaimonism and the negative concept of happiness inaugurated by Kant exerted a deep influence on Fichte, Hegel, Schopenhauer, and E. v. Hartmann.[54] Hegel's claim that "world-history is not the soil for happiness," is just another expression of the "betrayal of joy" characteristic of Prussia's ethos.

Scheler analyzes the genealogy of Prussia's joyless ethos under three aspects: (a) the tradition of the tribe, (b) the spirit of the state, and (c) the landscape, climate and people.[55]

[52] "Vom Verrat der Freude," in *Schriften zur Soziologie und Weltanschauungslehre,* pp. 73-76. This essay is also printed in Scheler's *Liebe und Erkenntnis* (Bern: Francke Verlag, 1955), pp. 69-72. The following quotations are from the former edition.

[53] *Ibid.,* p. 73.

[54] *Ibid.,* p. 74.

[55] *Ibid.,* pp. 74-75.

The tradition of the tribe is that of a strict and ascetical knight-hood colonizing the soil of Prussia. All energies are directed toward action, achievement, order and domination. A poor, unwieldy and resisting nature had to be brought under control, and this demanding task formed, in turn, the colonizing tribe. In sharp contrast, the tribes along the Rhine and in the southern part of the country were blessed with a friendlier nature and a richer culture; thus, they did not have to expend all their energies on will-power, hard work and domination, but could afford to develop also their emotional dimensions and the whole richness of their humanity.[56]

The second stream in the genealogy of the Prussian ethos is the spirit of the state, a spirit which finds its true incarnation in the mentality of Frederic the Great. The Prussian king despised happiness and personally was a joyless man. He took a deeply pessimistic view of human nature and even despised his own people. Dominated by a high sense of duty, Frederic, in the last analysis, did not know why and for what purpose he was doing his duty. His idea of duty seemed almost purposeless.[57]

Landscape, climate [58] and peoples constitute the third factor in the genealogy of the Prussian ethos. The lean and meager

[56] *Ibid.,* p. 74.
[57] *Ibid.,* pp. 74-75.
[58] Tetsuro Watsuji, the leading moral philosopher of modern Japan, was deeply influenced by Scheler and developed systematically the interrelationship between *fuudo* (the natural geographical setting conditioned by climate) and the way of life of peoples in different countries. In particular, he analyzed three characteristic climate zones, the monsoon, the desert and the pastoral zone. Watsuji shows how they have formed the ethos, the approach to reality and the life-style of their respective inhabitants. A passive attitude of receptivity (*juyoo*) and submissive resignation (*ninjuu*) are characteristic of people in the monsoon climate. India is the most typical example. The Buddhist doctrines of compassion (*jihi*) and benevolence (*jin*) which originated in India, express the basic attitude of the inhabitants of the monsoon climate. North-Africa and the Moslem culture were formed by the desert climate. A continuous battle with a meager soil and struggles for possession of rare oases and water sources have given a combative spirit to these people. Greece and Europe are examples of the pastoral zone. Rational spirit, order and the conquest of nature characterize the people of this region. Cf. Tetsuro Watsuji, *Fuudo* (Tokyo: Iwanami, 1933). English translation: *A Climate* (Tokyo: Japanese National Commission for UNESCO, 1961).

environment made man's life hard, offered little reward and thus led to a "betrayal of joy." In other parts of Europe, nature was more generous to its inhabitants and allowed them to rejoice in life. But with regard to Prussia, Scheler quotes approvingly Werner Sombart's witty and pertinent remark: "In such frugal and poor environment where nothing invites one to love and to joy, what else can one do but 'one's duty?' " [59]

Rejecting the truncated ethos of Prussia, Scheler emphasizes the importance of joy in man's moral life. Joy, although not the goal or aim, is the source and necessary concomitant of every good and noble life. Only the happy man is a good man, only the man who experiences bliss in God can be a good man. According to Scheler, Schiller's "Ode to Joy" which Beethoven took up in the fourth movement of his Ninth Symphony might be considered an antidote against the one-sided ethos of Prussia with its "betrayal of joy." [60]

The Franciscan Ethos

Scheler describes the Catholic ethos of St. Francis of Assisi and contrasts it with the Protestant ethos of Prussia. Whereas the Protestant ethos, according to Scheler, tends to "subjugate nature into an exclusive preserve for human control and activity," [61] the Catholic ethos of St. Francis emphasizes man's unity and identification with nature and his love of all created beings. [62] It was the remarkable achievement of St. Francis to unite within a single life-stream the Christian's personal love of God, his fellow man, and the cosmos. [63] St. Francis addresses sun and moon, fire and water, animals and plants, as his "brothers" and "sisters." Thus, he expands the traditional Christian

[59] "Vom Verrat der Freude," p. 75.
[60] Ibid., p. 76.
[61] SYM, p. 104; Sympathy, p. 94.
[62] SYM, pp. 96-104; Sympathy, pp. 87-95.
[63] SYM, p. 96; Sympathy, p. 87.

concept of personal love to include all the lower orders of nature. At the same time he achieves a subsuming of nature into the light and glory of the supernatural.[64] Nature is not primarily something to be dominated and exploited by man, as the Protestant ethos would have it. Rather, according to the vision of St. Francis, all creatures are regarded "as self-subsistent beings having, even in relation to man, intrinsic value of their own." [65] With Eros as the ultimate source of his union with nature, St. Francis turns with sympathy and love to all creatures.

His feeling toward nature is thus characterized:

> His loving soul discerns in every created thing a work of the invisible spiritual Creator, a stepping-stone from Nature towards God, a footstool for His feet, a manifestation of His glory—a visible and audible "Glory to God the Father. . . ." [66]

Scheler attaches a unique importance to the ethos of St. Francis. Never again in history, he says, have the emotional forces of sympathy been expressed in the same harmonious pattern. In the ethos of the great saint the emotional forces of sympathy achieve a unity and harmony of simultaneous activity in religion, love, social endeavor, art and knowledge such as we see nowhere else in human history.

Environmental studies of recent years have shown that the ethos of St. Francis has contributed richly to the new assessment of nature which is urgently needed if we want to save life on our planet earth from imminent doom. Some modern ecologists present Francis of Assisi as a patron saint of ecology [67] and propose his ethos as an antidote to the one-sided Calvinist ethos of modern

---

[64] *Ibid.*

[65] SYM, p. 98; *Sympathy,* p. 89.

[66] SYM, pp. 98-99; *Sympathy,* p. 89.

[67] Warren G. Hansen, *St. Francis of Assisi: Patron of the Environment* (Chicago: Franciscan Herald Press, 1970). Edward B. Fiske, "The Link between Faith and Ecology," *The New York Times,* January 4, 1970.

technology with its dominion-oriented approach to nature and environment.[68]

The Ethos of Modern Industrialism

In his essay on resentment, Scheler describes the ethos of modern industrialism.[69] Typical of this ethos is the tendency to place utilitarian and instrumental values over vital and organic values.[70] The same rule of preference permeates all value-judgments of this ethos: the "useful" is always placed higher than values of vitality and life. This reversal and falsification of the true hierarchy of values is ultimately due to the resentment of the slave revolt.[71] People of weaker vitality revolt in resentment against the stronger and reverse the hierarchy of values.[72]

The subordination of the "noble" (vital values) to the "useful" (utility values) manifests itself in numerous ways. The professional values of the merchants and industrialists, the qualities that enable this type of man to succeed in his business, are set up as the highest moral values.[73] New cardinal virtues appear: cleverness, quick adaptability, calculation, steadiness in work, industriousness and thrift. Less esteemed are now virtues like courage, bravery, loyalty and humility.[74] These virtues and

[68] The universal appeal of the ethos of St. Francis has been brought out in a recent study on the role of St. Francis in Japanese literature. A surprising number of non-Christian authors in Japan have written with great sympathy about St. Francis. There seems to exist a close affinity between the traditional Japanese love of nature and the similar attitude in the Christian saint. Maurus Heinrichs, *Der grosse Durchbruch. Franziskus von Assisi im Spiegel japanischer Literatur* (Werl: Dietrich-Coelde Verlag, 1969).

[69] "Das Ressentiment im Aufbau der Moralen," in *Vom Umsturz der Werte,* pp. 126-138. English translation: *Ressentiment,* ed. with an introduction by Lewis A. Coser, trans. by William W. Holdheim (New York: The Free Press of Glencoe, 1961), pp. 149-164. Henceforth, we shall quote the English translation as *Ressentiment* and the German original as UMST.

[70] *Ressentiment,* p. 162; UMST, p. 137.

[71] *Ibid.*

[72] Scheler adopts here ideas which were earlier expressed by Nietzsche.

[73] *Ressentiment,* pp. 155-156; UMST, p. 132.

[74] *Ibid.*

qualities are rated lower in the hierarchy of values because they are less important in a society in which a utilitarian and pragmatic outlook dominates and decides the relative significance of virtues and values.

In a proper hierarchy of values, life should rank high on its own merits. The sheer existence of a person, the expression of life through the arts, in sports, in play and in simple enjoyment without any reference to utility or purpose—these are to be treasured highly for their own intrinsic value. Medieval asceticism, knightly games and tournaments, the training of a Japanese samurai and the intricate style of Confucian education in ancient China—all of these approaches to life embodied a similar ethos: that life and the abundance of its forces deserves to be developed for its own sake, without reference to external purpose and usefulness.[75]

The ethos of today's utilitarian civilization, however, demands that there be a usefulness or a purpose to justify the value of life. Pure existence as such is not considered a value in itself; everything valuable must be "earned" through man's effort.[76] Bodily training has value only as recreation from work or the gathering of strength for renewed useful work. The pure play of vital forces as found, for example, in the arts is no longer considered of value. Sports are no longer an expression of free vitality but become a mere preparation for further work. Utility, purpose and external achievement dominate man and his evaluation of reality. This is the ethos of modern industrialist society.

The Esthetic Ethos of Japan

Scheler frequently refers to the ethos of Asia, contrasting it with that of Europe and America. Since his knowledge of Asia was, however, rather sketchy and limited, his pronouncements on the ethos of Asia tend to be somewhat superficial and, at times, inaccurate. He had intended further Asian studies that

[75] *Ressentiment,* p. 159; UMST, p. 134.
[76] *Ressentiment,* p. 159-160; UMST, pp. 134-135.

would have enabled him to concretize his general theory of ethos by historical illustrations from various Asian societies, but his premature death intervened. It would seem to be more in accord with Scheler's own basic concern, then, to present in place of his defective views concerning Asia a characteristic example of the ethos of Asia which contemporary scholarship has brought to light.

An informative example which stands in sharp contrast to the ethos forms of both Europe and America is the esthetic ethos of Japan. The cult of beauty has nowhere been so earnestly pursued as in Japan. The Japanese have been governed by a "rule of taste" and have cultivated an extraordinary esthetic sensibility. The later Heian period (967-1167) has been the one epoch in human history when an ethos of beauty was the absolute norm and ideal. Shikibu Murasaki, in her novel *Genji Monogatari* (*The Tale of Genji*),[77] has depicted the life of the Japanese artistocracy at the court of Kyoto, and the one overwhelming impression one receives from this great classic is that of a society completely dedicated to the pursuit of the beautiful. The main preoccupation of the aristocracy was the discovery, cultivation and creation of beauty.[78] Every aspect of the lives of the upper classes was governed by the rule of taste. Even Buddhism lost its distinctly religious character and was cultivated as an esthetic pursuit. "Sincerity in seeking salvation was totally emasculated, so that the Pure Land of Amida was interpreted purely from aesthetic and sentimental viewpoints without any reference to its ethical, doctrinal, and philosophical content." [79] Or as the great historian Sir George Sansom has put it, religion turned into an art and art into a religion.[80] Taste in color and the art of combining colors, especially as applied to clothing, was devel-

[77] Shikibu Murasaki, *The Tale of Genji*, trans. by Arthur Waley (New York: Modern Library, 1960). *The Tale of Genji*, written about 1010 A.D., was the world's first novel.

[78] Ray F. Downs, *Japan Yesterday and Today* (New York: Bantam, 1970), p. 52.

[79] Joseph M. Kitagawa, *Religion in Japanese History* (New York: Columbia University Press, 1966), p. 80.

[80] George Sansom, *A History of Japan* (3 vols.; Stanford: Stanford University Press, 1958-1963), I, Chapter IX: "The Rule of Taste."

oped to an extraordinary degree. A sophisticated esthetic code governed the smallest details of everyday life. The overwhelming interest in the esthetic side of life reached such extremities that even "the Intendant of the Imperial Police was chosen for his good looks as much as for his family connections." [81]

The whole-hearted pursuit of artistic sensibility and the single-minded cult of beauty created, during the Heian period, an esthetic ethos which has been unequalled in history. A potentiality in man which has to a large extent lain dormant in other peoples was here cultivated to the highest degree. The one-sided emphasis on one particular value, the esthetic, contained, however, a grave danger which was pointed out by Japanologist Ivan Morris in the following description:

Not only did the rule of taste extend to every sphere of life and apply to the smallest details, but (with the single exception of good birth) it took primacy over all else. Artistic sensibility was more highly valued than ethical goodness. Despite the influence of Buddhism, Heian society was on the whole governed by style rather than by any moral principle, and good looks tended to take the place of virtue. The word *yoki* ("good") referred primarily to birth, but it also applied to a person's beauty or to his aesthetic sensibility; the one implication it lacked was that of ethical rectitude. [82]

Logic, reasoned analysis and systematic ethics have never been fully developed in Japan, as they were in the West. [83] Consequently, the Japanese language lacks both rich expressions

[81] Ivan Morris, *The World of the Shining Prince: Court Life in Ancient Japan* (London: Oxford University Press, 1964), p. 194.

[82] *Ibid.,* p. 195.

[83] Hajime Nakamura, *Ways of Thinking of Eastern Peoples: India-China-Tibet-Japan*, rev. trans. by Philip P. Wiener, (Honolulu: East-West Center Press, 1968), pp. 531-576. F. S. C. Northrop, *The Meeting of East and West* (New York: The Macmillan Company, 1946). Edwin O. Reischauer, *The United States & Japan* (3rd ed. rev.; New York: The Viking Press, 1967), p. 118: "Emotional expression in art or poetry is more their forte than a reasoned analysis."

and precise technical terms in the realm of strict philosophical thought. In esthetics, however, that language offers such rich and varied expressions that no truly equivalent ones can be found in any Western language. Here, the poverty of European languages would seem to reflect a deficiency of esthetic experience, while the richness of the Japanese language reveals a highly-nuanced perception and appreciation of esthetic values which remain hidden to the eyes and the mind of Western man.

One example may suffice to illustrate this point. There exist four Japanese words denoting "beautiful": *shibui, miyabi, hade* and *iki*. They represent four different esthetic systems with contrasting norms and operational values, and there are no equivalent concepts in any European language.

Elizabeth Gordon has attempted to analyze these four untranslatable esthetic concepts:

Shibui: This means beauty that is understated, never obvious, deceptively simple while really being complex. The *shibui* object never proclaims itself—in color or line or material. It must wait for its depths to be discovered. This value applies to almost everything in Japanese life: architecture, gardens, foods, clothing, ceramic and lacquer ware, straw goods, etc. Even manners! In short, *shibui* is the main, most-sought-after value in Japanese esthetic life.

Miyabi: It means high aristocratic elegance and deliberate splendor. It reveals itself instantly because of its splendor, or by its high cost of upkeep. It associates with the richness of gold, of mother-of-pearl inlay, intricacy of pattern intertwined with pattern of sand gardens which must be raked every day. . . . *Miyabi* means restrained, highly disciplined, sophisticated elegance.

Hade: It means brightly colored, with a complexity of color combinations. *Hade* carries no connotations about intrinsic quality, for it can be paper decorations for festivals, or clothing for young girls (up to the age of marriage) or a bridal kimono of great expense and luxury, or the costumes of apprentice geishas. Kabuki costumes are considered *hade,* whereas the costumes of Noh plays are considered, in the main, to be *shibui.* The temples of Nikko are *hade.* There is only one *hade* temple in Kyoto —all the others are *shibui.*

Iki: It means refined but personalized originality in style of dress, in architecture, in landscape design, in food presentation, in hair styles, in arrangement of an *obi,* or in almost anything which can be personalized. But, it means personalized within the framework of Japanese tradition. It does not mean going over to Western ways to be personally original.[84]

The English language has, of course, a great variety of words like pretty, cute, chic, a la mode, stylish, beautiful, handsome, lovely, etc.—all referring to beauty. But these are not precise concepts and they do not correspond to well-defined esthetic categories or specific types of beauty.[85]

Max Scheler maintained that through a study of various ethos forms and value systems each culture could heighten the awareness of its own limitations and discover manifold new possibilities for self-enrichment. The highly developed esthetic ethos of Japan could fulfill the function of disclosing to Europeans and Americans profound human potentialities that have remained largely dormant in Western cultures. Recent studies [86] have confirmed that the esthetic ethos is still very much alive in Japan. The cult of beauty and the esthetic ethos may well be Japan's "greatest contribution to the world." [87]

[84] Elizabeth Gordon, *The Culture of Japan: Esthetics* (San Francisco: JAL, 1966), pp. 4-6.

[85] *Ibid.,* p. 6.

[86] Ezra F. Vogel, *Japan's New Middle Class* (Berkeley: University of California Press, 1967), pp. 158-160. Edwin O. Reischauer, *op. cit.,* pp. 117-125; 176-177. Joseph J. Spae, *Christianity Encounters Japan* (Tokyo: Oriens Institute, 1968), pp. 196-200.

[87] Ivan Morris, *op. cit.,* p. 194.

IV
Kairos—The Demand
of the Present Hour

In the manuscript of the preface to the third edition of his *Formalismus*, Scheler added a remark which brings out strongly his growing emphasis on the historical dimension of ethics. Although it was not published in the printed text of the preface, it does exist in the original manuscript:

> After all, ethics is a damned bloody affair, and if it cannot give me directions on how I ought to be and to live now in this social and historical context—well, what meaning does it have then? [1]

Scheler added a further remark in the margin of the manuscript:

> The path from eternity or from the *amor intellectualis sub specie quadam aeternitatis* in which a glimmer of eternity becomes visible, to "Today and Here" is immeasurably

[1] Maria Scheler, the editor of Scheler's collected works, published this quote in the annotations to the text and to the footnotes of *Formalismus*. FORM, p. 591: "Schliesslich ist Ethik eine verdammt blutige Sache, und wenn sie mir nicht Direktiven geben kann, wie ich jetzt in diesem sozialen und historischen Zusammenhang sein und leben soll—ach, was ist sie dann?"

long. But it is precisely the task of philosophy to bridge, however indirectly, this gap.[2]

I

SCHELER'S THEORY OF KAIROS AS THE MORAL
DEMAND OF THE PRESENT HOUR

In the preface to the third edition of his *Formalismus,* Scheler defines kairos as the "demand of the hour of our human and historical humanity and life." [3] The term "demand of the hour" (*Forderung der Stunde*) occurs also in the first edition of the *Formalismus,*[4] although the equivalent concept of kairos does not yet appear. In this first edition Scheler develops the idea that good-in-itself is adequately represented only by the synthesis of supratemporal, universal values with temporal historical values, values that emerge from the concrete situation.[5] This is meant as a critique of rationalist systems of ethics which look only for universality in ethics, while they ignore the modifying aspects of history and time. Scheler singles out Henry Sidgwick as one of his adversaries who, in *The Methods of Ethics,* contends that a volition is good only when it is independent of the differences and changes of time. Scheler holds that man must always have a composite view, both a vision of the totality of life and a fine ear for the unique "demand of the hour" (*Forderung der Stunde*).[6] Thus, the "demand of the hour" takes on the characteristic of "an essential category of ethics." [7]

Scheler places his ideas on the demand of the hour, which he will later call "kairos," within the broader context of the proper relationship between "value-universalism" (*Wertuniversalismus*) and "value-individualism" (*Wertindividualismus*).[8] A balanced

[2] FORM, p. 591.
[3] *Ibid.,* p. 23: " . . . zum Kairos, d.h. zu der Forderung der Stunde unseres menschlichen und historischen Menschseins und Lebens. . . ."
[4] *Ibid.,* p. 485.
[5] *Ibid.*
[6] *Ibid.*
[7] *Ibid.* At this place, Scheler acknowledges that he has borrowed the term "Forderung der Stunde" from Goethe.
[8] *Ibid.,* p. 484.

proportion between these two dimensions is needed. It is achieved only when each individual moral subject realizes and cultivates those values which are comprehensible and available to him alone, and if at the same time he does not neglect the values which are universally valid for all. Both individuals and groups (families, tribes, peoples and nations) have to strive for this kind of balance between the realization of universal values and the cultivation of their specific individual values. Only a harmonious synthesis between these two ethical dimensions will lead to the realization of the good-in-itself.

The demand of the hour, or kairos, represents an essential aspect of the totality of man's moral "oughtness." Every hour in the historical development of an individual person offers the possibility of insights into certain unique values and consequently a call to certain moral tasks and actions. If the person misses the opportunities which are, in a sense, predetermined for this particular moment of his life, they will never return. Consequently, the demand of the hour is of utmost importance for the moral life and growth of the individual.

The rationalist systems of ethics failed to do justice to the dimension of kairos. They denied the variety and multiplicity of historically changing moral values. Scheler attempts to correct this one-sidedness by pointing out that essentially and characteristically they can be known and realized in their whole variety and abundance only in successive stages of history. It is a basic error of rationalism to maintain that the multitude of values can ever be grasped by one individual, one people, one nation, or one period of history.[9]

The ethical content contained in the demand of the hour (*Forderung der Stunde*) and in the specific call to an individual (*Ruf an diese Person*) is termed the "good-in-itself for me" (*das An-sich-Gute für mich*).[10] At first sight, this concept may appear to be a logical contradiction. However, the phrase "for me" is not meant in a subjective sense. Rather, the good in question is an objective good, independent of the subject (the

[9] *Ibid.,* p. 485.
[10] *Ibid.,* p. 482.

aspect of the *"An-sich-Guten"*), but which at the same time is directed to a specific subject calling it to moral action (the aspect of *"für mich"*).[11]

> There exists the possibility of an insight into a good which contains in its essence and value-content a pointing to an individual person. It also possesses a corresponding oughtness that emerges as a "call" to this person and to this person alone, regardless of whether or not the same "call" is also addressed to other persons. . . . [The good in question] is the good-in-itself for me in the sense that in the particular material content of this good-in-itself (descriptively said) lies a pointer to me, an experienced hinting, which emerges from this content and points toward me. It says and whispers, so to speak, "For you." Thus, this content offers me a unique place in the moral cosmos. It also orders me to perform acts, deeds and works which, if I fancy them in my imagination, all call to me: "I am for you" and "You are for me." [12]

In a critique of Kant, Scheler states that in ethics apriority does not always imply universal validity. Universal validity is not a necessary concomitant of an essence, for there are also individual essences. "There can exist an *a priori* into which only one person possesses the insight." [13]

According to Scheler, it is quite possible that at one particular moment in history one particular individual alone comprehends new moral values.[14] The evidence perceived by this individual need not be corroborated by the fact that a multitude of persons share the same insight or that these values have a universal validity and place a moral demand on any other persons.[15] With this view, Scheler may be considered a precursor of the

[11] *Ibid.*
[12] *Ibid.*
[13] *Ibid.*, p. 94.
[14] *Ibid.*, p. 277.
[15] *Ibid.*

existential ethics which would later be developed more systematically by Karl Rahner.[16] Scheler writes:

It is quite possible that one individual person alone possesses full evidence of a moral demand which points to this individual alone and which holds validity solely for this unique case.[17]

Here, Scheler explicitly rejects as erroneous Kant's view that universal validity ought to be a criterion for the justification of moral imperatives.[18] Universality is not required, either in the sense of being valid for all situations and cases or in the sense of binding all human beings. According to Scheler, there is a moral oughtness or moral demand which is in no way fit to become a universal law for all men and all similar situations, but which is nevertheless binding on one individual person in one specific situation.[19] This does not lead to subjectivism, as Scheler hastens to add, for the unique, individual demand is of an objective nature. Besides, the objective nature of general moral demands remains intact. The cases we are dealing with here are individual moral imperatives that do not invalidate any germinal norms but go beyond the realm of universally valid moral norms.

In the midst of World War I, Scheler published a lengthy essay in which he concretized his ideas of kairos and "demand of the hour." The essay is entitled "Sociological Re-Orientation and the Task of German Catholics after the War." [20] Scheler tries to show

---

[16] Karl Rahner, *The Dynamic Element in the Church,* trans. by W. J. O'Hara (New York: Herder and Herder, 1964). Karl Rahner, *On the Question of a Formal Existential Ethics,* in *Theological Investigations,* vol. II: *Man in the Church,* trans by Karl H. Kruger (Baltimore: Helicon, 1963), pp. 217-234. Karl Rahner, "Situation Ethics in an Ecumenical Perspective," in Karl Rahner, *The Christian of the Future* (New York: Herder and Herder, 1967), pp. 39-48. Anita Röper, *Objektive und subjektive Moral. Ein Gespräch mit Karl Rahner* (Freiburg: Herder, 1971).

[17] FORM, p. 279.

[18] *Ibid.*

[19] *Ibid.*

[20] Max Scheler, "Soziologische Neuorientierung und die Aufgabe der deutschen Katholiken nach dem Krieg," *Hochland,* XIII (January, 1916), pp. 385-406; (March, 1916), pp. 682-700; (May, 1916), pp. 188-204; (June, 1916), pp. 257-294.

that the experience of the war offers Europeans a unique opportunity for reorientating the meaning and essence of human society.[21] At the outbreak of the war Scheler had been swept along
with the winds of patriotism, but gradually he became disillusioned with the nationalistic temper of the time. He now began
to see the present moment in history as a kairos,[22] a unique
opportunity for an intellectual and spiritual-religious reorientation of the peoples of Europe.

The first step must be a common repentance for the collective guilt resulting from the war.[23] In another essay, "Repentance and Rebirth," [24] Scheler explained the creative function of
repentance in the life of an individual. In the present essay he
applied the idea of repentance to whole peoples and to whole
periods of human history.[25]

Past events in history, of course, cannot be changed in their
objective reality. But the ultimate meaning of past history
can still be altered; it depends, in fact, on our decisions and actions.[26] Past historical reality remains, in its meaning and worth,
incomplete and is, so to speak, still "redeemable" through our
redeeming acts.[27] Repentance is the transforming power in the
life of an individual as well as in the life of a community. The
meaning of an individual's culpable action can be altered if
the person repents. Similarly, the meaning of a whole period
in human history, like the present time of war and hatred can be
transformed through a universal repentance. The present generation can, through repentance, impose a new meaning on the
past years of history. In this way, out of this evil period can
sprout the seed of a better phase of human history.

---

[21] *Ibid.*, p. 386.

[22] Scheler does not yet use the word kairos in this essay but he
describes the historical situation in the same way as he will in later years
talk about kairos.

[23] *Ibid.*, p. 190.

[24] "Reue und Wiedergeburt," in *Vom Ewigen im Menschen*, pp.
27-59.

[25] "Soziologische Neuorientierung und die Aufgabe der deutschen
Katholiken nach dem Krieg," pp. 190-191.

[26] *Ibid.*

[27] *Ibid.*

Scheler proposes a fundamental sociological reorientation of European society. This reorientation consists primarily in overcoming the present individualism and nationalism, and replacing it with a new spirit of Christian solidarity. It will be a specific task for Catholics to bring about a rebirth of the idea of Christian solidarity out of the blood-bath of present-day Europe.[28] Since for Catholics the principle of solidarity and collective responsibility are an essential part of their intellectual and spiritual heritage, Catholics at this moment must feel a special responsibility in shaping a new future for Europe. The present war and the experience of hatred and division offer a unique opportunity—an opportunity which may not be granted a second time—to reactivate the opposite spirit of solidarity and co-responsibility. Thus, it is an "imperative of the present hour" (*Gebot der Stunde*) to work for unity and solidarity among the divided nations.[29]

Toward the end of his essay on "The Sociological Re-Orientation and the Task of German Catholics after the War" Scheler's vision goes beyond the immediate post-war years and he foresees the dawn of another kairos which he calls

the most mysterious hour that the historical future of civilized man harbors, the hour of encounter between the metaphysical and religious life-foundations of Europe and Asia.[30]

In this encounter Scheler attributes a specific role and task to Catholics. In a slightly simplified manner, he characterizes the religious approach of Asia and that of the Protestant West as two extremes. Asians tend to be very active in their relationship to the sacred, even to the extent of self-redemption through knowledge or through other spiritual, cultic or ascetical practices. On the other hand, they show a rather passive attitude toward this world. In sharp contrast, Protestant Christianity,

[28] *Ibid.,* p. 386.
[29] *Ibid.,* pp. 386-387.
[30] *Ibid.,* p. 289.

especially in its Calvinist form, is passive and receptive in its relationship to God—God plays the active part in the redemptive process. Protestants are, however, extremely active in their relationship to this world—work becomes the new worship.[31]

Scheler considers the Catholic Church a harmonious synthesis of these two extremes.[32] The Catholic view of the relationship between freedom and grace, between liturgy and work, points in the direction of harmony. Catholicism appears as a natural bridge between Asia and Europe. Consequently, Catholics are called to function as leaders and mediators in the coming kairos of East-West encounter.[33]

Immediately after the end of the First World War, Scheler published a moving essay in *Hochland,* "On Religious Renewal," [34] in which he summoned all Europeans to recognize the kairos situation and to make a new beginning in unity and solidarity. Scheler challenges the war-torn European countries to face their common guilt for the late war and to arise out of the ashes of destruction to a creative religious renewal. In poetic language he addresses the people, "The cry goes out to all men: Arise! Set your feet to the holy mountain of your consciences. . . . From its sunbathed peak you may look' down into the maelstrom of Europe's common guilt, as into a valley of fearfulness, of sin and tears!" [35] The call to a religious renewal carries with it a special urgency at this particular moment in European history. "Today," writes Scheler, "this call takes on a singularly historic character." [36] It is the religious moral principle of solidarity which must be at the heart of the present religious renewal.[37] Individualism had torn modern Europe apart. A new

[31] *Ibid.,* pp. 290-291.
[32] *Ibid.,* p. 291.
[33] *Ibid.*
[34] Max Scheler, "Zur religiösen Erneuerung," *Hochland,* XVI (October, 1918), 5-21. This essay was later reprinted in Scheler's *Vom Ewigen im Menschen* (Bern: Francke Verlag, 1968), pp. 103-124. I will quote from and refer to this version in *Vom Ewigen im Menschen,* English translation: *On the Eternal in Man,* pp. 107-128.
[35] VEIM, p. 121; *Eternal,* p. 125.
[36] VEIM, p. 104; *Eternal,* p. 107.
[37] VEIM, p. 121; *Eternal,* p. 125.

solidarity can make people aware of their collective guilt for the recent war, can awaken in all peoples a spirit of reconciliation, of mutual pardon, collective repentance and atonement for the past guilt. The principle of solidarity teaches us that "this world is rising to God or falling from God as a *single,* indivisible whole, a morally compact mass, and that all therein answer for all, and all for the whole, before the highest judge." [38]

During the years of war the primordial longings of man's heart had been suppressed. With the beginning of peace, a powerful bursting forth of these primordial longings, of love, tenderness, compassion and rejoicing with others (*Mitfreuen*), is the most significant ferment in man's new outlook on the world.[39] The ice in men's souls has begun to melt, a new era has been ushered in. In this kairos situation, philosophy is confronted with the important task of reflecting anew on the nature of religion and its role and function in the structure of human reason and in the spiritual and religious renewal taking place in the post-war years.

In December of 1926, a year and a half before his death, Scheler formulated in his preface to a third edition of his *Formalismus* his ideas about the future development of the material value ethics. Nicolai Hartmann, who in his monumental *Ethik* [40] had tried to carry further and expand the work initiated by Scheler, was criticized for not paying sufficient attention to the historical and social nature of every living ethos.[41] "Even as spiritual being, man breathes only in history and society," writes Scheler.[42] Consequently, the further development of material value ethics did not lie in an individualistic analysis of virtues nor in an analysis of supra-temporal values which are abstracted from the concrete historical community experience. What was now needed was a philosophy of the development of the moral consciousness in history and society.[43] A central

---

[38] *Ibid.*
[39] VEIM, p. 122; *Eternal,* p. 126.
[40] Nicolai Hartmann, *Ethik* (Berlin: Walter de Gruyter, 1926).
[41] FORM, p. 22.
[42] *Ibid.*
[43] *Ibid.*

point of this history-conscious ethics was to be a philosophy of the kairos, i.e. of the ethical demand of the hour and its significance for the moral life of man.

II
THE IDEA OF KAIROS
IN POST-SCHELERIAN THINKERS

Subsequently, a good number of philosophers and theologians have taken up Scheler's challenge and have developed a philosophy and theology in which the idea of kairos and of the demand of the hour—although the terminology may differ—play an important role.

Martin Heidegger, who was profoundly influenced by Scheler, developed the idea of the "mittence (*Geschick*) of Being" as an ontology of ethics.[44] Heidegger proposed as the provisional aim of his *Sein und Zeit* to interpret time as the possible horizon for any understanding of Being.[45] Accordingly, every epoch of history is characterized by a finite mittence (*Geschick*) of Being or by the way Being reveals itself and conceals itself. Responsiveness to the historical mittence of Being is the basic moral act, or the act that is good in itself.[46]

Heidegger wrote:

. . . If, according to the fundamental meaning of the word ethos, the name "ethics" is supposed to say that it meditates upon the sojourn (*Aufenthalt*) of man, then that type of

[44] William Richardson, S.J., "Heidegger and the Quest of Freedom," *Theological Studies*, XXVIII (June, 1967), pp. 286-307. Giles Driscoll, "Heidegger's Ethical Monism," *The New Scholasticism*, XLII (Autumn, 1968), pp. 497-510. Bernard J. Boelen, "The Question of Ethics in the Thought of Martin Heidegger," in *Heidegger and the Quest for Truth*, ed. by Manfred S. Frings (Chicago: Quadrangle Books, 1968), pp. 76-105. Reuben Guilead, *Etre et Liberté: Une étude sur le dernièr Heidegger* (Louvain, 1965).

[45] Martin Heidegger, *Sein und Zeit* (Tübingen: Max Niemeyer, 1970), p. 1.

[46] Giles Driscoll, "Heidegger's Ethical Monism," *The New Scholasticism*, XLII (Autumn, 1968), p. 510.

thought which thinks the truth of Being as the originating element of man [conceived] as an ek-sistent being is in itself the original Ethics. . . .[47]

William Richardson relates this idea that foundational thinking is "in itself the original Ethics" to another basic insight of Heidegger, i.e. "that Being in its mittences is likewise the original Moral Law that Ethics normally meditates." [48]

Another text in Heidegger's *Über den Humanismus* addresses itself to this point:

Only insofar as man, ek-sisting in the truth of Being, is an attend-ant (*gehört*) of Being, can come the dispensation of those intimations which are to become law and rule for man. The Greek word *nemein* means "to dispense." The *Nomos* is not only law but more originally the dispensation of Being hidden in [its] mittence [to *Dasein*].[49]

It would seem that there exists a certain affinity between Scheler's idea of kairos or "demand of the present hour" and the ethical implications of Heidegger's "mittence of Being." One might reasonably surmise that in this question Heidegger took over a key insight of Scheler and developed it within the framework of his own fundamental ontology. However, since Heidegger has never developed a systematic treatise on ethics and since his scattered references to ethics remain somewhat ambiguous, it is only with considerable hesitation that I present this comparison between Scheler and Heidegger. Among interpreters there exists a good deal of disagreement on the problem of Heidegger's ethics. Some critics even assert that Heidegger had denatured the moral dimension of Scheler's insight. A definitive statement on this question has to await further clarifications by

[47] Martin Heidegger, *Über den Humanismus* (Frankfurt: Klostermann, 1949), p. 41.
[48] William Richardson, S. J., "Heidegger and the Quest of Freedom," *Theological Studies*, XXVIII (June, 1967), p. 304.
[49] *Über den Humanismus*, p. 44.

Heidegger himself on his understanding of moral philosophy.[50]

Another thinker who has taken up the challenge of Scheler is Karl Rahner who has developed an existential ethics.[51] In Rahner's ethical system, the objective and universal norms retain their validity. The existential ethics deals with an added norm, the specific demands and calls made to an individual person or to a certain nation or age. According to Rahner, there is more in a moral action than the mere fulfillment of universal norms. Rahner bases his existential ethics on his conception of man. Man is both nature and person. Nature refers to the universal and common element in man, and as nature, man is bound by universal, moral laws. Person denotes the individuality and uniqueness of a specific man, and as a person man is confronted with unique ethical prescriptions and calls which cannot be reduced to a mere fulfillment of universal laws.

Rahner distinguishes between principles (*Prinzipien*), i.e. universal moral norms, and prescriptions (*Imperative*), i.e. "ethically important precepts, addressed to the conscience and the practical creative power of an individual, a nation or an age." [52] Rahner does not quote Scheler in this connection but the close

---

[50] On the affinity between the philosophy of Max Scheler and Martin Heidegger see Manfred S. Frings, *Person und Dasein. Zur Frage der Ontologie des Wertseins* (Den Haag: Martinus Nijhoff, 1969). In the introduction (p. XII), Frings quotes Heidegger who had sent a copy of *Sein und Zeit* right after publication to Scheler: "Scheler was one of the very few, if not even the only one who then immediately understood the problem of *Sein und Zeit*. . . . M. Scheler was primarily concerned with the themes: *Dasein*, temporality and death. . . ." During the winter semester of 1927/28 Heidegger lived for three days at Scheler's house in Cologne at which time the latter recognized his own profound influence on Heidegger. Shortly before his death he wrote: ". . . Heidegger is, of course, influenced by my anthropology. . . ." (quoted in Frings, *Person und Dasein*, p. XIII).

[51] Karl Rahner, *The Dynamic Element in the Church*, trans. by W. J. O'Hara (New York: Herder and Herder, 1964). Karl Rahner, *On the Question of a Formal Existential Ethics*, in *Theological Investigations*, vol. II: *Man in the Church*, trans. by Karl H. Kruger (Baltimore: Helicon, 1963), pp. 217-234. Karl Rahner, "Situation Ethics in an Ecumenical Perspective," in Karl Rahner, *The Christian of the Future* (New York: Herder and Herder, 1967), pp. 39-48. Anita Röper, *Objektive und subjektive Moral. Ein Gespräch mit Karl Rahner* (Freiburg: Herder, 1971).

[52] Karl Rahner, *The Dynamic Element in the Church*, p. 14.

affinity of the two thinkers is here evident, as the following passage of Rahner indicates:

> The distinction between principles and prescriptions holds good not only for individual men one by one, but also for historical entities like states and other collective historical factors. These have their intrinsic individuality in time and place, their definite moment in history. Each has its kairos, its historical task and so on. Consequently they also have their definitive normative "prescriptions" and these are not to be confused with general moral principles, for the two things have different ontological grounds and are not known or put into effect in the same way. In short, collective entities on the large scale such as nations, ages and epochs, historical situations, all have their own quite definite imperative "prescriptions" which cannot be reduced to the sum-total of abstract general principles.[53]

A theologian whose whole thinking centers around the root-term kairos is Paul Tillich.[54] Tillich distinguishes between chronos which is measured time or clock time and is of an exclusively quantitative character, and kairos which has a qualitative meaning—"the right time, the time in which something can be done." [55] Tillich takes the concept kairos from the New Testament where it signifies the "fulfillment of time" when history "had matured to the point of being able to receive the breakthrough of the central manifestation of the Kingdom of God." [56] There occurred one "great kairos" in history, the coming of the New Being in Jesus Christ, the moment when time was invaded by eternity. The breakthrough of the eternal into the finite which

[53] *Ibid.*, pp. 22-23.
[54] Erich Przywara, S. J., "Christian Root-Terms: Kerygma, Mysterium, Kairos, Oikonomia." in *Religion and Culture. Essays in Honor of Paul Tillich,* ed. by Walter Leibrecht (New York: Harper & Brothers, 1959), p. 113.
[55] Paul Tillich, *Systematic Theology* (3 vols.; Chicago: University of Chicago Press, 1951-53), III, p. 369.
[56] *Ibid.*

originated in the first kairos is re-experienced again and again "through relative 'kairoi,' in which the Kingdom of God manifests itself in a particular breakthrough." [57] Kairos, or eternity in time, becomes for Tillich the key to a new understanding of time and history, and also of the nature of man's being.

There exists a surprising similarity between Tillich's teaching on kairos and the reflections that Scheler developed on the same theme a few years earlier. Tillich introduced the term kairos into the theological discussion in connection with the religious socialist movement after World War I. What Scheler had written in 1916,[58] Tillich repeated in the post-war years: that the time after the First World War was for the people of central Europe a unique kairos situation, that for them "a moment of history had appeared which was pregnant with a new understanding of the meaning of history and life." [59]

Again, as Scheler had done before, Tillich went beyond a new interpretation of history and applied the idea of kairos also to his understanding of man. In the concrete situation of the kairos, man becomes aware of his being bound into history, and of his finitude; yet at the same time he experiences his freedom, his personal uniqueness and the creative possibilities that the kairos offers him. Human finitude and human freedom, historicity and creativity become key concepts for the understanding of man's being—both for Scheler and for Tillich.[60]

E. Schillebeeckx, in an attempt to overcome a morality that is either merely situational or purely abstract, emphasized equally the importance of the concrete historical situation (the kairos aspect) and of general norms.[61] General norms express a real, albeit limited, aspect of concrete reality. Therefore, the concrete moral decision must never fall outside of the framework of these

[57] *Ibid.*, p. 370.
[58] Max Scheler, "Soziologische Neuorientierung und die Aufgabe der deutschen Katholiken nach dem Krieg."
[59] *Systematic Theology*, III, p. 369.
[60] Walter Leibrecht, "The Life and Mind of Paul Tillich," in *Religion and Culture. Essays in Honor of Paul Tillich*, ed. by Walter Leibrecht (New York: Harper & Brothers, 1959), pp. 13-15.
[61] E. Schillebeeckx, O.P., *God the Future of Man*, trans. by N. D. Smith (New York: Sheed and Ward, 1968), pp. 151-152.

norms. But since general norms can never adequately reveal the totality of a concrete situation another dimension must be taken into consideration:

> There is only one source of ethical norms, namely the historical reality of the value of the inviolable human person with all its bodily and social implications. That is why we cannot attribute validity to abstract norms as such. Moreover, no abstract statements can produce a call or invitation. . . . Therefore, these abstract, generally valid norms are an inadequate yet real *pointer* to the one real, concrete ethical norm, namely, this concrete human person living historically in this concrete society. Ethical norms are requirements made by reality, and the so-called abstract general norms are but the essentially inadequate expression of this. Therefore, it is not the inadequate expression which, by itself, constitutes the ethical norm, but it is a pointer to the one and only norm: these persons who must be approached in a love that demands justice for all.[62]

With his emphasis on historicity in ethics and on the importance of kairos, Scheler has exerted a profound influence on many moral philosophers and theologians, inspiring them to broaden their ethical thinking by including the dimensions of time and history. Bernhard Häring, Werner Schöllgen, Johannes Hessen, Theodor Steinbüchel, Johannes Messner, Joseph de Finance and many others acknowledge their indebtedness to Max Scheler. Even the neo-scholastic proponents of a natural law approach to ethics—an approach which at first sight would seem to be rather static and less open to the dynamic changes of history—have in recent years become increasingly aware of the need to illuminate the supra-historical dimension of unchangeable laws in the light of concrete historical situations.[63] Josef Fuchs, for

---

[62] *Ibid.*
[63] There is, of course, warrant for such an interpretation of the natural law in the writings of St. Thomas. Some critics attribute the static approach which can be found in certain neo-scholastic textbooks

example, dedicates a chapter of his *Natural Law* to the question
of "Natural Law and the Situations of History." [64] As he expresses it in one subtitle, there is a "conditioning of the natural
law by time and situation." [65] With regard to the ideal state, the
ideal economy and ideal laws, the absolute natural law can make
certain statements. But, according to Fuchs, these statements
are "relatively general, formal and scanty in content." [66] Consequently, there is needed "a more precise determination produced by the historical situation." [67] Although man's nature is
substantially unchangeable, it is accidentally in constant movement; and since natural law is based on man's nature, it also
shares in the historicity of changing and evolving man. Fuchs
can thus conclude that "the natural law possesses historicity in
the same way in which human nature is historical and unique
and peculiar at every moment." [68]

Kairos has become a key concept not only for moral philosophers and theologians. Some psychotherapists, too, have recently
emphasized the importance of kairos for the success of therapy.
James C. Crumbaugh, for example, calls kairos and encounter
"complementary integrals of psychotherapy." [69] He distinguishes between a kairos in the patient, an event of basic personal significance, and a kairos in the therapist, a sharing with

---

to St. Thomas but without justification. In the *Summa Theologica*, I-II,
q. 97, a.1 we read: "There may be two causes for the just change of
human law: one on the part of reason; the other on the part of man
whose acts are regulated by law. The cause on the part of reason is
that it seems natural to human reason to advance gradually from the
imperfect to the perfect. . . . On the part of man, whose acts are regulated
by law, the law can be rightly changed on account of the changed
condition of man, to whom different things are expedient according to
the difference of his condition."

[64] Josef Fuchs, *Natural Law* (New York: Sheed and Ward, 1965),
pp. 85-122.
[65] *Ibid.*, p. 110.
[66] *Ibid.*, p. 100.
[67] *Ibid.*
[68] *Ibid.*, p. 118.
[69] James C. Crumbaugh, "The Relation of Kairos to Encounter in
Psychotherapy," *Review of Existential Psychology and Psychotherapy*,
III (Winter, 1963), p. 35.

the patient the feeling that the present moment is of great immediate significance. According to Crumbaugh,

> the effects of therapy occur for many only at points of at least some degree of kairos. Many patients are ready only in such experiences to enter into the encounter—that deeply personal and often nonverbal mode of communication of feeling . . . which is frequently considered to be the heart of the therapeutic process.[70]

With his reflections on kairos, Scheler has stimulated numerous thinkers in various fields to explore the significance of kairos for man's moral and religious life as well as for the areas of psychology, sociology and political science. In concluding this chapter one might point out that Scheler's idea of kairos could also enrich the ongoing discussion of situation ethics. The situation-ethics controversy could receive new light and become more fruitful if a study of kairos and ethos were to precede the usual discussions on law, norm and context. Scheler has made a valuable contribution by showing that, besides the extremes of legalism and situationism, there is a third approach possible. This approach, as we have seen in this chapter, takes full account of the "situation" by evaluating it in the broader context of ethos and kairos, and yet avoids the pitfall of moral relativism by holding fast to an unchangeable realm of eternal values.[71]

[70] *Ibid.*

[71] For an exposition of the "situationist" viewpoint cf. Joseph Fletcher, *Situation Ethics* (Philadelphia: The Westminster Press, 1951); Joseph Fletcher and Thomas A. Wassmer, *Hello, Lovers! An Introduction to Situation Ethics* (Washington: Corpus Books, 1970). A critique of situation ethics is offered in the following books and articles: Harvey Cox, ed. *The Situation Ethics Debate* (Philadelphia: The Westminster Press, 1958). John C. Bennett, ed. *Storm over Ethics* (Philadelphia: United Church Press, 1967). Thomas E. Davitt, *Ethics in the Situation* (New York: Appleton-Century-Crofts, 1970). Robert L. Cunningham, ed. *Situationism and the New Morality* (New York: Appleton-Century-Crofts, 1970). James M. Gustafson, "Context Versus Principles: A Misplaced Debate in Christian Ethics," in *New Theology No. 3*, ed. by Martin E. Marty (New York: The Macmillan Company, 1966), 69-102. Paul Ramsey, *Deeds and Rules in Christian Ethics* (New York: Charles Scribner's Sons, 1967).

V

"Resentment" and the Historicity of Ethics: Resentment as a Source of Value-Deception

W hen he discusses the different variations of ethos, Scheler is primarily concerned with the growth and development of ethos and with the discovery of new and higher values. But looking back over history, he cannot ignore the fact that there have been frequent falsifications of the hierarchy of values. Value-deception is a common phenomenon. Of the many possible sources of value-deception, Scheler studies *one* such form in greater depth, namely "resentment."[1] He

[1] Both Nietzsche and Scheler used the French word "ressentiment" which has since become generally accepted in the German language. There exists no equivalent term in English. For lack of a better word we shall use "resentment" but this word does not possess the breadth and depth of meaning of "ressentiment" as should become evident in the course of this chapter. Helmut Schoeck has called our attention to the difference by pointing to an interesting linguistic comparison. In English one frequently hears the expression: "I resent that," or "I resent your action, your remark," etc. These phrases do not indicate genuine "ressentiment" but only a feeling of indignation or annoyance. In German one cannot even say: "I resent you," for there is no such verb. And nobody would dare to say in German "I have a 'Ressentiment' against you," —a phrase which would be grammatically correct—because since Nietzsche and Scheler the noun "Ressentiment" has such profound and negative meanings which the English word "resentment" does not possess. Cf. Helmut Schoeck, *Der Neid: Eine Theorie der Gesellschaft* (Freiburg: Verlag Karl Alber, 1968), pp. 16-17.

admits his indebtedness to Nietzsche who preceded him with a study on the phenomenon of resentment as a source of value-deception. Since Scheler presupposes and builds upon Nietzsche's theory, modifying and developing it in the process, we have first to delineate the theory of resentment as put forth by Nietzsche.

I

NIETZSCHE'S THEORY OF RESENTMENT

Master-morality and Slave-morality

Nietzsche distinguishes two basic types of morality, master-morality and slave-morality.[2] The aristocrat or noble creates his own values and is "beyond good and evil." Good and evil, however, do not here mean good and bad.[3] Bad signifies weakness and inferiority, whereas evil refers to a conscience-stricken sense of immorality. Bad conscience, sin and evil are inventions of the slaves; the aristocratic masters are beyond such traditional moral concepts.

Nietzsche claims to find some confirmation of his theory in etymology. In the ethics of the aristocracy, good meant noble, brave, strong, generous and chivalrous. Bad, in the understanding of the master race, signified common, base or plebeian. An interesting example of the latter: up till the 16th century *"schlecht"* (bad) and *"schlicht"* (simple) had the same meaning.[4] The term *"schlecht"* was used interchangeably with

---

[2] Friedrich Nietzsche, *Zur Genealogie der Moral* (Munich: Goldmann Verlag, 1966), pp. 23-25 (I, 7-10). Friedrich Nietzsche, *Jenseits von Gut und Böse* (Munich: Goldmann Verlag, 1966), pp. 149-153 (IX, 259-260). The works of Nietzsche have been published in many different editions with varying pagination. For easier reference I shall also add to the pagination of the Goldmann edition the number of chapters and sections. The Roman numerals refer to *Abhandlungen* in *Zur Genealogie der Moral* and to *Hauptstücke* in *Jenseits von Gut und Böse*. The Arabic numerals indicate the sections within the *Abhandlungen* and *Hauptstücke*. All references are based on the Goldmann edition.

[3] *Zur Genealogie der Moral*, p. 40 (I, 17).

[4] *Ibid.*, p. 18 (I, 4).

"schlicht" simply to distinguish the common man from the noble. When the aristocracy employed the term "bad," they meant inferior or cowardly. On the other hand, the term "evil," when employed by the slave, referred to precisely those qualities that were valued by the noblemen, like the powerful, beautiful, strong and noble. In self-defense, the weak people designated as evil what in the eyes of the strong was good.

Slave-morality is essentially a morality of utility, taking as its moral standard what is useful or advantageous to the inferior, the cowardly and the weak. The weak will extol humility, sympathy, love of enemies, and kindness as virtues. By imposing their own values on the strong and healthy, the slaves try to protect themselves against the superior master race.

Resentment and the Transvaluation of Values

"The revolt of the slaves in morals begins with resentment becoming creative and giving birth to values."[5] Whereas the aristocrat creates his values out of the fullness of his own strength, and is thus positive and affirmative, the slave is basically negative, starting out with a "no" to that which is outside himself. This "no" becomes precisely the creative act of the slave morality. Full of resentment at his own powerlessness, the slave cannot act on his own; he needs objective stimuli, and thus his action is fundamentally a re-action.[6]

A concrete example of resentment coming into being is, according to Nietzsche, to be found in the origin of the Christian ethic. This ethic of pity and sympathy is rooted in Jewish resentment. The Jews, living under the occupation of powerful Rome and being weak themselves, inverted the values of their oppressors. What was beautiful in the eyes of the Romans became ugly in the eyes of the Jews. The power of Rome was depicted as the "world" with all its negative connotations.[7] The Jewish race defeated its enemies by downgrading their values.

[5] *Ibid.*, p. 25 (I, 10).
[6] *Ibid.*, p. 26 (I, 10).
[7] *Jenseits von Gut und Böse*, p. 82 (V, 195).

The oppressed and the suffering, envious of the virtues of the powerful, try to persuade themselves that the happiness of the masters is not genuine; at the same time they transvaluate their own miserable deeds into splendid virtues:

> Weakness is turned to merit . . . the impotence which requites not, is turned to "goodness," craven baseness to meekness, submission to those whom one hates, to obedience (namely, obedience to one who they say ordered this submission—they call him God). The inoffensive character of the weak, the very cowardice in which he abounds, his standing at the door, his forced necessity of waiting, gain here fine names, such as "patience," which is also called "virtue"; not being able to avenge one's self is called not wishing to avenge one's self, perhaps even forgiveness (for they know not what they do—we alone know what they do). They also talk of the "love of enemies" and sweat thereby.[8]

The creative transvaluation of values brought about by the resentful weak of the earth consists, therefore, in this twofold process of downgrading the values of the strong and healthy, and of propounding their own wretched deeds as virtues. "Rich" becomes, in the language of the Jewish prophets, a synonym for "evil," and the "poor" are praised as saints.[9]

Asceticism and Resentment

Asceticism is, according to Nietzsche, a clear expression of resentment. The ascetic is said to be "hostile to life," [10] and, therefore the extreme opposite of Nietzsche's ideal man. For the latter the crucial question in all moral judgments is: to what extent does this judgment further and preserve life? to what extent

[8] *Zur Genealogie der Moral*, p. 34 (I, 14).
[9] *Jenseits von Gut und Böse*, p. 82 (V, 195).
[10] *Zur Genealogie der Moral*, p. 97 (III, 11).

does it preserve and promote the human race? [11] Since the "self" is seen as essentially "body," and the soul as nothing but a "name for something pertaining to the body," [12] it follows that the ascetical life is a self-contradiction.[13]

> Here rules resentment without parallel, resentment of an insatiate instinct and ambition that would be master, not over some element in life, but over life itself, and over life's deepest, strongest, innermost condition.[14]

How did man happen to turn to a life of asceticism which, since it is hostility to life, seems to be so strongly opposed to the basic drive of man toward full development of life? First, there is the historic origin of asceticism in the Pauline form of Christianity which Nietzsche tries to sever from the original teaching of Jesus. Through the influence of Paul and the "ascetical priests," bad conscience, a strong feeling of guilt, and a general devaluation of nature and of all natural values spread among the peoples of Europe. "Paul," Nietzsche claims, "is the incarnation of the type opposite to the 'Messenger of Glad Tidings,' the genius of hate." [15]

Besides describing the historical origin of resentful asceticism, Nietzsche also proposes another explanation of why men turned to the ascetical life. Originally, man saw no meaning in life. Feeling this tremendous void, he started searching for a purpose for his life and especially his suffering. The ascetical ideal offered precisely such a meaning.[16] Suffering was now seen under the perspective of guilt, and so, was given an explanation. The previous suicidal nihilism had thus been overcome; man had found a new purpose and, in the ideal of asceticism, something to

---

[11] *Jenseits von Gut und Böse,* p. 9 (I, 4).

[12] Friedrich Nietzsche, *Also sprach Zarathustra* (München: Goldmann Verlag, 1966), p. 27.

[13] *Zur Genealogie der Moral,* p. 97 (III, 11).

[14] *Ibid.,* pp. 97-98 (III, 11).

[15] Friedrich Nietzsche, *Der Antichrist,* in *Werke in Drei Bänden* (München: Carl Hanser Verlag, 1960), II, p. 1204.

[16] *Zur Genealogie der Moral,* pp. 135-136 (III, 28).

strive for. It is true that this new sense of purpose and goal-oriented striving furnished by the newly discovered ascetical ideal brought with it new sufferings and even led man to hate the human and to fear happiness and beauty; but nonetheless the ascetical ideal gave meaning and purpose to life. And "he who has a why to live for can bear with almost any how."

Resentment in Morality and the Will to Power

The intemperate diatribes against slave-morality and resentment-ethics create the impression, at times, that Nietzsche intends its complete condemnation and opts for a radical replacement of it by a superior master-morality. But this is *not* his intention. A peaceful coexistence of the two types of morality would be acceptable, albeit under the condition that the "slaves" do not try to impose their values universally and thus corrupt the masters.

Unfortunately, far from being satisfied with a mere peaceful coexistence, the "slaves" have always tried to make the strong weak in order to subdue them and to bring them down to the same level with the pariahs of the earth. The strong have been victimized by the weak, the aristocrats have been tyrannized by a majority of cripples. For almost two thousand years Christian ethics, a morality of pity and resentment, has dominated Western civilization.

The constant struggle between the two types of morality has a profound metaphysical basis. The world "viewed from within," human life [17] and all human effort, are ultimately a striving motivated by a will to power [18] and nothing else. Consequently, it comes as no surprise that slaves and masters should try to impose their set of values on all men. Both the morality of resentment and the "ethics beyond good and evil" of the masters are, each in its own way, manifestations of life itself and there-

[17] *Jenseits von Gut und Böse*, p. 17 (I, 13); p. 150 (IX, 259).
[18] *Ibid.*, p. 25 (I, 23).

fore manifestations of the same basic principle, the will to power. The difference is, of course, that in the one case it is the will to power on the part of the healthy, and in the other case the will to power on the part of the sick.

The Judeo-Christian ethic expresses its will to power in striving to make all mankind sick, turning the valuable into valueless, devaluating and desecrating nature and all that is good and strong. The priests use the concept of sin to gain control over all people. "The priest lives on sin, it is essential for him that people 'sin,' his supreme principle is: 'God forgives those who repent' which in plain language means: those who submit to the priest." [19]

The aristocrats, the noble or the strong have to "prevent the sick ones from making the healthy ones sick, too—this ought to be [their] highest aim in the world." [20] Since man is "something that is to be surpassed," the masters have to transform themselves into fathers and forefathers of the Superman. Power is the criterion of their moral values. "What is good? Everything that heightens the feeling of power in man, the will to power, power itself." [21] The great task is, then, a "revaluation of all values," or, specifically, the transformation of a negative Christian ethic of pity and resentment into a positive master morality.

II

SCHELER'S DEVELOPMENT OF THE
THEORY OF RESENTMENT

Scheler pays generous tribute to the extraordinary achievement of Nietzsche's theory of resentment. "Among the scanty discoveries which have been made in recent times about the origin of moral judgment, Friedrich Nietzsche's discovery that resentment can be the source of such value judgments is the most

[19] *Der Antichrist,* p. 1188 (No. 6).
[20] *Zur Genealogie der Moral,* p. 104 (III, 14).
[21] *Der Antichrist,* p. 1166 (No. 2).

profound." [22] At the same time he severely criticizes and rejects some of Nietzsche's concrete applications, notably his characterization of Christian love as "the most delicate flower of resentment." [23]

Scheler developed and advanced considerably the theory of resentment and thus went far beyond Nietzsche. We might summarize his specific contribution in the following four points. First, Scheler offers an incisive description of the phenomenon of resentment and develops a systematic theory of the role of resentment in the origin of moral value judgments. Secondly, he illuminates his own philosophy of values, of value-preference and ethos forms, as well as the question of the historicity of ethics in the light of resentment. Thirdly, he refutes Nietzsche's accusation that Christian love has its roots in resentment. Instead he shows that it is modern humanitarian love (*allgemeine Menschenliebe*) which proceeds from resentment. Fourthly, Scheler analyzes four characteristic traits of the "bourgeois mentality"—humanitarian love, the labor theory of value, subjectivism of values, and utilitarianism—and shows that their origin can be traced back to resentment.[24]

[22] Max Scheler, *Ressentiment,* ed. with an introduction by Lewis A. Coser, trans. by William W. Holdheim (New York: The Free Press of Glencoe, 1961), p. 43; UMST, p. 37. Henceforth, we shall quote the English translation as *Ressentiment* and always add the page number of the German original as UMST. The German text is contained in Scheler's *Vom Umsturz der Werte.*

[23] *Ibid.*

[24] For an "ontology of resentment" based on a comparative study of Heidegger and Scheler see Manfred S. Frings, *Person und Dasein: Zur Frage der Ontologie des Wertseins* (Den Haag: Martinus Nijhoff, 1969), pp. 62-68. Frings writes: "Das dem Ressentiment zugrunde liegende Vergleichen bezieht sich auf die zwischenpersonale Wertmässigkeit. . . . Wie sehr auch das Ressentiment in seinem psychologischen Effekt in der Geschichte wirksam sein mag, so ist es ontologisch doch nur durch Differenzwertigkeiten des Mitseins zu klären. . . . Es zeigt sich gerade beim Ressentiment, dass der interessenehmende Akt so beschaffen ist, dass er ontologisch zum Mitsein gehört. . . . Dies macht uns auch verständlich, dass Scheler, der immer wieder die Vorgegebenheit des Du betonte, die eigentliche "Qual des Konfliktes" des Ressentiment nicht in der faktisch vorgegebenen positiven Wertperson sieht, der das Ressentimentsubjekt ausgeliefert ist, sondern in der "Transparenz" der echten Wertrangverhältnisse (ordo amoris), die durch die Illusionswerte des Ressentiment noch hindurchscheinen" *Ibid.,* pp. 65-67.

The Phenomenology of Resentment

Scheler characterizes the phenomenon of resentment as follows:

> Resentment is a self-poisoning of the mind . . . caused by the systematic repression of certain emotions and affects which, as such, are normal components of human nature. Their repression leads to the constant tendency to indulge in certain kinds of value delusions and corresponding value judgments. The emotions and affects primarily concerned are revenge, hatred, malice, envy, the impulse to detract, and spite.[25]

If hostile feelings can be acted out or if they are overcome by moral self-conquest, no resentment results. Resentment arises when a man is unable to release his negative emotions against other persons, institutions or situations, and when he repeatedly re-experiences and relives a particular emotional reaction against someone or something.[26] Etymologically, *ressentiment* means repeating or reliving a feeling over and over again. The continual reliving of a negative emotional reaction eventually saturates the entire personality with repressed feelings of hatred, revenge, envy and the like. It also leads to a tendency to downgrade genuine values and their bearers to the level of one's own factual desire or ability. Out of a sense of impotence and weakness the man of resentment will try to construe an illusory hierarchy of values in accordance with the structure of his own personal moral condition.

Since there exists no appropriate word in German, Scheler—like Nietzsche before him—adopted the French term *ressentiment*. He suggests that the German word which most nearly approximates the meaning of *ressentiment* is *Groll* or rancor.

[25] *Ressentiment*, pp. 45-46; UMST, p. 38.
[26] *Ressentiment*, p. 39; UMST, p. 36.

"Rancor is just such a suppressed wrath, independent of the ego's activity, which moves obscurely through the mind. It finally takes shape through the repeated reliving of intentionalities of hatred or other hostile emotions." [27]

Scheler considers thirst for revenge to be the most important source of resentment.[28] Revenge is not an active but a *re*active impulse that presupposes an attack or an injury. In this regard it resembles resentment which, as the very term indicates, expresses a *re*action. Revenge is based upon an experience of impotence and weakness. The revengeful person usually postpones his response to a later time and a more suitable occasion because he does not feel strong enough to act immediately. In this way, revenge becomes a fertile breeding-ground for resentment. One can distinguish different stages in the progression of feelings as these evolve toward resentment. The progression starts with revenge, and there follow consecutively, the feelings of rancor, envy, the impulse to detraction (*Scheelsucht*), spite (*Hämischkeit*) and, finally, resentment. Whereas revenge and envy usually have specific objects, the impulse to detract (*Scheelsucht*) is not tied to definite objects. "It likes to disparage and to smash pedestals, to dwell on the negative aspects of excellent men and things, exulting in the fact that such faults are more perceptible through their contrast with the strongly positive qualities." [29]

Scheler points to the feelings of revenge and resentment in political and social life whenever a publicly professed legal equality of all citizens goes hand-in-hand with wide factual discrepancies in property, power and education. Revenge tends to turn into resentment the more it is directed against lasting situations of injustice or inequality. Prejudices based on the very nature and quality of a certain group or race usually nurture resentment in the people suffering such injustices. Physical or other natural defects, especially if they are easily visible, will often create feelings of revenge and resentment, as can be seen in the familiar resentment of cripples. "Impulses of revenge lead

[27] *Ressentiment*, pp. 39-40; UMST, p. 36.
[28] *Ressentiment*, pp. 46-52; UMST, pp. 38-44.
[29] *Ressentiment*, p. 47; UMST, p. 40.

to resentment the more they change into actual vindictiveness, the more their direction shifts toward indeterminate groups of objects . . . , and the less they are satisfied by vengeance taken on a specific object." [30]

Envy, jealousy and the competitive urge are another important source of resentment. Envy originates from the desire for a certain good or a quality which another person possesses and from the inability to acquire it. It is thus an expression of impotence and weakness. The tension between desire and nonfulfillment creates a feeling of powerlessness and consequently results in a state of envy and resentment. In most cases, envy is directed toward innate characteristics or the acquired qualities of others; for example, envy of beauty, of high character, of race, social status, reputation, or honor. Such envy often produces an illusory devaluation of the envied values.

The most intense form of envy, which in turn brings forth the strongest type of resentment, is the one directed against the very being of another person:

> The most powerless envy is the most terrible. Therefore existential envy, which is directed against the other person's very nature and being, is the strongest source of resentment. It is as if it whispers continually: "I can forgive everything, but not that you are—that you are what you are—that I am not what you are—indeed that I am not you." This form of envy strips the opponent of his very existence, for this existence as such is felt to be a "pressure," a "reproach," and an unbearable humiliation.[31]

According to Scheler, the "noble man" (*der Vornehme*) has a healthy awareness of his own value and he can, therefore, freely rejoice in the virtues and values of others. He experiences values prior to any comparison and has no need to compare himself constantly with others. The common man (*der Gemeine*), however, experiences values only *in* and *through* a com-

[30] *Ressentiment*, pp. 48-49; UMST, p. 41.
[31] *Ressentiment*, pp. 52-53; UMST, p. 45.

parison. He feels a painful tension between the higher values of other people and his own inferiority and impotence. "To relieve the tension, the common man seeks a feeling of superiority or equality, and he attains his purpose by an illusory devaluation of the other man's qualities or by a specific 'blindness' to these qualities." [32] He falsifies the values themselves and lowers them to the level of his own factual desire or ability. Out of value blindness or value delusion he construes his own illusory hierarchy of values in accordance with his own desires and his inferior moral condition.[33]

At this point, Scheler develops an idea that sharply differs from Nietzsche's interpretation of resentment. According to Nietzsche, certain economic, political or psychological situations seem of necessity to create a feeling of resentment, leading to a poisoning of man's value judgments. Scheler, however, tries to show that revenge, envy and hatred need not necessarily blossom into resentment but can be overcome by moral self-conquest. Genuine forgiveness in the case of revenge would be a striking example of such moral self-conquest.[34] Scheler stresses man's moral responsibility with regard to his negative and hostile emotions. If these are simply suppressed or are allowed to dominate man, they will poison the person, falsify his value judgments and eventually lead to resentment. But man has the freedom to

[32] *Ressentiment,* p. 58; UMST, p. 49.

[33] Helmut Schoeck has explored in a more systematic way the important role of envy in society and culture. Cf. Helmut Schoeck, *Der Neid: Eine Theorie der Gesellschaft* (Freiburg: Verlag Karl Alber, 1968). English translation: *Envy: A Theory of Social Behavior,* trans. by Michael Glenny and Betty Ross (New York: Harcourt, Brace & World, 1969). Schoeck is greatly inspired by Scheler and incorporates his ideas on envy and resentment. However, he expands the doctrine of envy, developing it—as the German subtitle indicates—into a general "theory of society." Schoeck shows both the creative and the disruptive functions of envy in the life of society. Envy of others can be a positive driving force in the creation of culture and society. Without envy there would be no evolution of society and no movements for social justice. In its negative form, envy is at the root of an egalitarian utopianism which reduces all citizens to the same level and strangles human creativity and social progress.

[34] *Ressentiment,* p. 48; UMST, p. 41.

positively control his emotions and thus can prevent a self-poisoning of the soul by resentment.

Some Types of Resentment

Scheler tries to concretize his theory of resentment by describing some types of persons who, as experience seems to indicate, are more predisposed than others toward resentment. Although nobody is necessarily gripped by resentment, certain social roles and certain recurrent situations in which individuals find themselves, are charged with the danger of resentment. Types of persons who, because of their particular place within the social structure or for some other reasons, have a propensity toward developing resentment are, for example, women, old maids, the elderly, mothers-in-law, priests, apostates and romantics (*romantische Seelentypen*).

In Scheler's view, women are more likely to engage in resentment than men. The feminine role in society is weaker and more passive than that of the male role. Woman is always forced to compete with other women for man's favor. If she is rejected, her feelings of revenge are usually repressed, because pride and modesty do not allow her to speak out and recriminate. Customs and conventions impose great restrictions and reserve on woman's work and speech and, in the case of injustice and injury, on her desire for reparation and satisfaction. All these factors collaborate to place a woman in such a disposition that she will more easily nurture feelings of resentment.[35]

What is true of the feminine role in general applies even more so to the role of the spinster. "The 'old maid' with her repressed cravings for tenderness, sex, and propagation, is rarely quite free of resentment." [36] Spinsters tend to ferret out sexually significant events in their surroundings in order to condemn them. Scheler interprets this behavior as a pursuit of sexual gratification under the guise of resentment-satisfaction.[37] The prudery

[35] *Ressentiment*, pp. 60-61; UMST, pp. 52-53.
[36] *Ressentiment*, p. 61; UMST, p. 53.
[37] *Ibid.*; cf. also NACH, p. 99.

of the old maid is not genuine modesty but a typical expression of sexual resentment.[38]

The older generation frequently develops a feeling of envy and resentment in its relationship to the young. Aging people feel threatened because they imagine that maturing youths are just waiting to oust them from positions of eminence and power. Certain values which can be enjoyed by the young are no longer accessible to the old. This awareness often becomes a source of envy and resentment in aging persons. It is only when the elderly have freely renounced the values proper to an earlier stage of life and have discovered the new horizons which an older age alone can offer, that they will successfully overcome their grievances and resentments against the young.

Scheler points to the great historical variations of the roles of the elderly. In earlier cultures, old age as such was honored and respected for the experience and wisdom which accompanied it. Today, education and the modern mass media are progressively depriving the elder and more experienced of their prerogative as dispensers of wisdom. Because the old can no longer keep up with their highly-trained and progress-oriented juniors, the problem of resentment in old age seems to be growing ever more acute in modern society.[39]

The tragic figure of the mother-in-law exemplifies another common type of resentment.[40] A mother who has loved her son since birth and has cared for him in everything must suddenly surrender him to another woman who has done nothing for him and yet demands everything. Heroic virtue, indeed, is needed here not to feel any jealousy or grudge. A mother is even expected to offer a warm welcome to the young competitor for her son's affection. "Her situation is one which the devil might have invented to test a hero." [41] No wonder that such severe emotional strain predisposes a mother-in-law to develop feelings

[38] Scheler has discussed at great length the nature of true modesty and its difference from prudery in his essay "Über Scham und Schamgefühl," in *Schriften aus dem Nachlass. Band I: Zur Ethik und Erkenntnislehre* (Bern: Francke Verlag, 1957), pp. 65-154.

[39] *Ressentiment,* pp. 62-64; UMST, pp. 54-55.

[40] *Ressentiment,* p. 64; UMST, p. 55.

[41] *Ibid.*

of envy and resentment. The songs and sagas of all nations seem to confirm this view, for they all describe the mother-in-law as an invidious and resentful creature.

Because of the special requirements of his profession, the priest is more than any other human type exposed to the creeping poison of resentment.[42] The priest is placed in the midst of earthly struggles and yet must stand above the battle. He is always expected to control his emotions and to represent the image of peace and harmony. He must serve a concrete institution and yet may not wield any secular power. Thus, his situation and social role are particularly apt to give rise to resentment.

The apostate is another type of person who is eminently predisposed to resentment.[43] An apostate, in Scheler's description, is not a man who once in his life radically changes his political, philosophical or religious convictions, or one who is "reborn" in and transformed by a new faith. Rather, he is basically a negative person who is motivated primarily by a struggle against the old belief. "The apostate does not affirm his new convictions for their own sake, he is engaged in a continuous chain of acts of revenge against his own spiritual past. . . . The new faith is merely a handy frame of reference for negating and rejecting the old." [44]

Both Nietzsche and Scheler cite Tertullian as a prime example of an apostate motivated by resentment. Tertullian asserted that the sight of Roman officials burning in hell was one of the main sources of heavenly bliss. Resentment against his own pagan past seems to have been a driving force in Tertullian's defense of the Church. After his subsequent apostasy from Catholicism and conversion to Montanism it was again resentment that motivated him to ridicule and deride the rejected Church. Johann Adam Möhler's characterization of Tertullian corroborates Scheler's view: "He was bitter and gloomy by nature, and even the mild light of the Gospel could not brighten his gloom." [45]

[42] *Ressentiment,* pp. 65-66; UMST, pp. 56-57.
[43] *Ressentiment,* pp. 66-67; UMST, pp. 57-58.
[44] *Ressentiment,* pp. 66-67; UMST, p. 57.
[45] Johann Adam Möhler, *Patrologie* (Regensburg, 1840), p. 703. Quoted in UMST, p. 58.

According to Scheler, the romantic type of mind (*romantischer Seelentypus*), the person whose preoccupation has shifted from the present to an historical past, is usually to some extent motivated and directed by resentment.[46] There exists, of course, also a genuine romantic love for the past based on the positive values of a certain historical period. Hölderlin's love for Hellas, for example, was authentic devotion to the Greek mind and mentality. But in most cases, the romantic nostalgia for a past era originates from a desire to escape from the unpleasant situation of the present time. A well-known example is Friedrich Schlegel's nostalgia for the Middle Ages. Schlegel's praise of medieval culture had the implied purpose of downgrading contemporary civilization and was thus tinged with resentment.

Scheler gives us this key to recognize resentment:

The formal structure of resentment expression is always the same: A is affirmed, valued, and praised not for its own intrinsic quality, but with the unverbalized intention of denying, devaluating, and denigrating B. A is "played off" against B.[47]

Resentment and the Falsification of Moral Value Judgments

Maurice Mandelbaum has called Scheler's analysis of the influence of resentment a classical example of the "ways in which psychological inquiry is relevant to the problem of error in moral judgment." [48] In his essay on resentment Scheler strongly asserts that there exists an "eternal hierarchy of values" and that the rules of value preference are objective and evident. However, history teaches us that there have been different moralities and types of ethos in different periods of mankind. In Scheler's view,

[46] *Ressentiment,* p. 68; UMST, pp. 58-59.
[47] *Ressentiment,* p. 68; UMST, p. 59.
[48] Maurice Mandelbaum, *The Phenomenology of Moral Experience* (Baltimore: The John Hopkins Press, 1969), p. 312.

resentment is one important key for the understanding of these developments and changes in moral judgments.[49] It was often resentment that subverted the eternal order in man's value-consciousness.

The psychological law underlying the origin of resentment is man's tendency to overcome any strong tension between desire and impotence by depreciating or denying the positive value of the desired object.[50] Scheler distinguishes two basic effects of resentment. The first one is a mere denial that a certain thing or a person possesses a value that one cannot oneself attain. When someone fails to gain another person's friendship he will often comfort himself with the thought that the other person is not really so intelligent or so good as one had thought. The old story of the fox and the sour grapes expresses the same idea. But this is not yet a falsification of values, since the values as such are not denied. "The fox does not say that sweetness is bad, but that the grapes are sour." [51]

Frequently, resentment becomes more radical and perverts the sense of values itself or—as Nietzsche puts it—falsifies the tables of values. Now the positive values themselves are inverted and become negative. Personal experience of moral failure combined with the inability to endure and tolerate other peoples' moral success is a frequent source of such resentment. It brings about a transvaluation of values by denying the very existence of objective goodness and of an objective hierarchy of values. A person always begins with the natural intention of willing the objective good as presented in the objective and eternal hierarchy of values. "But as his efforts are less and less successful and as his envy and hatred for those who are objectively 'good' grows by necessity, he increasingly tends to devaluate the idea of 'goodness' itself by degrading it to the mere X of his factual desire and condition." [52] In his attempt to escape the tormenting conflict between desire and impotence, man tends to depreciate and

[49] FORM, p. 310.
[50] *Ressentiment*, p. 73; UMST, p. 63.
[51] *Ressentiment*, p. 74; UMST, p. 64.
[52] *Ressentiment*, p. 145; UMST, p. 123.

belittle whatever he can; he will even go so far as to falsify his world-view and slander life itself.

The creative role of resentment in the history of value systems nowhere manifests itself more clearly than when the sense of values shifts so completely that it produces new moral value judgments. In the eyes of the resentful man, the strong, the healthy, the rich, the handsome people are no longer enviable or worthy of revenge. Rather they are considered to be unfortunate and pitiful. Even those who are endowed with positive values are affected themselves by this process of falsification of values.

> When the reversal of values comes to dominate accepted morality and is invested with the power of the ruling ethos, it is transmitted by tradition, suggestion, and education to those who are endowed with the seemingly devaluated qualities. They are struck with a "bad conscience" and secretly condemn themselves. The "slaves," as Nietzsche says, infect the "masters." Ressentiment man, on the other hand, now feels "good," "pure," and "human"—at least in the conscious layers of his mind.[53]

This transvalution of values affects a man at such a deep level of his personality that the false moral judgments cannot even be interpreted any longer as a conscious lying. We are dealing here with an "organic mendacity" (*organische Verlogenheit*) [54] which lies beyond all conscious lying and falsifying Scheler characterizes "organic mendacity" as the situation where "a man's mind admits only those impressions which serve his 'interest' or his instinctive attitude." [55]

As we shall show later in this chapter, resentment has profoundly affected the formation of various moralities in European history.

[53] *Ressentiment*, p. 77; UMST, p. 67.
[54] *Ibid.*
[55] *Ressentiment*, pp. 77-78; UMST, p. 67.

Christian Love and Resentment

It was noted earlier that Nietzsche argued that the Christian morality of love originated in repressed hatred and fear and that it was but an attempt to transform weakness into positive merit. He even characterized Christian love as "the most delicate flower of resentment." [56] Scheler strongly rejects this contention and shows that Nietzsche failed to distinguish between a Christian love which is not stained by resentment and numerous other interpretations of love which, in varying degrees, deserve Nietzsche's critique.[57]

To bring out the distinctive features of Christian love Scheler compares and contrasts it with the concept of love in ancient Greece:

The most important difference between the ancient and Christian views of love lies in the direction of its movement. All ancient philosophers, poets and moralists agree that love is a striving, an aspiration of the "lower" toward the "higher," the "unformed" toward the "formed," the $μὴ$ $ὄν$ towards the $ὄν$.[58]

Plato's statement that "we would not love if we were gods," clearly expresses the Greek idea of love and its direction, namely a movement in which the lower strives for and is attracted by the higher.

The Christian idea of love differs radically from the Greek conception. It is characterized by what Scheler calls "a reversal in the movement of love" (*Bewegungsumkehr der Liebe*).[59]

[56] *Ressentiment*, p. 83; UMST, p. 70.
[57] Maurice Merleau-Ponty subsequently took up this discussion and basically restated Scheler's position. Cf. Maurice Merleau-Ponty, "Christianisme et Ressentiment," *La Vie Intellectuelle*, VII (1935), pp. 278-306. English translation: "Christianity and Ressentiment," *Review of Existential Psychology and Psychiatry*, IX (Winter, 1968) pp. 1-22.
[58] *Ressentiment*, pp. 84-85; UMST, p. 71.
[59] *Ressentiment*, p. 86; UMST, p. 72.

The Christian view boldly denies the Greek axiom that love is an aspiration of the lower towards the higher. On the contrary, now the criterion of love is that the nobler stoops to the vulgar, the healthy to the sick, the rich to the poor, the handsome to the ugly, the good and saintly to the bad and common, the Messiah to the sinners and publicans.[60]

Far from being a manifestation of weakness, of need or desire, love in the Christian understanding is an expression of fullness and strength. Christian love is a spontaneous overflowing of forces proceeding from plenitude, abundant vitality and magnanimity.

The true meaning of Christian love becomes even more manifest when compared with a widespread counterfeit, namely the concept of pity (*Mitleid*) and love in Schopenhauer. Schopenhauer reduces love to pity and interprets both emotions as "the supposed recognition that the will which suffers from itself, is metaphysically identical in all individuals." [61] This is not genuine love but is, as Nietzsche correctly noted, an emotion rooted in resentment. Christian love, however, is based on an entirely different metaphysical basis. It is not self-identification with suffering and weakness which is at its root; rather, an awareness of positive values, of objective goodness and strength. Scheler acknowledges that what was presented as "Christian" love in history did not always deserve this name. Much of the effeminate type of love-ethics, which was preached in the nineteenth century, rightly deserved Nietzsche's biting criticism. Christian love in its genuine form, however, is entirely free of resentment.

Scheler also refutes Nietzsche's assertion that Christian asceticism is rooted in resentment. In presenting asceticism as basically negative, destructive and hostile to life, Nietzsche was confusing a gloomy, Schopenhauer-Buddhist type of asceticism with the joyful, harmonizing self-discipline of the genuine Christian ascetic. Far from advocating hostility to the body and suppression of life, Christianity fosters the full and harmonious develop-

[60] *Ibid.*
[61] *Ressentiment*, p. 183; UMST, pp. 78-79.

ment of the whole man. Christian asceticism proceeds from an awareness of inner strength and vital plenitude. It "serves primarily to liberate the spiritual personality, secondarily to exercise the vital functions independently of the mechanisms that serve them, so that the living being becomes largely independent of the momentary external stimuli." [62] Not suppression or extirpation of the natural instincts is the goal of ascetical practices but rather their control and their infusion by spirit and mind (*Durchdringung mit Seele und Geist*).[63] Ultimately, asceticism is "concerned with liberating the highest forces of the personality from blockage by the automatism of the lower instincts." [64]

Resentment as the Root of the "Bourgeois Mentality"

Max Scheler was an incisive and severe critic of bourgeois civilization. In his book on resentment he analyzed a number of ideas which he considered to be characteristic of the bourgeois mentality and traced them back to their roots and origin in resentment. The four main ideas are: humanitarian love, the labor theory of value, subjectivism of values, and utilitarianism. We shall now briefly delineate these characteristic features of bourgeois civilization and present them as concrete examples of the transvaluation and subversion of values brought about by the resentment of an entire social group, the bourgeois of modern Europe.

Humanitarian Love

Nietzsche criticized and rejected Christian love as the most refined blossom ever grown on the tree of resentment. In Scheler's view, Nietzsche completely misunderstood the genuine meaning of Christian love, falsely equating it with modern "humanitarian love." [65] Scheler asserts that resentment is the real

[62] *Ressentiment,* p. 134; UMST, p. 113.
[63] UMST, p. 114.
[64] *Ressentiment,* p. 135; UMST, p. 114.
[65] Scheler uses different concepts and phrases to describe this "humanitarian love" which he considers to be rooted in resentment:

root of humanitarian love, but not of Christian love.

How, then, do the two types of love differ? There is a basic difference in their objects as well as in the subjective side of the process of loving. Christian love is directed toward the individual as a unique person, toward his spiritual core and the personal values incarnated in him.[66] The object of humanitarian love is not the individual but mankind as an undifferentiated whole and its impersonal welfare.[67] On the subjective side, Christian love is essentially an active, creative and spiritual activity. Humanitarian love is characterized by passive feelings which arise largely through psychic contagion.[68]

The transformation of personal Christian love into mere benevolent sentiment for mankind in general was inspired by the resentment of the spiritually impotent. It was especially during the 17th and 18th centuries that this change took place. Scheler cites moral philosophers like Hutcheson, Adam Smith, David Hume and Rousseau as having elaborated the theoretical formulation of the new ethos.[69]

The negative character of modern humanitarian love is thus characterized:

The humanitarian movement is in its essence a ressentiment phenomenon, as appears from the very fact that this socio-historical emotion is by no means based on a spontaneous and original affirmation of a positive value, but on a protest, a counter-impulse (hatred, envy, revenge, etc.) against ruling minorities that are known to be in the possession of positive values. "Mankind" is not the immediate object of love (it cannot be, for love can be aroused only by concrete objects)—it is merely a trump card against a hated thing. Above all, this love of mankind is the expres-

---

allgemeine Menschenliebe, Humanitarismus, Liebe zur Menschheit, Liebe zu allem, was Menschenangesicht trägt, etc. Cf. UMST, p. 96.

[66] Ressentiment, pp. 108, 115; UMST, pp. 91, 97. Cf. also Scheler's Wesen und Formen der Sympathie, passim.

[67] Ressentiment, p. 121; UMST, p. 101.

[68] Ressentiment, pp. 116-117; UMST, pp. 97-98.

[69] Ibid.

sion of a repressed rejection, of a counter-impulse against God. It is the disguised form of a repressed hatred of God.[70]

Scheler points out that his philosophical observations are strikingly illustrated in the value-judgments and world-view of Ivan in Dostoievsky's *The Brothers Karamazov*.

The new ethos of humanitarian love was announced to a wider audience through the powerful literary expression of Rousseau. "Scarcely any great German of that time, except for Goethe, escaped the contagious power of Rousseau's pathos." [71] It was Goethe who recognized as early as 1787 the grave dangers inherent in the new "humanism" (*Humanität*) of Rousseau. He wrote in his *Italienische Reisen:* "I think it is true that humanism will triumph at last; only I fear that the world will at the same time be a vast hospital, where each will be his fellow man's humane sick-nurse." [72]

Love of "mankind" as a resentment against love of God found its philosophical expression and formulation most clearly in modern positivism. August Comte put "mankind" as *Grand-Etre* in the place of God and thus contributed to the radical transformation of the meaning of love. Nietzsche lived in a period when "modern humanitarianism" was flourishing in Europe and, according to Scheler, he was right in interpreting it as an historical accumulation of resentment. His basic mistake lay in equating this modern ideology with Christian love.

Scheler describes two additional phenomena that explain modern man's resentment and his transformation of Christian love into humanitarian love.

The first is the repressed hatred of one's family and one's immediate surroundings; the second is self-hatred and the attempt to escape from one's own self.

"Universal love of mankind" has sprung from resentment . . . as a manifestation of inner protest and aversion against

[70] *Ressentiment*, p. 122; UMST, p. 103.
[71] *Ressentiment*, p. 121; UMST, p. 102.
[72] *Ibid.*

the immediate circle of the community and its inherent values—against the "community" which has physically and mentally formed a man.[73]

Scheler points here to the frequent experience that children who vainly sought their parents' tenderness and love express out of inner protest an intense emotional enthusiasm for "mankind." Resentment and repressed hatred of the family are here at the root of humanitarian love. A similar phenomenon can be observed on a large scale in certain periods of history; for example, during the declining years of the Roman Empire. People felt alienated and severed from the nourishing and sustaining force of the city state. The experience of loneliness and emotional deprivation gave rise to a new love of "mankind" and to a "cosmopolitan" feeling. The writings of the later Stoics, especially Epictetus and Marcus Aurelius, display strong feelings of resentment. Scheler claims that a similar experience underlies modern humanitarian love. A protest against the immediate community and a repressed hatred of one's native country produced a vague emotional concern for "mankind" in general.[74]

The second phenomenon that frequently lies at the root of resentment and humanitarian love is self-hatred and the attempt to escape from one's own self. If a man is afraid of facing himself and his own inferiority and weakness, he is easily inclined to turn away from himself and to give himself to others. "This love is not directed at a previously discovered positive value, nor does any such value flash up in the act of loving: there is nothing but the urge to turn away from oneself and to lose oneself in other people's business." [75] By way of contrast, genuine Christian love always springs from an abundance of vital power and from strength and security. But here, love, or "altruism," is only a euphemism for escape or for the inability to remain at home with oneself. Scheler points to the familiar type of man with an ever-ready "social conscience" whose social activism "is quite clearly prompted by inability to keep his attention

[73] *Ressentiment,* pp. 123-124; UMST, p. 104.
[74] *Ressentiment,* pp. 124, 187; UMST, p. 104.
[75] *Ressentiment,* p. 95; UMST, p. 81.

focused on himself, on his own tasks and problems. Looking away from oneself is here mistaken for love." [76] This attitude seems to take, at times, the form of a collective delusion. Scheler illustrates this by pointing to the Russian intelligentsia and its morbid urge for self-sacrifice. It was self-flight (*Selbstflucht*) and a hidden nihilism that led many to a sick preoccupation with sacrificing themselves for some socio-political goal. Scheler agrees with Nietzsche's critique that such behavior originates from morbid feeling and resentment and that it is an expression of a declining life.

This type of self-escaping love has nothing to do with genuine Christian love. Scheler points to Pascal's work as a valuable illustration of man's flight from self under the delusion of love.

In his *Pensées,* Blaise Pascal has drawn the classic picture of a type of man who is entangled in many worldly activities (games, sports, hunting, also "business" or unceasing work for the "community"), and all this merely because he cannot look to himself and continually tries to escape from the vacuum, from his feeling of nothingness.[77]

In his book on sympathy [78] Scheler modified his critical view of modern humanitarian love (*allgemeine Menschenliebe*) and partly retracted it. Here he still maintains that there exists a clear distinction between the Christian idea of love and that of modern humanitarianism:

The essential characteristic of the Christian conception of spiritual love is that it is love of the individual as a person. . . . In this it is sharply distinguished from humanitarian love, which regards individuals as lovable merely qua "specimens" of the human race.[79]

According to Scheler's earlier view, modern humanitarian love

[76] *Ressentiment,* p. 96; UMST, p. 82.
[77] *Ressentiment,* pp. 125-126; UMST, p. 105.
[78] SYM, pp. 108-111; *Sympathy,* pp. 99-101.
[79] SYM, p. 111; *Sympathy,* p. 101.

originated entirely from resentment against the Christian love of God and person. Thus, it was not considered to be a genuine movement of love but rather a mere gesture of defiance and protest. In his modified view Scheler maintains that only the ranking of humanitarian love *above* the Christian love of persons proceeds from resentment. Humanitarian love as such is no longer linked to resentment as its origin; rather it is recognized as a positive force. But even in making this retraction, Scheler emphasizes again that there exists an unchangeable objective order of higher and lower values, that humanitarian love must be ranked below the Christian love of God and person and that any attempt to reverse this hierarchy of values could be due only to resentment.[80]

The Labor Theory of Value

The labor theory of value is another characteristic of the bourgeois morality that can be traced back to its psychological roots in resentment. Its basic principle says: "Moral value pertains only to those qualities, actions, etc., which the individual has acquired by his own strength and labor." [81] This new estimation has its basis in a different stance toward apprehending values. The emphasis has shifted from the objective qualities of values to the subjective process of work. Man no longer has the ability to see and accept ungrudgingly values as given by God. Rather he attaches all values to work and considers work and thus himself alone to possess the power of endowing being and action with value.

This transvaluation, or better devaluation, orginates from the resentment of the "moral proletarian." According to Scheler, all human beings are not equal in moral value and talents. Christianity has always recognized that there are differences in natural moral gifts as well as different "gifts of grace" and individual *virtutes infusae*. The labor theory of value was invented by "moral proletarians" who resented the superior endowments of their betters. Out of envy and resentment they desired "to degrade the superior persons, those who represent a higher value,

---

[80] SYM, p. 109; *Sympathy,* p. 100.
[81] *Ressentiment,* p. 138; UMST, p. 115.

to the level of the low." [82] The new axiom expressing the moral equality of all men says: "There is moral value only in that which *everyone*—even the least gifted—can do." [83] By degrading all innate higher qualities and by dragging the gifted down to their plebeian level, the morally weak have achieved an equality in which the least gifted set the criterion of value for all.

What he could not bear, the surpassing importance of the "superior nature," has now been devaluated. The sweat and tears of his moral "toil" are now shining in the light of highest value! Through this transvaluation, his secret thirst for revenge against the better man has now been quenched. [84]

As the above description clearly indicates, Scheler's sympathy lay rather with aristocracy than with an egalitarian democracy. Accordingly, he has been criticized for his aristocratic bent of mind. One can, it would seem, be critical of Scheler's insufficient understanding of modern democracy and still acknowledge the validity and importance of his thesis on the close link between resentment and the labor theory of value. [85]

Subjectivism of Values

The tendency to subjectify values is a third characteristic of the bourgeois mind and is also a product of resentment. The objective hierarchy of values makes definite claims on the individual man. If man fails to respond to these claims, the experi-

---

[82] *Ressentiment*, p. 143; UMST, p. 121.
[83] *Ressentiment*, p. 139; UMST, p. 117.
[84] *Ibid.*
[85] Many historical examples seem to corroborate and strengthen Scheler's assertions and analyses. Scheler quotes two examples in footnotes. Werner Sombart, in his book *Der Bourgeois,* claims that "resentment is the basic trait" in the family records of the Florentine Leon Battista Alberti, the first typical representative of the bourgeois spirit and morality. Again, Marcus Porcius Cato, an ancient bourgeois, has been described as a typical man of resentment. The historian Friedrich Leo attributed Cato's moralism to his feeling of being excluded from the old Roman nobility. Cf. Scheler, *Ressentiment*, pp. 190-191; UMST, pp. 115-117.

ence of his weakness and failure easily nurtures in him resentment against the values which he did not attain. This leads to the denial of any objective order of values and to a substitution of merely subjective personal standards. The man of resentment avenges himself on the good he cannot reach by dragging it down to the level of his factual condition.[86]

> The resentment-laden man, who in his insufficiency is oppressed, tormented, and frightened by the negative judgment on his existence which flows from an objective hierarchy of values—and who is secretly aware of the arbitrary or distorted character of his own valuations—"transvalues" the idea of value itself by denying the existence of such an objective hierarchy.[87]

All values are now considered as subjective and relative, as projections of man's desires and feelings.

Since, however, the man of resentment is a weakling and does not have the courage to live by his own judgment, he turns for support to his fellow men. Thus, he tends to follow the general trend of his community and the conventions and traditions that are generally accepted. Present community standards become his substitute for any objective hierarchy of absolute values, and all forms of morality that rise above the level of common standards are objects of his envy and resentment.

Utilitarianism

Utilitarianism is, according to Scheler, the basic philosophy of bourgeois man. It is also one of the chief manifestations of the transvaluation of values in modern morality proceeding from resentment.

> The most profound perversion of the hierarchy of values is the subordination of vital values to utility values, which gains force as modern morality develops. Since the victory of the industrial and commercial spirit over the military and

[86] *Ressentiment,* p. 145; UMST, p. 123.
[87] *Ibid.*

theological-metaphysical spirit, this principle has been penetrating ever more deeply, affecting the most concrete value judgments.[88]

The subordination of the noble (*das Edle*) to the useful is one important manifestation of this modern mentality. Scheler defines noble as standing for those qualities that constitute the value of life in living organisms.

Since the French Revolution, the merchants and representatives of industry have brought about a radical shift in values. The qualities that enable the businessman to succeed have been set up as generally valid moral values, indeed as the highest values. Utilitarian considerations triumph as the supreme criteria of morality in general. Consequently, the new cardinal virtues are cleverness, quick adaptability, a calculating mind, industriousness and thrift. These are set above the virtues that ranked high in an earlier period, virtues like "courage, bravery, readiness to sacrifice, daring, high-mindedness, vitality, desire for conquest, indifference to material goods, patriotism, loyalty to one's family, tribe, and sovereign, power to rule and reign, humility, etc." [89]

A change in meaning of certain concepts clearly indicates an underlying transformation of basic values. Earlier in this chapter we observed such a transformation in the concept of love that changed its meaning radically from "Christian" love to "humanitarian" love. A change in meaning can also be observed in concepts like self-control and loyalty. Originally, self-control meant primarily the sovereignty of the spiritual person over the chaos of sensuous impulses, without any further utilitarian considerations. Now, self-control is considered as a mere means for success in business which requires soberness, solidity and moderation.[90] The cult of the useful has also changed the meaning of loyalty (*Treue*). Formerly, it signified "the natural continuity and permanence of a disposition of love

[88] *Ressentiment*, p. 154-155; UMST, p. 131.
[89] *Ressentiment*, p. 156; UMST, p. 132.
[90] *Ressentiment*, pp. 156-157; UMST, p. 133.

and confidence." [91] Now, loyalty is nothing but a disposition to fulfill promises and agreements.

Modern utilitarianism has also succeeded in changing man's attitude toward life itself. In the Middle Ages, life was considered as an intrinsic value (*Leben als Selbstwert*). It deserved to be developed for its own sake, without any reference to professional usefulness. The modern cult of the useful has changed all that. "Now life itself—the sheer existence of an individual, a race, a nation—must be justified by its usefulness for a wider community." [92] A utilitarian civilization does not see any value in a purposeless self-expression (*zweckfreie Ausdrucksbetätigung*) of life. Even modern sports are no longer considered a manifestation of free vitality, pure play, or the exercise of vital functions for the sake of life, but rather as surcease from work and gathering of strength for renewed useful labor. Everything is now done for the sake of work.

The cult of the useful and the resulting exaltation of utility values over vital values are rooted in the "resentment of the vitally weaker against the stronger (*im Ressentiment der Lebensuntüchtigeren gegen die Tüchtigeren*), of those who are partially dead against the living!" [93] Guided by resentment, the modern world-view subverts the true hierarchy of values. "It seeks to understand the living by analogy with the dead. . . . The eye is explained by analogy with spectacles, the hand by analogy with the spade, the organ by analogy with the tool." [94] Life itself is seen as a mere accident in a universal mechanical process. It is ultimately the resentment of those "who got the worst of it" (*Schlechtweggekommene*) [95] who brought about this shift of values and fostered the cult of the useful.

It is the vitally inferior, relatively stagnant man—he who "got the worst of it"—who places the tool above the vital values he lacks! The near-sighted man will praise his eye-

91 *Ibid.*
92 *Ressentiment*, p. 158; UMST, p. 134.
93 UMST, p. 137.
94 *Ressentiment*, p. 171; UMST, pp. 144-145.
95 *Ibid.*

glasses, the lame man his stick, the bad mountain climber will extol the rope and climbing iron.[96]

Modern utilitarian civilization as a product of resentment marks, in Scheler's view, a decline in the evolution of mankind. The cultural decline manifests itself in the "rule of the weak over the strong, of the clever over the noble, the rule of mere quantity over quality." [97] Scheler discerns signs of decadence in the "weakening of man's central, guiding forces as against the anarchy of his automatic impulses. The mere means are developed and the goals are forgotten. And that precisely is decadence!" [98]

Scheler concludes his book on resentment, however, on a positive note, pointing to the healthy effects that a return to the proper hierarchy of values would offer mankind. He even presents some remarkable "ecological" considerations, long before the importance and urgency of ecology received general recognition.

How differently do things look when this basic error is abandoned! Then the further development of industrialism is not unconditionally valuable, but only if it inflicts no permanent damage on vital values. Then we must say, for example: preserving the health of the race as a whole— and of the groups within it in proportion to their vital fitness and their vitally valuable, "noble" qualities and forces —is an intrinsic value and should be placed above useful achievements even if the industrial evolution is thus slowed down. Units such as the family and the nation need support and care, even if it demonstrably delays industrial progress and the expansion of civilization. . . . The same applies to the preservation of plant and animal life, and the woods, and to the protection of the landscape against the devastating tendencies of industrialism.[99]

[96] *Ibid.*
[97] *Ressentiment,* p. 174; UMST, p. 147.
[98] *Ibid.*
[99] *Ressentiment,* pp. 173-174; UMST, pp. 146-147.

VI
Repentance and the Historical Nature of Man

Sigrid Wilhelm, in his study on the image of man in Max Scheler, interprets the phenomenon of repentance as the decisive foundation for the understanding of man's historicity. "We are convinced that the theory of the historicity of man—a theory which was enunciated but not proved by Dilthey and which was taken over by Heidegger—can be founded within the framework of value-ethics in Scheler's phenomenon of repentance." [1] Wilhelm demonstrates that the experience of the triad of guilt, repentance and rebirth enables us to understand "history as a specific human mode of existence." [2] On the same basis we can comprehend the essence of man under the aspect of historicity. It is in the realization and experience of repentance—in the experienced time-flux which spans the past, present, and future—that man's historicity discloses itself. Scheler attached extraordinary importance to repentance as a pivotal phenomenon for the understanding of man. This is evident, for example, in the following statement: "If anybody should say, 'I am not conscious of any guilt in

[1] Sigrid Wilhelm, *Das Bild des Menschen in der Philosophie Max Schelers* (Dresden: Franke, 1937), p. 66.
[2] *Ibid.*, p. 67.

myself, therefore I have nothing to repent'—he must surely be either a god or an animal." [3]

I

THE PHENOMENON OF REPENTANCE AND
THE HISTORICITY OF MAN

Scheler developed his theory of repentance primarily in the essay "Repentance and Rebirth." [4] This essay must be counted among his most widely acclaimed writings. Johannes Messner has called it "the most profound and most ingenious non-theological investigation on the essence of repentance ever written." [5] Hans-Eduard Hengstenberg wrote as recently as 1969 that "Scheler's statements on repentance are still unsurpassed." [6] Psychiatrist Ernest Keen, a professor at Bucknell University, acknowledges that he finds Scheler's theory of repentance "a great help in working with patients." He further states that Scheler's essay "really presents a view of man in which the therapeutic power of confronting one's guilt becomes intelligible." [7]

In Scheler's theory, repentance is "the mighty power of self-regeneration of the moral world." [8] Repentance conquers the moral evil of the past, brings renewal and rebirth to the present, and works joyfully for a better future. In this way, "repentance is the most revolutionary force in the moral world." [9]

In the past, repentance has often been misunderstood as a futile and meaningless attempt to undo a past deed. Scheler

[3] VEIM, p. 51; *Eternal*, p. 57.

[4] VEIM, pp. 27-59; *Eternal*, pp. 33-65.

[5] Johannes Messner, *Widersprüche in der menschlichen Existenz* (Innsbruck: Tyrolia, 1952), p. 157.

[6] Hans-Eduard Hengstenberg, *Grundlegung der Ethik* (Stuttgart: W. Kohlhammer Verlag, 1969), p. 90: "Im übrigen sind Schelers Aussagen über die Reue immer noch unübertroffen."

[7] Ernest Keen, "Scheler's View of Repentance and Rebirth and its Relevance to Psychotherapy," *Review of Existential Psychology and Psychiatry*, VI (Winter, 1966), 84.

[8] VEIM, p. 49; *Eternal*, p. 55.

[9] VEIM, p. 50; *Eternal*, p. 56.

sees one of the principal causes for this misconception in a false notion of the internal structure of man's intellectual and spiritual life. An analysis of the concept of time and of the specific characteristics of the temporal life-stream of man reveals that there exists a basic difference between objective time and human time. This distinction is of central importance for the understanding of repentance.

In his discussion of past guilt Scheler starts with the question whether something that was done in the past can be undone now, whether an evil deed can be blotted out. It seems that the passing of time is an irreversible process and that what is past is simply past. This is true with regard to *objective time* within which physical events take place. But it is not so with *human time*. Man's existence is not like a river which flows by and cannot turn back and alter a part that has gone before and is past. In contrast to the continuous flux of inanimate nature, which knows only one dimension and one direction, man still has power over the meaning and value of his past acts. He cannot alter the physical fact that a certain deed was done by him, nor can he change the external effects of his actions. But man can alter their internal meaning and value. Every event of our past remains somehow indeterminate in significance, incomplete in its value, and still redeemable. In every moment of man's life the whole of his past is still present and in his power. In the act of repentance man has the capability of imprinting on past deeds a new meaning and value. In repentance man reappraises part of his past life and shapes for it a new worth and significance. *Human time* differs from objective time precisely in this, that the former is not bound to the one-directional flux of inanimate nature. Man can still lay hold of the meaning and worth of his past deeds. Thus, repentance is an incursion into our own past life and an encroachment upon it. Every moment of man's past history can still be redeemed and will remain redeemable as long as man lives. Repentance is a form of self-healing of the soul, a great power of self-regeneration. Since through repentance man really does have power over the meaning and value of his past acts, he can drive guilt out of the vital core of his personality. "In so doing repentance relieves the pressure of the guilt which spreads in all directions from that wickedness, and at the same time deprives evil of that power of reproduction by which it must always bring forth more evil." [10]

Repentance liberates man from the shackles of evil forces which have bound him slavishly in the past. Scheler attaches great importance to this liberation as an essential aspect of repentance. He recognizes man's negative determination by his historical past as the major obstacle for any genuine improvement in the future. This explains why for Scheler repentance always includes a twofold movement of turning both to the past and to the future. Some authors writing on repentance, even recent ones, have failed to recognize the importance of turning to the past as a necessary process of self-liberation. Maria Otto, for example, states in her recent book, *Reue und Freiheit,* that repentance is not a turning back to past deeds but is only concerned with the task of making a new beginning.[11] Scheler scoffs at the naive popular attitude that advises people to ignore their evil past and to simply resolve to do better in the future:

> The jovial gentlemen say, "No repentance!—just resolve to do better in the future." But what these jovial gentlemen fail to tell us is where we may find strength to make those resolutions, still less the strength to carry them out, if repentance has not first liberated the personal Self and empowered it to combat the determining force of the past.[12]

It is, therefore, only after the liberation of our moral self from the determining power of past evil deeds that we can truly and effectively resolve to improve our moral conduct in the future. The first movement must always be the debilitation (*Ent-*

[10] VEIM, p. 37; *Eternal,* p. 44. In the German wording Scheler seems to allude here to the famous poetic lines of Schiller: "Das eben ist der Fluch der bösen Tat, dass sie, fortzeugend, immer Böses muss gebären." (Such is the curse of an evil deed that constant evil it must bear.)

[11] Maria Otto, *Reue und Freiheit—Versuch über ihre Beziehung im Ausgang von Sartres Drama* (Freiburg: Verlag Karl Alber, 1961).

[12] VEIM, p. 36; *Eternal,* pp. 42-43.

mächtigung) of the continuing influence and effectiveness of past guilt, and the inner striving to drive guilt out of the vital core of the person. Only then will repentance effect moral rejuvenation and enable life to begin anew. In this way man can make his personality whole again and bring about his own moral rebirth.

In popular opinion repentance has often been interpreted and then brushed aside as a mere impotent regret or a sorrowful looking back to past failures. For Scheler, repentance is more; it is a great paradox whereby man turns powerfully to the past to extinguish the quality of evil in past actions and at the same time works joyfully for the future, for liberation, renewal and rebirth.

Hans Urs von Balthasar, in an illuminating chapter on the nature of time, concurs with Scheler's interpretation of the reversibility of time. But as a theologian he raises some difficulties regarding the viability of a merely philosophical approach to repentance. He writes:

> The *conversio* of a man as a reversal of the direction of his time—that which Max Scheler has described as "repentance and rebirth"—is an act which is understandable in terms of the philosophy of religions, because it is truly, as Augustine's *Confessions* show, an act of man as such. But this insight into the reversibility of time and of the judgment upon us which it involves is only understandable if it is on God's initiative; otherwise God would be compelled to forgive because man repents.[13]

As a philosopher Max Scheler conducted his research into the phenomenon of repentance on a strictly philosophical level. However, at the end of his essay "Repentance and Rebirth," he clearly indicates that the philosophical reflections need to be complemented by a theological interpretation of repentance. He acknowledges that ultimately man experiences the strength for

[13] Hans Urs von Balthasar, *A Theological Anthropology*, trans. from the German (New York: Sheed and Ward, 1967), p. 35.

the realization of repentance as a gift of God's love and grace.[14]

At this point we must briefly discuss a critique of Scheler's theory put forth by Albert Esser. In his penetrating study on repentance *Das Phänomen Reue*,[15] Esser integrates the basic insights of Scheler and tries to further develop and systematize them. He approaches the phenomenon of repentance from the experience of conscience in which guilt discloses itself as a discrepancy between what should be and what in fact is, or as a conflict between the "ideal" and the "real" self.[16] Esser offers here a perceptive and illuminating analysis of guilt. Equally valuable is his description of the five possible responses to a situation of guilt. The first is characterized as an attempt to simply forget and ignore one's guilt; a second response is resignation. Defiance and simple regret are two other modes of reacting to guilt. The fifth and only appropriate response is genuine repentance.[17]

On the whole, Esser's book is an excellent philosophical treatise on repentance. It is, therefore, surprising that the author should accuse Scheler, to whose philosophy he is so deeply indebted, of misunderstanding both the ideas of guilt and repentance. He claims that Scheler failed to grasp the basic idea of guilt as a discrepancy between the moral ought and the actual deed, or as a conflict between the ideal and the factual self. Scheler's theory of repentance fails, according to Esser, because it does not come to grips with the phenomenon of guilt.[18]

Esser's analysis of guilt is accurate and illuminating, but he is altogether mistaken in his interpretation of Scheler. His basic problem would seem to be his unfamiliarity with Scheler's numerous writings other than "Repentance and Rebirth." A reading of *Vorbilder und Führer, Ordo Amoris,* and *Der Forma-*

---

[14] VEIM, p. 59; *Eternal,* p. 65.

[15] Albert Esser, *Das Phänomen Reue* (Cologne: Jakob Hegner, 1963).

[16] *Ibid.,* pp. 56-61; 143.

[17] *Ibid.,* pp. 79-106: "Die Antwortmöglichkeiten auf die Schuldsituation: Das Vergessen, die Resignation, der Trotz, das Bedauern, die Reue."

[18] *Ibid.,* p. 143.

lismus in der Ethik und die materiale Wertethik clearly shows that Scheler has an accurate understanding of guilt and of the ought-is conflict as the basic situation underlying both the process of repentance and rebirth. But even in his essay on repentance, the one at issue in Esser's critique, Scheler speaks repeatedly of the tension and conflict between the "ideal" and the "real" self as the area in which the dynamism of repentance is at work:

> Thus the continuous dynamic of repentance enables us to glimpse the attainment of an altogether higher, ideal existence—the raising through firm self-revision of the whole plane of our moral existence—and lays open to our gaze, far below us, the whole condition of the old Self. This is the deepest mystery of that vital, deeper act of repentance. . . .[19]

In the process of repentance man ascends to a higher plane of life and envisages the ideal value-image of himself. This image was hidden from him in his state of guilt, but he discovers it in the liberating act of repentance and is drawn to it in love.[20]

II
REPENTANCE OF DEED (TATREUE)—
REPENTANCE OF BEING (SEINSREUE)

Repentance is usually concerned with a particular deed. But besides this "repentance of deed" (*Tatreue*) there is also a type of repentance that looks beyond the individual negative act of the past and is concerned with one's own personal being which has disclosed itself negatively in such a deed. Scheler calls this "repentance of being" (*Seinsreue*).[21] The "repentance of

[19] VEIM, p. 41; *Eternal,* pp. 47-48.
[20] VEIM, p. 46; *Eternal,* pp. 52-53.
[21] VEIM, pp. 40, 42, 49; *Eternal,* pp. 46, 48, 55. For a discussion of the differences between "repentance of deed" (*Tatreue*) and "repentance of being" (*Seinsreue*) see Manfred S. Frings, *Person und Dasein: Zur Frage der Ontologie des Wertseins* (Den Haag: Martinus Nijhoff, 1969), pp. 73-79. Also Manfred S. Frings, "Insight-Logos-Love (Lonergan-Heidegger-Scheler)," *Philosophy Today,* XIV (Summer, 1970), pp. 113-115.

deed" expresses itself in a statement such as "how could I ever have *done* this or that." When man goes a step further and evokes a "repentance of being" he might say: "How could I ever have *been* such a person who could perform that deed." However, repentance of being does not refer to the total being of a person. We cannot repent our whole person as such or our essential self, but only certain levels of our being that are the source of our evil deeds.[22]

Although the repentance of deed is primarily concerned with the moral deficiency of an individual act, it also should always turn its attention beyond the single deed to the person himself and his guilt. But it is only in the repentance of being that man is directly concerned with the renovation of the person as a whole. In one dynamic act man expels and leaves behind, so to speak, the old self and rises to a new height of a more perfect existence. Scheler illustrates this with the experience of a mountain-climber who in the process of climbing sees at the same time the summit approaching and the valley sinking beneath his feet. Thus, in repentance of being the person ascends to new heights of being and, in rising, sees the negative levels of his old self receding from view.

Scheler's idea of repentance of being must be seen in the context of his theory of value-person-types or ideal model persons.[23] In the act of repentance man experiences the call of the ideal model person which draws him from his present level toward fuller self-realization. Every man sees before him the image of the person he ought to be, and the cognition of the value-difference between his present factual being and his potential ideal being challenges him and moves him in the act of repentance toward the realization of his own higher self.

To the extent that man moves from a mere repentance of deed to repentance of being he will seize the very root of guilt

[22] To bring out this dimension and to avoid any misunderstanding, Manfred Frings translates *Seinsreue* as "repentance of levels of one's being." Cf. Manfred S. Frings, "Insight-Logos-Love (Lonergan-Heidegger-Scheler)," *Philosophy Today*, XIV (Summer, 1970), p. 113.

[23] For an exposition of Scheler's theory on value-person-types or ideal model persons see chapter VIII.

and evil and pluck it out of his own being, thus regaining his full moral freedom. At the same time he will stir up the in-dwelling force of regeneration which can create in him a new heart and a new man. Repentance of being thus takes on the character of a genuine repentance of conversion which brings about a transformation of outlook and a "rebirth" (*Wiederge-burt*) of man. In this rebirth, the spiritual core of the person as the ultimate root of all moral deeds turns wholly away from its former negative inclinations and builds itself anew.[24]

III
COLLECTIVE REPENTANCE

So far we have discussed repentance as the response of in-dividual man to his personal guilt. Scheler expands the idea of repentance and applies it also to whole social groups.[25] "Re-pentance is not only a process in the individual soul; like guilt it is basically also a social, historical, collective phenomenon." [26] The principle of solidarity and the ideal of collective responsi-bility lie at the root of such collective repentance. As there can be group responsibility for guilt, there can also be group re-sponsibility for repentance. According to Scheler, each individual does in fact share a certain responsibility for *all* events of the moral cosmos. There is a form of collective responsibility which expresses itself in the awareness "that even the *total* moral world of all past and future, of all stars and heavens, could be radi-cally different if 'I' were only 'different.' " [27]

[24] VEIM, p. 42; *Eternal*, p. 48.

[25] In his *Kulturethik,* Johannes Messner has a chapter entitled "On the Possibility of Spiritual Rebirth of Nations" in which he appropriates Scheler's ideas on collective repentance as a regeneration and rebirth of communitives and nations. Messner laments the fact that this dimen-sion of cultural philosophy is scarcely ever touched in works on the philosophy of culture. He states that Scheler is the only philosopher to have explored this question. Cf. Johannes Messner, *Kulturethik* (Inns-bruck: Tyrolia-Verlag, 1954), pp. 617-620: "Möglichkeit seelischer Wiedergeburt der Völker."

[26] VEIM, p. 51; *Eternal*, p. 57.

[27] *Ibid.*

The principle of solidarity is one of the distinguishing features of Scheler's philosophy in general—a sharp contrast to the rampant individualism reigning in those days. Scheler applies the principle of solidarity to various areas of philosophy and ethics. With regard to moral responsibility, for example, he writes: "This fundamental sense of collective responsibility is just as essential to the subsistence of a moral subject as the sense of responsibility for itself." [28] Scheler rejects the idea that collective responsibility arises only from a mutual pledge or contract. Rather, it is a basic phenomenon of the moral cosmos that antecedes and conditions all explicit human agreements.

It follows then that repentance must be equally concerned with the collective guilt of our community and our share in it, and with our own individual culpability. The principle of solidarity implies that we must feel genuinely implicated in the collective guilt of our community and our historical era. Consequently we must regard such guilt also as our own and share in the repenting of it.

Scheler describes in moving words the powerful rejuvenating effect of communal repentance in history:

> We see in history how repentance can grow into a mighty torrent; how it rushes for generations through whole peoples and civilizations; how it opens obdurate hearts to compassion; how it endeavors to drive the accumulated guilt of ages out of the life of communities; how it historically illumines the past of nations which was hidden by racial pride; how it broadens the once ever-narrowing future into a broad, bright plain of possibilities—and so prepares the way for the regeneration of a collective moral existence.[29]

Scheler further illustrates the historical role of communal repentance with three examples: the movement of repentance in early Christianity, the medieval renewal under the leadership of St. Bernard of Clairvaux, and the collective repentance after

[28] VEIM, p. 51; *Eternal*, p. 58.
[29] VEIM, p. 52; *Eternal*, p. 58.

World War I as a creative response to the collective war guilt of the European nations.

> It was not least through the countless tears of its repentance that early Christianity renewed the outgoing world of antiquity, hardened by pleasure-seeking, by lust for power and glory, and poured into that world a feeling of rejuvenation.[30]

Again, after the moral decadence and brutality of the 11th century another powerful wave of repentance ran through the peoples of Europe and, under the leadership of Bernard of Clairvaux, brought about a moral renewal and religious rebirth.

The third historical example of communal repentance is the creative response of many Europeans to the collective guilt of World War I. Immediately after the war Scheler published an article in *Hochland* under the title "On Religious Renewal," which contained an urgent plea for collective repentance and for solidarity:

> The cry goes out to all men: Arise! set your feet to the holy mountain of your consciences. . . . From its sunbathed peak you may look down into the maelstrom of Europe's common guilt, as into a valley of fearfulness, of sin and tears! . . . this world is rising to God or falling from God as a *single,* indivisible whole, a morally compact mass, and all therein answer for all, and all for the whole, before the highest judge. . . . only this perception of collective guilt can awaken in us . . . the great pathos of mutual pardon with collective repentance and atonement for this guilt.[31]

In the midst of the war Scheler had published his book *Krieg und Aufbau* (1916) [32] in which, among other things, he reflected on a possible meaning of the war. He saw only one, that the war could help all Europeans to acknowledge their co-

[30] *Ibid.*
[31] VEIM, p. 121; *Eternal,* p. 125.
[32] Max Scheler, *Krieg und Aufbau* (Leipzig: Verlag der Weissen Bücher, 1916).

responsibility in the moral downfall and so lead to collective repentance and a genuine change of heart. Thus, there could be hope for a moral rebirth of Europe.

During the war and the immediate post-war years, Scheler addressed himself time and again to the question of Europe's future. He warned against the naive belief that mere diplomatic good will and pragmatic wisdom could create a new and better future for the nations of Europe. It is only by genuinely coming to grips with Europe's past failures and by true repentance, he writes, that a better future can emerge from the ruins of the murderous war. In a series of articles published during 1916, "Sociological Reorientation and the Task of German Catholics after the War," [33] Scheler forecasts "an era of great repentance." He then specifies this repentance as not being simply concerned with the war in general but with the types of models and ideals that the preceding era had worshipped and which were ultimately responsible for the moral downfall and the war.[34] Although writing in the midst of the war, Scheler sounds a hopeful note in these articles. However hellish an event of world history may be, he says, it always contains the seeds of renewal and rebirth. Any moment of history remains redeemable and men can imprint a new meaning on it if only they repent and start anew.[35] In his lecture "The Reconstruction of European Culture" (1917) he said:

A cultural reconstruction is only possible if an increasingly large proportion of the European population learns to

[33] Max Scheler, "Soziologische Neuorientierung und die Aufgabe der deutschen Katholiken nach dem Krieg," *Hochland,* XIII (January, 1916), 385-406; (March, 1916), 682-700; (May, 1916), 188-204; (June, 1916), 257-294.

[34] *Ibid.,* p. 698: "Und es wird—sehe ich recht—die Zeit einer grossen Reue und einer grossen Busse kommen—ja nicht über den Krieg an sich, wie die Pazifisten meinen, wohl aber über Sein und Werden der menschlichen Gesinnungen und über den Wert der 'vorbildlichen' führenden Menschentypen der vorangehenden Zeiten, die diesen Krieg als letztes Sympton ihres Fiebers aus sich hervortrieben, die ihm vor allem den ihm eigentümlichen moralischen Gesamtcharakter erteilten." For a more detailed discussion of Scheler's ideas on *Vorbilder* see chapter VIII: "Value-Person-Types (Ideal Model Persons)."

[35] *Ibid.,* pp. 190-191.

look upon this cataclysm as resulting from a collective guilt of the European peoples, resting on their moral solidarity —as, therefore, a guilty evil which can only be removed and inwardly conquered by common expiation, common repentance and common sacrifice. . . . There is no psychic power more clairvoyant than repentance, none which more deeply sounds the well of past being, no greater power of healing than this liberating light of our history, which illumines our quintessential self. It is repentance indeed which enables man to acquire that kind of historical knowledge which not only describes the past but does the most important thing that historical knowledge can do—unburden from the past, free and strengthen the soul for a new future, a new power of action.[36]

One cannot but feel a certain sadness when reading the urgent pleas for repentance and rebirth that Scheler addressed to the nations of Europe in their hour of darkness. The bright new hope and the enthusiasm with which Scheler tried to renew the cultural and political life of Europe assume a melancholic touch in view of the subsequent course of history. But then, the insight on collective repentance retains validity and may even take on a heightened relevance at a later time. "It is a dreadful thing that we can win life only on the dark and painful way of repentance. But the simple truth that there is a way for us to obtain life at all is glorious." [37]

[36] VEIM, pp. 416-417; *Eternal,* pp. 416-417.
[37] VEIM, p. 55; *Eternal,* pp. 61-62: "Es ist furchtbar, dass wir das Leben nur gewinnen können auf dem dunkeln Schmerzensweg der Reue. Aber es ist herrlich, *dass* es überhaupt einen Weg zum Leben für uns gibt."

VII
Love and the Historical Nature of Man

The *ordo amoris* is a central idea of Scheler's value ethics which explains and illumines numerous aspects of his moral philosophy and unifies, in a sense, the whole of his creative thought. In the *ordo amoris* we find the coincidence of objectivity and subjectivity, of universality and individuality.[1] The *ordo amoris* elucidates the objective moral order as well as man's knowledge and pursuit of values. It also explains the falsifications of the order of values, for such falsifications mean precisely a confusion or distortion of the *ordo amoris*.[2] Scheler describes at great length the phenomenon of resentment as a prime example of how man can distort the objective *ordo amoris*.

I

ORDO AMORIS—MICROCOSM OF THE
WORLD OF VALUES

If the *ordo amoris* is of such eminent importance for the understanding of Scheler's moral philosophy it is surprising, indeed, that most critics of Scheler have failed to recognize and evaluate the centrality of this idea.[3] This neglect seems to be

[1] NACH, pp. 347, 351, 352.
[2] *Ibid.*, p. 355.
[3] Manfred S. Frings has drawn attention to this anomaly. He singles out for his criticism the works of such distinguished Scheler scholars as Maurice Dupuy, Wilfried Hartmann, Johannes Hessen, Heinrich

one important reason for the numerous misinterpretations of Scheler's moral philosophy. At best, such neglect has resulted in literally correct but one-sided expositions of Scheler's philosophical thought.

The term *ordo amoris* has two basic meanings, one normative, the other descriptive.[4] In its normative meaning, *ordo amoris* signifies the objective right order of love or the ordered counterpart of the hierarchy of values reflected in the heart of man. When used descriptively, *ordo amoris* means the system of actual valuations and value-preferences operative in an individual man's life. The *ordo amoris* is thus the basic structure of a person's moral makeup and the foundation from which all the individual acts of his moral behavior arise. It is, so to speak, the basic moral formula (*sittliche Grundformel*)[5] according to which a person lives and exists on a moral plane.

In an unusually profound and insightful passage Scheler describes the *ordo amoris*, its importance for the understanding of man, and its significance for the moral life of the individual.

Whoever understands the *ordo amoris* of a man understands the man. He possesses for him as a moral subject that which the crystal formula is for the crystal. He sees through the man as far as one can see through a man. He sees— behind all empirical multiplicity and complexity—the simple basic structure of his heart (*Gemüt*), which is more deserving of being called the center of man as a spiritual being than are the processes of knowing and willing. He possesses in a spiritual schema the inner spring that secretly feeds all that emanates from this man; even more, the primordial, determining factor (*das Urbestimmende*) of that which unceasingly sets about placing itself around man—his moral environment in space, and his fate in time,

Lützeler and Erich Rothacker. Cf. Manfred S. Frings, "Der Ordo Amoris bei Max Scheler. Seine Beziehungen zur materialen Wertethik und zum Ressentimentbegriff," *Zeitschrift für Philosophische Forschung,* XX (January, 1966), p. 57.

[4] NACH, pp. 347-348.
[5] *Ibid.,* p. 348.

that is, the quintessence of the possibilities that can happen to this man, and to him alone.[6]

The hierarchy of values has, according to Scheler, an objective and immutable nature, ultimately based on the eternal love of God. Consequently, there must also exist an objective order of appropriate responses to these levels of values. Values ought to be loved and realized in man's life according to their higher or lower rank. The higher ones must take precedence over the lower.

The objective order of values is reflected in every man's heart. The human heart is the seat of the *ordo amoris* and thus, so to speak, a microcosm of the whole objective world of values. The heart of man is not a chaos of blind emotional states but an ordered counterpart of the world of values.[7] Scheler disagrees here strongly with Kant's presupposition that the heart and feelings of man are an original chaos that needs the practical reason to instill order. According to Scheler, the heart of the morally good man is already basically in accord with the objective hierarchy of values. The emotive dimension of man is "in-formed" by the *ordo amoris*. The human heart is, so to speak, a subjective sounding-board of the objective order of values.

As the snail carries with it its shell, so man carries with him his *ordo amoris* wherever he may go. The objective structure of values existing around him and residing within him remains forever the same. However, this does not exclude the possibility of man's distorting the objective order of love. Love can conform to the objective realm of values and can oppose it. The distortion and confusion of the *ordo amoris* is a recurring theme in Scheler's writings. The classical example of such distortion is the value-deception created by resentment.[8] Resentment is a

[6] NACH, p. 348.

[7] NACH, p. 361: "Denn das, was wir 'Gemüt' oder in bildhafter Weise das 'Herz' des Menschen nennen, ist kein Chaos blinder Gefühlszustände. . . . Es ist selbst ein gegliedertes Gegenbild des Kosmos aller möglichen Liebenswürdigkeiten—es ist insofern ein Mikrokosmos der Wertewelt. 'Le coeur a ses raisons.' "

[8] Cf. chapter V: " 'Resentment' and the Historicity of Ethics: Resentment as a Source of Value-Deception." Resentment and *ordo amoris* are closely related in Scheler's philosophy.

self-poisoning of the soul which results in a falsification of man's value-judgments.

The distortion of the *ordo amoris* is also exemplified by a person's "metaphysical aberration." [9] This takes place when a person loves an object of relative value as if it were an absolute value. Making an idol of a relative value-object—for example, knowledge, money, power, one's country—is a typical case of falsifying and distorting the *ordo amoris*. A process of disillusionment is necessary, and false idols must be destroyed if a man is to free himself from the self-delusion of putting finite goods in the place of God. Only thus can he recover in his heart the objective *ordo amoris*.[10]

In a penetrating analysis of the origin of hedonism Scheler lays bare an important reason why man distorts and falsifies the *ordo amoris*. He traces hedonism to a false direction of love which in turn results in a general *désordre du coeur*. Scheler entitles his analysis "Law of the tendency to search for substitutes in the case of a negative determination of the emotional 'depths' of the ego." [11]

Whenever a man finds himself thwarted on a more central and more profound level of his being, his natural tendency is to replace immediately that unpleasant state by an intentional direction towards a pleasure belonging to a more peripheral level, that is, to the level of those sentiments or feelings that are easier to evoke. The very desire for lust is an indication of inner unhappiness. . . . Also for whole historical periods intensified practical hedonism is always a sure indication of vital decadence. . . . The use of external means to evoke pleasure and to get rid of physical pain (for example, drugs) is usually proportionate to the absence of real joy . . . in a certain society.[12]

[9] NACH, p. 367.
[10] VEIM, pp. 261-263.
[11] FORM, p. 347.
[12] *Ibid.*

Scheler shows a strong awareness of the aberrations of the human heart and of the possible distortions of the *ordo amoris*. Nevertheless, in developing the doctrine of the *ordo amoris* his main emphasis is always on the positive order of love in man and on the objective counterpart of the value-cosmos mirrored in every man's heart.

II
LOVE AS A DYNAMIC MOVEMENT AND
DISCOVERER OF NEW VALUES

Love, according to Scheler, is an "emotion" in the literal sense of the term, that is, a motion and a movement that leads us out of our own ego and beyond our limited selves. Love is not a static state of feeling but a dynamic movement toward higher values and toward other persons. At times, Scheler speaks of love as a response to values. But more important than the "response" character of love is its "creative" aspect in terms of a spontaneous, dynamic movement in which man discovers new and higher values. The higher values with which love is concerned are not previously "given" but rather disclose themselves only in the process and movement of love.[13] "It is *in* the exercise of love that goodness shines forth in the lover in the most original way." [14] Love thus plays a creative role in the discovery of values. It is in its nature as a spontaneous act that love differs basically from sympathy. Sympathy as well as fellow-feeling (*Mitfühlen*) are *re*-active attitudes or *re*sponsive functions expressing an affective reaction to another person. Love, however, is always characterized by spontaneity.[15]

Love is that movement of intention whereby, from a given

---

[13] SYM, pp. 170-171; *Sympathy,* pp. 157-158.
[14] SYM, p. 176; *Sympathy,* p. 164.
[15] SYM, p. 155; *Sympathy,* p. 142: "Vor allem aber ist die Liebe ein spontaner Akt." Cf also FORM, p. 266.

value A in an object, its higher value is visualized. Moreover, it is just this vision of a higher value that is of the
essence of love. In its ultimate nature, therefore, love is not
just a "reaction" to a value already felt . . . nor yet an
attitude to a pair of previously given values, such as "preference." . . . Those who treat love as a merely consequential "reaction" to a value already felt, have failed to recognize its nature as a movement. . . .[16]

Scheler's characterization of love as a dynamic movement
must be seen within the framework of his general understanding
of man. In his essay "On the Idea of Man" [17] Scheler establishes
two constitutive marks of man: self-transcendence and an unceasing dynamic movement. Man is essentially a being "that
transcends itself." [18] Scheler is continually groping for new words
and images to describe the dynamic character of man. Man is a
"transition" from one realm to another; he exists only as a
"bridge" or a "passage" from one kingdom to a higher one.[19]
"The fire, the passion of moving beyond himself—whether the
goal be called 'superman' or 'God'—that is his only genuine
humanity." [20] It is precisely because of his dynamic character
that man cannot be defined. He exists only as a "between" and

[16] SYM, p. 165; *Sympathy,* p. 153.
[17] "Zur Idee des Menschen," in UMST, pp. 171-195.
[18] *Ibid.,* p. 186.
[19] Scheler's choice of concepts manifests a remarkable similarity to
some paragraphs in Nietzsche's *Zarathustra.* Scheler, however, wrote
"Zur Idee des Menschen" during his Catholic period, and the concepts
are clearly used within a theistic framework, thus differing basically
from the meaning Nietzsche meant to convey. Nietzsche writes in *Also
sprach Zarathustra:* "Man is a rope, tied between beast and overman—
a rope over an abyss. A dangerous across, a dangerous on-the-way, a
dangerous looking-back, a dangerous shuddering and stopping. What is
great in man is that he is a bridge and not an end; what can be loved
in man is that he is an overture and a going under." Friedrich Nietzsche,
Also sprach Zarathustra (Munich: Goldmann Verlag, 1966), p. 13.
English translation from Friedrich Nietzsche, *Thus Spoke Zarathustra,*
trans. by Walter Kaufmann (New York: The Viking Press, 1966), pp.
14-15.
[20] UMST, p. 195: "Und nur als ein 'Hinüber' von dem einen dieser
Reiche zum anderen, als 'Brücke' und Bewegung zwischen ihnen hat er
seine Existenz. . . . Das Feuer, die Leidenschaft über sich hinaus—
heisse das Ziel 'Übermensch' oder 'Gott'—das ist seine einzige wahre
'Menschlichkeit.' "

a "transition," a "crossing" from one land into another. He is
an eternal transcending of life beyond itself. Or, from God's
vantage point, man is the epiphany of God in the stream of
life.[21]

> "Man" in this new sense is the intention and gesture of
> "transcendence" itself; he is the being that prays and seeks
> God. We do not say "man prays," but rather "he is the
> prayer of life transcending itself." We do not say "he seeks
> God" but rather "he is the living seeker of God." . . . God
> is the sea, and men are the rivers. And from their original
> gushing forth from their very origin the rivers are aware of
> the sea towards which they are flowing.[22]

Scheler never tires of stressing that self-transcendence is not a
mere optional endeavor of man, or something that he may do
or may refuse to do. It is so essential to the whole makeup of
man that it belongs to the very definition of what a man is. "A
being that begins to transcend himself and to seek God—that is
man. . . ."[23]

In his continuous quest for self-transcendence and the attainment of his ideal self, man is driven by the power of love. The
subjective dimension of the *ordo amoris,* that is, the objective
order which resides in man's heart, impels a person to reach out
for the ideal value-perfection attainable to him. Love is the
primordial driving force and the energy from which all other
acts derive their energy to grow and penetrate more deeply
into the archetypal image of man's ideal self. Through love we
participate in the power of divine love which is present and
active throughout the whole universe. Love is a "dynamic becoming, growing, and welling forth of all created beings in the
direction of the prototype (*Urbild*) of themselves existing in

[21] *Ibid.,* p. 186: "Der Mensche . . . ist nur ein 'Zwischen,' eine
'Grenze,' ein 'Übergang,' ein 'Gotterscheinen' im Strome des Lebens
und ein ewiges 'Hinaus' des Lebens über sich selbst.
[22] *Ibid.,* p. 186.
[23] *Ibid.,* p. 189.

the mind of God." [24] Love brings about a gradual growth of values, and each phase of growth is, so to speak, a "station of the universe on its pilgrimage to God." [25]

A popular proverb has it that love is blind. In Scheler's view the very opposite is true. "Genuine love opens our spiritual eyes to ever-higher values in the object loved." [26] What blinds people is infatuation or sensual impulses, not genuine love. Love instills vision and deeper knowledge. "Love is the awakener to knowing and willing—she is, in fact, the mother of spirit and reason itself." [27]

Commenting on the widely accepted opinion that the lover tends to idealize the beloved, Scheler reverses the argument and strongly questions the alleged objectivity of the so-called "detached observers." The "detached observers" (die "kalten Anderen") assert a lack of objectivity in the lover because they themselves "fail to recognize the particular *individual* values present in the object which are discernible only to the sharper eye of love. The 'blindness' then, is all on the side of the 'detached observers.' " [28] Scheler insists that the essence of another person is always a unique value which cannot be expressed in conceptual terms. The essence of individuality ". . . is *only* revealed in its full purity by love or by virtue of the insight it provides." [29] In a critique of Kant's one-sided emphasis on universality and general validity, Scheler tries to recover the dimension of uniqueness and individuality in every human person. With regard to the personal uniqueness of another person, "it is the lover who actually sees *more* of what is present than the others, and it is *he* and not 'others,' who therefore sees what is objective and real." [30]

[24] NACH, p. 355: "Immer war uns dabei die Liebe dynamisch ein Werden, Wachsen, Aufquellen der Dinge in die Richtung des Urbildes, das in Gott von ihnen gesetzt ist."

[25] *Ibid.*, p. 356.

[26] SYM, p. 170; *Sympathy,* p. 157.

[27] NACH, p. 356: "Also ist Liebe immer die Weckerin zur Erkenntnis und zum Wollen—ja die Mutter des Geistes und der Vernunft selbst."

[28] SYM, p. 173; *Sympathy,* p. 160.

[29] *Ibid.*

[30] *Ibid.*

In his writings Scheler returns time and again to the problem of how love and knowledge are related to one another and, more precisely, how love is related to man's perception of values. The realm of values is inexhaustible and no individual person can grasp and realize all possible values. Each person will select and focus upon a finite sector of values cut out of an infinite richness. The question arises then as to how the axiological viewpoint of a particular individual originates and develops. How does a person expand his axiological horizon, how does he discover new values?

It is the *ordo amoris* that functions as the ultimate foundation and source of man's knowledge and value perception. Werner Stark describes this *ordo amoris* of Scheler as "the axiological layer of the mind—this a priori system of social valuations or prejudgments which enables us to form, out of the infinitude of the knowable, the finite and hence comprehensible universe of the known." [31] A self-transcending interest (*Teilnahme*) in or a love of a larger or smaller sector of reality and of values determines the horizon of an individual's knowledge and perception of values. It is, then, the measure of man's love that determines the depth of his knowledge and the extent of his value perception.

The following passage is of crucial importance for understanding the relationship between love and knowledge in Scheler's thought:

> Knowledge is an existential relationship, and one which presupposes the ontological forms of whole and part. It is the relation of participation (*Teilhabe*) of an existing being in the essence (*Sosein*) of another existent entity by which no change is brought about in the latter. What is "known" becomes a "part" of the "knower," but without moving in any way from its place or being otherwise transformed. This ontological relationship is not a spatial, temporal or causal relationship. "*Mens*" or "mind" we call

[31] Werner Stark, *The Sociology of Knowledge* (Glencoe, Ill.: The Free Press, 1958), p. 113.

the X or the sum and substance of the acts in the "know-ing" being by dint of which such a participation is possible; by which a thing, or rather the essence (*Sosein*)—and only the essence—of an existing thing becomes an "*ens inten-tionale*" in contradistinction to a mere existence (*Dasein*) ("*ens reale*") which always and necessarily remains outside and beyond the relationship of knowing. The root of this X, the direction-giving moment for the realization of acts which lead to some form of participation (*Teilhabe*), can only be that self-transcending interest (*Teil-nahme*) in it which, in its most formal sense, we call "love." Knowledge is there, and only there, where the essence (*Sosein*) is, in strict identity both *extra mentem*, i.e. *in re*, and at the same time also *in mente*—as *ens intentionale* or as "object." [32]

Scheler continues to explain that there can be no knowing without the knowing subject going out of himself and partici-pating in another being. This self-transcending movement is love or self-surrender, "a bursting open of the boundaries of one's own being and essence through love." [33]

For Scheler, love is not a mere response to values already known, but rather it discovers new values and thus precedes value-feeling.

Love . . . plays the role of a discoverer in our perception of values. Love is a movement in the course of which new and higher values flash forth and reveal themselves, i.e. values hitherto unknown to this person. Hence, love does not follow after value-feeling or value-preference, but precedes them as their pioneer and leader.[34]

The expansion or narrowing of an individual's realm of values depends on the degree and intensity of his love and hatred. If a

[32] "Erkenntnis und Arbeit," in *Die Wissensformen und die Gesellschaft*, pp. 203-204. The English translation is taken, with slight alterations, from Werner Stark's *The Sociology of Knowledge*, pp. 111-112.
[33] *Ibid.*, p. 204.
[34] FORM, pp. 266-267.

man loves, his vision of values widens and deepens; if he allows himself to be dominated by hatred, hatred will limit the range of his perception of values and, in extreme cases, even blind entirely his vision of values.

"Man is first and foremost a loving being (*ens amans*) before he is ever a knowing (*ens cogitans*) or willing being (*ens volens*)." [35] This statement sums up Scheler's theory on the primacy of love over knowledge. Scheler maintains this primacy of love in the field of ethics as well as in the philosophy of religion. He elaborates his theory especially when he treats man's knowledge of God. The primacy of love over knowledge in our cognitive approach to God signifies that genuine knowledge of God always presupposes a threefold love, a loving self-disclosure of God, man's loving response to him, and man's love for his fellow human beings. First comes the loving dialogue between God and man:

It is in the nature of a personal God that knowledge of his existence is only possible by grace of this fundamental act of self-disclosure. . . . It is in love of the divine and holy, a love which has to move towards its goal before it recognizes itself as the response to a pre-existent love directed toward the loving soul, that God has located, in the final analysis, that mysterious driving-wheel which sets in motion all our cognitive knowledge of him as a person.[36]

But this loving encounter between God and man does not yet by itself suffice to bring about a genuine knowledge of God. The principle of the primacy of love over knowledge means also that "love for God as a condition of knowing him necessarily implies love for one's brothers." [37] In other words, there can be no true knowledge of God without man's prior turning in love to his fellow men. It is in this broad and comprehensive sense

[35] NACH, p. 356: "Der Mensch ist, ehe er ein ens cogitans ist oder ein ens volens, ein ens amans."
[36] VEIM, p. 333; *Eternal*, pp. 336-337.
[37] VEIM, p. 206; *Eternal*, p. 210.

that love occupies a position that is prior to and more fundamental than knowledge.

Scheler states repeatedly that his teaching on the primacy of love over knowledge is akin to that of St. Augustine. "What is called primacy of will in Augustine is, in fact, a primacy of love; primacy of the act of love before knowing as well as before striving and willing. . . ." [38] Scheler erred in this interpretation of Augustine.[39] It is true that Augustine held an ontic primacy of love over knowledge, but not a primacy of origin. Augustine teaches explicitly that nothing is loved that is not previously known.[40] He expressed the interplay of knowledge and love most profoundly in his commentary on St. John: "We do not love what we do not in some way know, but when we do love what we in some way know, it is by love itself that which is known is known better and more fully." [41]

If love is so much concerned with the "higher value," with the dynamic growth of the loved person and his highest image of values, is there then not a danger that love turns, in fact, to a non-existing ideal phantom instead of to the concrete, real person? Scheler sees this problem. He finds the answer in the dialectical relation that exists between the empirical and the ideal dimension of man. First he states emphatically that we love, indeed, the concrete empirical person as he *is*. Love is not some pedagogical technique according to which the other person's improvement is the prerequisite or condition for our loving him. Scheler cites here the idea of love in the Gospels. In his meeting with Mary Magdalene, Jesus did not tell her "You must sin no more; promise me this, and I shall love you and forgive your sins." Rather, Jesus first gave her a sign of his

---

[38] Max Scheler, *Liebe und Erkenntnis*, p. 24.

[39] Cf. Erich Przywara, S.J., *Religionsbegründung: Max Scheler—J. H. Newman* (Freiburg: Herder, 1923), p. 59. Also Josef Malik, "Wesen und Bedeutung der Liebe im Personalismus Max Schelers," *Philosophisches Jahrbuch*, LXXI (Spring, 1963), p. 112.

[40] St. Augustine, *De Trinitate*, VIII, 4; X, 1 and 2.

[41] St. Augustine, *In Joannem evang.*, tract. 96, 4; PL 35, 1876. "Non enim diligitur quod penitus ignoratur. Sed cum diligitur quod ex quantulacumque parte cognoscitur, ipsa efficitur dilectione ut melius et plenius cognoscatur."

love and forgiveness of sins and then told her to go and sin no more.[42]

Love is not a pedagogical technique that is primarily interested in "changing" the other person. One loves another as he *is*. But this does not mean that love is a mere response to the values already actualized in the other person. This would deprive love of its essential character as a dynamic and creative movement. Love does not consider the other person as a static object, finished and complete, but as a dynamic presence of inexhaustible richness and possibilities. For Scheler, the person is always a task, and the task to be fulfilled is the creative self-actualization of the personal being in loving dialogue with other persons. Love is concerned with the other person's fullness of being. This includes the "ideal" dimension of his personality, or the inner dynamism that is operative in his very being and impels him toward his own full self-realization. Our love for another person turns to the totality of his being, both actual and potential. By encouraging one's partner to move beyond the "empirical" being toward the "ideal" level we do not intend to tell him "you should do this or that" but we simply express the idea "become what you are." [43]

Scheler is here basically concerned with "a dialectical relation between what is given empirically and what is given phenomenologically." [44] The factual or empirically given is always limited and unfinished. But it contains a sphere of value potentialities or possibilities, as yet unrealized. Phenomenologically, the factual discloses itself as an indeterminate reality which is always open to an unceasing process of creative transformation and fulfillment. In his interpretation of Scheler's philosophy of love, M. C. D'Arcy writes:

I think it fair to Scheler to say that what he means is that,

[42] SYM, p. 172; *Sympathy*, p. 159.
[43] SYM, p. 172; *Sympathy*, p. 159.
[44] I am here indebted to A. R. Luther's interpretation of Scheler. Cf. A. R. Luther, *Persons in Love: A Study of Max Scheler's "Wesen und Formen der Sympathie"* (The Hague: Martinus Nijhoff, 1972), pp. 112-116.

when one truly loves, the ideal and the actual meet mysteriously in the loved object, and that love unconsciously always seeks to reduce the gap between the actual and the ideal. It makes the best always of what is really there, and, thank heaven, a lover does seem to see in his beloved treasures of beauty, which are hidden from the gossip and the critic—and he often succeeds in bringing them out.[45]

Love is directed toward the whole (*Ganzheit*), that is, toward the person as a dynamic reality which lives and moves out of the past through the present into the future. In the movement of love man sees always "more" than what is empirically given.[46] This "more" is characterized as "totality" or "wholeness" (*Ganzheitsstruktur*) and as "gestalt" (*Gestaltstruktur*).[47] Although Scheler clearly distinguishes the empirically given dimension of the person and its "ideal value image" (*ideales Wertbild*),[48] this is not a phenomenon-noumenon distinction in the Kantian sense. For Scheler, the "more" or the "whole" is present in what is empirically given, albeit as a reality that is still in the process of being fully actualized. Love presupposes the "gestalt" or the "whole" and approaches the other person in his totality and "wholeness." As a "whole" the loved person appears in the process of love to be full of possibilities and endowed with inexhaustible richness. In his invitation to love, man invites his partner to break out of the incomplete structure of his empirical being and to open himself toward a fuller and deeper participation in the infinite realm of values.

The creative character of love, then, does not consist in "producing" a thing or in "changing" a person. Love discloses its

[45] M. C. D'Arcy, S.J., *The Mind and Heart of Love* (New York: Holt, Rinehart and Winston, Inc.; London: Faber and Faber Ltd., 1962), p. 297.

[46] NACH, p. 358: "Die Liebe liebt und schaut im Lieben immer etwas *weiter* als nur auf das, was sie in Händen hat und besitzt. . . . Die Bewegung entfaltet—im höchsten Falle der Personliebe—eben hierdurch die Person in der ihr eigentümlichen Idealitäts- und Vollkommenheitsrichtung prinzipiell ins Unbegrenzte."

[47] SYM, p. 166; *Sympathy*, p. 154.

[48] *Ibid.*

creative character as a dynamic movement towards deeper value participation and value fulfillment. It lets the other person be as he is and encourages him to become more fully himself. A wider fullness and a greater richness become actualized in the process of interpersonal love in both the lover and the loved person. The dynamism of love is directed more to the fuller realization of being than to this or that particular value. Scheler quotes with approval a statement of Karl Jaspers to the effect that it is not particular values which are discovered in love, but that "in the movement of love everything becomes more valuable." [49]

Scheler succinctly summarizes his insight into the dynamic and creative character of love in the following definition:

Love is that movement in which every concrete individual subject who is a bearer of values successfully achieves the highest values possible for that subject according to its ideal vocation. Again, love is that movement in which the individual attains the ideal value-essence compatible with his nature.[50]

Scheler has found a wide following for his interpretation of personal love. For example, Eduard Spranger, Karl Jaspers,[51] Dietrich von Hildebrand and Nicolai Hartmann have appropriated some of his basic insights into the nature of love. In his *Ethik*,[52] Nicolai Hartmann follows closely Scheler's idea of the function of personal love. He restates persuasively the dynamic

[49] SYM, p. 166. Karl Jaspers, *Psychologie der Weltanschauungen* (4th ed.; Berlin: Springer-Verlag, 1954), p. 124: "Es sind nicht 'Werte,' die entdeckt würden in der Liebe, sondern in der Bewegung der Liebe wird alles wertvoller."

[50] SYM, p. 174; *Sympathy*, p. 161: "Liebe ist die Bewegung, in der jeder konkret individuelle Gegenstand, der Werte trägt, zu den für ihn und nach seiner idealen Bestimmung möglichen höchsten Werten gelangt; oder in der er sein ideales Wertwesen, das ihm eigentümlich ist, erreicht."

[51] Karl Jaspers, *Psychologie der Weltanschauungen* (4th ed.; Berlin: Springer-Verlag, 1954), pp. 123-129.

[52] Nicolai Hartmann, *Ethik* (4th ed.; Berlin: Walter de Gruyter, 1962), pp. 532-544 *et passim*.

relationship between the empirical and the ideal dimension in man and describes the role of love in bringing about the full self-realization of the beloved person.

> The empirical personality never strictly corresponds to its own ideal value. But since love envisages precisely this ideal value in the other person, it is of the essence of personal love to pierce through the empirical person to the ideal value of his personality.[53]

This is the basic tendency of love. Love, therefore, can rightly be directed even toward a morally imperfect person. This does not mean, however, that love is indifferent to the empirical man and is only concerned with the not yet existing ideal image of him. Love turns genuinely to the empirical individual in his uniqueness but envisages at the same time the highest possibilities which are already present in him as an essential tendency or movement. Love is directed to the axiological uniqueness of the other person and accepts the value of his ideal self precisely as a reality that exists already in the beloved person, albeit as a tendency striving toward actuality.

In this sense, personal love lives by faith in the ideal self of the other person, that is, by faith in a reality which is somehow already present and is gradually emerging toward full realization. Hartmann refers to this love as "ethical divination." [54] Genuine love "divines" and foresees in the other person the full actualization of his ideal self. Love senses prophetically perfection in the imperfect, and infinitude in the finite. Personal love discovers the ideal in the empirical. By its anticipation and active encouragement of the ideal, love helps the other person to grow and to work toward the actualization of his own ideal selfhood.

Scheler's theory of love has been significantly advanced and complemented by some insights of Karl Jaspers. Jaspers concurs with Scheler's characterization of love as a dynamic movement

[53] *Ibid.,* p. 533.
[54] *Ibid.*

and with the idea of man's gradual growth in the process of love. He advances Scheler's insight on love by introducing two important ideas concerning the process of interpersonal growth through love. Jaspers describes the process of mutual love between two persons in terms of "existential communication" and of "loving strife" (*liebender Kampf*).[55] These two concepts are of great value in complementing and in fleshing out the somewhat sketchy theory of love in Scheler.

Jaspers distinguishes two different types of interpersonal communication. The first is the so-called pre-existential communication which is of a merely functional or useful character. An ordinary business transaction between two people is an example of such a functional communication. On this level, one person is interchangeable with other human beings. But besides these functional communications there is another type of interpersonal encounter which Jaspers calls *existential* communication. This refers to the deeper experiences of personal relationship which involve a man as an irreplaceable and unique being, and where two people encounter each other and commit themselves to one another as uniquely individual persons. In existential communication no functional goal outside of the true good for both persons is intended; they mutually evoke their potential energies and bring them to full development. In this way both persons, in a sense, create each other.[56]

The way toward deepening this existential communication—and here we come upon a special contribution of Jaspers to the problem of love—is "loving strife" (*liebender Kampf*).[57] This loving strife should not be misunderstood as a fight of each against the other. It is a particular sort of strife in which both partners fight *together,* challenging each other, evoking the hidden potential, eventually bringing forth a new being in each other. Jaspers calls it also a "strife for the truth of *Existenz,*" [58]

[55] Karl Jaspers, *Philosophie* (3 vols.; 3rd ed.; Berlin: Springer Verlag, 1956), II, pp. 50-117; 277-279.
[56] *Ibid.,* pp. 58, 70.
[57] *Ibid.,* pp. 65-67. Cf. also Karl Jaspers, *Psychologie der Weltanschauungen* (4th ed.; Berlin: Springer-Verlag, 1954), p. 126.
[58] *Philosophie,* p. 67.

where truth signifies the authentic uniqueness that is revealed and achieved in the two partners engaged in loving strife. He means quite literally that it should be a true struggle: "Each one should make things existentially as difficult as possible both for himself and for the other. Chivalry and making things easy may only be tolerated for a brief time. . . . If this becomes permanent, communication has ceased." [59]

Stressing aspects like strife, challenge and alternating solitude and self-assertion as integral parts of existential communication, Jaspers makes it quite clear that half-way houses like mere sentimental camaraderie, erotic love that does not grasp the whole man, reaching out for the other as an escape from one's own loneliness, or the will to possess another person, should not be confused with existential communication. In fact, such relationships with others will often prove to be real obstacles preventing genuine communication.

The struggle involved in true communication leading to genuine selfhood is, however, always a loving struggle, in which both partners are constantly concerned with the good of the other. "Love is self-becoming and self-giving. When I give myself truly, without reservation, I find myself. When I turn to myself and hold back, I become a man without love and lose myself." [60]

Existential love, for Jaspers, is not a blind immersion in the loved one. Such a love would end the necessary struggle or strife which presupposes firm self-assertion. Existential communication is a continuing dynamic process, and this process necessitates a continued fruitful tension between the twin poles of self-assertion in solitude and of reaching out to the other person in loving union. [61]

We cannot establish existential communication or an I-Thou relationship with everyone we meet. Yet it is essential that each man reach, in at least some of his everyday relationships, that depth which goes beyond the level of the merely functional or

[59] *Ibid.*, p. 66.
[60] *Ibid.*, p. 278.
[61] *Ibid.*, pp. 61-64.

useful. One of the more serious dangers of modern civilization lies precisely in its tendency to make the smooth and pleasant yet superficial type of functional dealing with others *the* pattern for all encounters with our fellow men. In this way, men deprive themselves of the in-depth relations that are not primarily geared toward a pleasant and smooth getting-along-with-one-another, but toward confronting one's partner and, through loving strife, challenging him to develop all the potentialities of a rich interpersonal relationship. Such encounters, which far transcend the merely functional relationships in communities of common interest, will frequently have to break the stifling mold of textbook etiquette and of established behavior patterns. A certain degree of severity and even of harshness may often be inevitable. But such experiences are an essential condition for our becoming fully human. In a civilization which dictates being nice and pleasant at all costs as a supreme law for human relations, it becomes increasingly boring to have so many "nice people" around. We begin to look out for people who are willing to go through the severer school of some kind of "loving strife" by which alone they can exhaust the full possibilities and depths of interpersonal relationships. A genuine friend must be ready to enter into such struggle. Without it friendship remains barren and grows stale.

III
FORMS OF LOVE AND "LOVE IN GOD" (AMARE IN DEO)— PARTICIPATION IN THE DIVINE LOVE AS THE PROTOTYPE AND APEX OF ALL LOVE

Scheler distinguishes three basic forms of love.[62] These forms of love correspond to the hierarchy of values as well as to the different types of human acts. Scheler declares that there can be no genuine love of the lowest rank of values, that is, of the merely pleasant things. Love implies always an enhancement of value, and since merely pleasant things are incapable of such

[62] SYM, pp. 181-184; *Sympathy*, pp. 169-171.

enhancement they are not suitable objects of love. The first form of true love is called vital or passionate love. It corresponds to the vital values of nobility, health and vigor. Love of the noble, sexual love and authentic friendship are examples of vital love. The second form of love corresponds to spiritual values and is called mental love (*seelische Liebe*). Mental love is directed toward beauty and aesthetic values, the realm of law and justice, and pure knowledge—in short, toward cultural values. In Scheler's hierarchy of values the highest rank is occupied by the values of the holy. The spiritual love of persons corresponds to this highest class of values and is, therefore, the third and highest form of love.

Scheler also correlates the forms of love with basic types of human acts. Vital acts of the body correspond to the vital or passionate love, purely mental acts of the self to mental love, and finally, spiritual acts of the person correspond to the supreme form of love, that is, the spiritual love of persons.[63]

The close correlation between forms of love, ranks of values and types of human acts, manifests a profound unity of vision in Scheler's philosophy of love. One might add to this correlation the corresponding types of knowledge [64] as well as the hierarchy of value-person-types.[65] There then emerges an impressive unity of Scheler's entire philosophical system, a wholeness that blends the otherwise disjointed and sometimes perplexing fragments of his thought into an organic system of striking harmony.

As we have seen above, the highest form of love is the spiritual love of persons. Scheler further elaborates his theory of personal love and offers some important reflections on man's participation in the divine love as the prototype and apex of all personal love. The essence of God himself is love. As *summum bonum* God is the source of all value, being and love. Man's love of God is not a benevolent love *for* God, as if he could enhance God's well-being. Rather, our love of God participates

[63] *Ibid.*
[64] Cf. chapter IX.
[65] Cf. chapter VIII.

in, and is co-executive with (*Mitvollzug*), God's own love of the world and his love of himself.

> The love of God in its highest form is not to have love "for" God, the all-merciful—for a mere object, in effect; it is to *participate* in His love for the world (*amare mundum in Deo*), and for Himself (*amare Deum in Deo*); in other words it is what the scholastics, the mystics and Saint Augustine before them, called "*amare in Deo.*" [66]

Scheler offers a profound reason why love in its highest form cannot approach another person as an object but must be a participation (*Mitvollzug*) in the acts of that other person. Love is a thoroughly "objective" attitude in the sense that in love we are not determined by "subjective" interests or desires. Nevertheless, it is not "objective" in the sense that the other as a person becomes "objectified." The personal dimension of man can never be disclosed to us as an "object." The essence of the person always eludes our rational analysis and can never be pinned down as an "object" (*Gegenstand*). "The person of another can only be disclosed to me by my joining in the performance of his acts, either cognitively, by 'understanding' and vicarious 're-living,' or morally, by 'following in his footsteps.' " [67]

If the above is true with regard to the knowledge of any finite person, it applies even more to the knowledge and love of the infinite person of God. Man can never "objectify" God, he can

---

[66] SYM, p. 177; *Sympathy,* p. 164. "Die höchste Form der Gottesliebe ist nicht Liebe 'zu Gott' als dem Allgütigen, d.h. einer Sache, sondern der *Mitvollzug* seiner Liebe zur Welt (amare mundum in Deo) und zu sich selbst (amare Deum in Deo), d.h. das, was die Scholastiker, die Mystiker und vorher schon Augustin 'amare in Deo' nannten."

[67] SYM, p. 180; *Sympathy,* p. 167. "Die Person kann mir nur gegeben sein, indem ich ihre Akte 'mitvollziehe'—erkenntnismässig im 'Verstehen' und 'Nacherleben,' sittlich aber in der 'Gefolgschaft.' " Cf. also SYM, p. 241: ". . . dass (geistige) Person qua Person überhaupt nichtobjizierbares Sein ist, sondern . . . dem Dasein nach nur durch Mit-vollzug (Mit-denken, Mit-wollen, Mit-fühlen, Nach-denken, Nach-fühlen usw) einer Seins-teilnahme fähiges Sein."

only draw near to him by participating in God's own divine life and love.[68]

> . . . the mystic, contemplative love for God as the highest good must necessarily lead to participation in, and emula- ion of (*Mit- und Nachvollzug*), God's infinite action of love towards himself and his creatures—so that the con- duct of us men towards our fellow-creatures is analogous to that of God towards us. Conversely, love "in" God, which is the active insertion of the nucleus of mental per- sonality into the core of the divine person, and a loving of all things with the love of God (*Mitlieben*), must of its own accord revert to God as the highest object of love and thus perfect itself mystically, contemplatively, in the *amare Deum in Deo*.[69]

Man's love for his fellow men must be mediated through God if it is to be love in the fullest and deepest sense possible. Human love ought to associate itself with the divine love for mankind. In this way, genuine love of other persons is ultimately rooted in the act of "loving all things in God" (*amare in Deo*).[70]

[68] SYM, p. 241; *Sympathy*, p. 224.
[69] VEIM, p. 220; *Eternal*, p. 226.
[70] SYM, p. 205; *Sympathy*, p. 191.

VIII
The Role of Value-
Person-Types
(Ideal Model Persons)

S ome critics have been misled by Scheler's pronounced emphasis on values and have completely overlooked his concretization of values in a value-personalism. Scheler has been criticized for being overly preoccupied with abstract values to the detriment and neglect of the human person. He has been accused of defending a priority and primacy of values over persons.

I

CONCRETIZATION OF VALUES
IN VALUE-PERSON-TYPES

It is regrettable that even a man like Emmanuel Mounier, who was himself one of the main spokesmen of a personalist philosophy, should have misinterpreted the value-personalism of Max Scheler. In his book *Personalism* he perpetuates the legend which erroneously attributes to Scheler an impersonal type of value philosophy:

Several contemporary thinkers speak of "values," conceived as realities in themselves apart from their relations, and recognizable a priori (Scheler, Hartmann). Personalists however cannot willingly surrender the person to anything impersonal, and most of them seek in one way or another to personalize these values.[1]

This indicates an astounding ignorance of Scheler's value-personalism, yet seems to reflect a rather widespread misinterpretation. Values are, of course, of central importance in Scheler's ethics, but this does not mean that the person is subservient to a system of abstract values. Time and again Scheler stresses the point that love is not directed to values as such, but to persons as bearers of values:

> Love and hatred . . . these attitudes are not directed intentionally towards value, let alone "higher" value, as when we prefer one value to another; they refer to objects inasmuch and insofar as these possess value. It is never values we love, but always something that possesses value.[2]

To describe Scheler's moral philosophy as an ethics of abstract values is certainly erroneous. Rather, one might characterize it as a value-personalism. For Scheler, "all values are founded upon the value of an infinite personal Spirit and of the cosmos of values which stands before Him." [3] We shall now discuss at greater length the intimate relation between value and person, and in particular, the concretization and incarnation of values in value-person-types.

Kaspar Hürlimann is one of the few critics of Scheler who has systematically investigated the close relationship between Scheler's value-ethics and his personalism.[4] According to Hürli-

---

[1] Emmanuel Mounier, *Personalism* (Notre Dame: University of Notre Dame Press, 1952), p. 68.

[2] SYM, p. 160; *Sympathy,* p. 148.

[3] FORM, p. 113. The atheist value ethics of Nicolai Hartmann is in this respect, of course, fundamentally different from that of Scheler. Since Mounier (see above quote) and numerous other critics of Scheler always juxtapose these two philosophers, as if their value ethics were identical, one might suspect that these critics have not adequately explored the ethics of either Scheler or Hartmann.

[4] Kaspar Hürlimann, "Person und Werte. Eine Untersuchung über den Sinn von Max Schelers Doppeldevise: 'Materiale Wertethik' und 'Ethischer Personalismus,' " *Divus Thomas,* XXX (September, 1952), pp. 273-298; (December, 1952), pp. 385-416.

mann, Scheler developed his value-personalism in order to give a concrete status to the otherwise abstract values.[5] A concern for the ethical a priori had led Scheler to an abstract conception of values. In order to overcome extreme abstraction, and to regain the concrete Scheler developed the idea of personalism. Values were now seen as concretized or incarnated in the person, the bearer of values. "The idea of personalism means a concretization of the order of material values by taking into consideration the bearers of values." [6]

Scheler's theory of value-person-types, then, must be seen in light of his endeavor to concretize values. The otherwise abstract values reveal themselves to us as incarnated in ideal model persons. As shall be explained later in greater detail, a hierarchy of value-person-types corresponds to the hierarchy of higher and lower values. Consequently, each rank of values is embodied in a corresponding rank of value-person-types. There is, therefore, nothing arbitrary or subjective in the ideal model persons. They are rooted in, and determined by, the objective hierarchy of values. This assures their objective character. The choice of a certain value-person-type as one's personal model is moral only if it corresponds to the a priori laws of preference which prevail in the objective order of values.

In developing his theory of value-person-types, Scheler is not merely answering the problem of his own axiological abstractions.[7] He is also attempting to provide an alternative to the abstract moral norms conceived by Kant. Mere norms are too abstract, too remote from the actual ethical situations, too disembodied and, ultimately, too impersonal. In Scheler's view, man is not really moved by abstract norms: he needs concrete examples and models, or values exemplified and concretized in such ideal model persons.

[5] Ibid., pp. 287ff: "3. Der Wertpersonalismus als Konkretisierung der materialen Wertethik."

[6] Ibid., p. 295.

[7] Scheler's theory on the relationship between values and persons also has, of course, important implications for the more general question of the relationship between values and being. Scheler often emphasizes the independence of values and being, but a close look at his value-personalism would seem to indicate that, at least on this level, values and being are intimately related.

Pure value-person-types are of an ideal nature and are only to a limited degree actualized in living persons. The question arises, then, whether values are truly concretized or incarnated if value-person-types have only an ideal existence. To answer this question we must consider two characteristics of value-person-types. First, pure value-person-types themselves are concretized and actualized, although only in a fragmentary way, in concrete model persons. Consequently, we can speak of value concretization on two levels, namely, in pure (ideal) types, and in empirical model persons. Secondly, value-person-types are given an ultimate metaphysical foundation and reality by their rootedness in the supreme value of God.

Scheler distinguishes between pure value-person-types and historically existing empirical model persons. The former are ideal models which correspond to the objective hierarchy of values. They are a priori intuited, universally valid and not affected by the fortuitous changes of history. They may never be "hypostatized" in actual historical figures.[8] Pure types are proto-models which, as such, never exist in history. They become partly actualized in historical model persons. Historical model persons are, therefore, only limited "examples" or specimens of pure value-person-types:

> We often say: This X is my exemplar (*Vorbild*). But what we mean or rather what is meant by the word exemplar is not at all this actual man of flesh and bone. Rather, we intend to say: This X is an "example" or a specimen of our actual exemplar—perhaps the only example possible. But as such, he is never more than an example. In a man who functions as an example, the exemplar himself is more or less adequately beheld and conceived—but is never gathered or abstracted from the man's empirical, accidental qualities and is never found in him as a real or abstract part.[9]

[8] FORM, p. 571.
[9] *Ibid.*, p. 568.

The pure value-person-types and their hierarchical order exist, like the hierarchy of values, outside of time and history. But they are, so to speak, immersed in time and history by their partial incarnation in historical model persons. These historical models are usually mixed types, representing different ideal types. St. Augustine, for example, was a mixture of the saint and the genius, Frederick the Great, a mixture of the hero and the genius.[10]

Pure value-person-types, like the saint, the genius, or the hero, possess universal validity and remain, therefore, the same in the midst of historical changes. But, in their incarnation in historical model persons, they take on different forms in different peoples and historical periods. Thus, the French, British, and Germans cherish different types of heros, geniuses and saints. There exist many different historical and national model persons, as is evident from the different images of exemplary men represented in ideas like "gentleman," *gentil homme, homme honnête, Biedermann, cortigiano,* and *bushido.*[11]

Value-person-types, as well as values themselves, are ultimately rooted in the supreme value of God. It is from this foundation that they receive their actuality. All values participate in the highest value of God and manifest, in a fragmentary way, the supreme value of the divine essence. Similarly, value-person-types are reflections and correlates of the Divine Spirit. Their metaphysical status must be understood from their relationship to the idea of God. Scheler explains this exemplarism as follows:

We must ask how such types are related to the idea of God as an idea of an infinite person. . . . The essential goodness of God constitutes an idea which "co-contains" (*'mit'enthalten*), in an infinitely perfect way, in the plenitude of their exemplarity and according to their hierarchical rank (but not *as* models) the universally valid person-value-types themselves. . . . It is only through the relationship of a finite person to the infinite person, a relationship of experi-

[10] *Ibid.,* p. 571.
[11] *Ibid.,* p. 572.

ence and knowledge, that the essential goodness of God is
divided into the unities of value-essences, that is to say, into
value-person-types along with their hierarchical degrees.[12]

Scheler's "value-personalism" must always be envisaged on
three different levels: that of the pure value-person-types, the
concrete finite person, and the infinite supreme person of God.
The realm of abstract values is concretized, to a certain extent,
in pure value-person-types. It is actualized, in a limited way, in
concrete human persons, and it is ultimately rooted and an-
chored, in its full plenitude, in the supreme value-person of God.

II

THE HIERARCHY OF VALUE-PERSON-TYPES: SAINT,
GENIUS, HERO, LEADING SPIRIT OF CIVILIZATION,
ARTIST OF ENJOYMENT

In his search for moral growth and development, man is not
primarily guided by a hierarchy of abstract values but rather by
a hierarchy of value-person-types in which the values are embodied and concretized.[13] The hierarchy of value-person-types
runs in descending order as follows: saint, genius, hero, leading
spirit of civilization, and artist of enjoyment.[14] These basic
types are not abstracted from the experience of empirical persons. Rather they pertain to the essential makeup of man and
are, therefore, intuited a priori. They constitute the basic values

---

[12] *Ibid.*, p. 573.

[13] Erhard Denninger, a scholar of jurisprudence, published an important work on "the legal person and solidarity" in Max Scheler. In
this book he calls it one of the most profound insights of Scheler's personalist ethics that in his moral life man does not encounter values as
mere abstract norms but rather as embodied in value-person-types and
in mythical, religious and historical model persons. Cf. Erhard Denninger, *Rechtsperson und Solidarität: Ein Beitrag zur Phänomenologie
des Rechtsstaates unter besonderer Berücksichtigung der Sozialtheorie
Max Schelers* (Frankfurt: Alfred Metzner Verlag, 1967), pp. 134-137.

[14] "Der Heilige, der Genius, der Held, der führende Geist der
Zivilisation, der Künstler des Genusses." Cf. NACH, pp. 274-318; also
FORM, p. 494. The fifth type is sometimes also called "artist of life"
(*Lebenskünstler*), for example, NACH, p. 268.

and thus correspond strictly to the hierarchy of values. However, we notice here a certain discrepancy between the number of value-person-types and that of the value modalities. Scheler usually speaks of five pure person-types but according to his *Formalismus* there are only four value modalities. Although Scheler never explains this inconsistency, the obvious reason lies in the fact that in his essay "Vorbilder und Führer" he treats utility-values as a separate modality,[15] whereas in *Formalismus* he considers them as consecutive values of the first modality.

In "Vorbilder und Führer" Scheler correlates the value-person-types to the hierarchy of values as follows: [16]

Values:	*Value-Person-Types*:
pleasure-values	the artist of enjoyment
utility-values	the leading spirit of civilization
vital values	the hero
spiritual values	the genius
the values of the holy	the saint

In the midst of all historical changes these hierarchies of values and of value-person-types remain unchanged and are the constant objective guide for man's moral life. Scheler calls these hierarchies "the pole-star of man." [17] However, since the pure person-types are of an ideal nature, they must be "incarnated in the empirical stuff of historical persons" [18] in order to become truly effective as exemplars. Thus, a living exemplar always consists of both an a priori and an empirical component. General ethics is dealing only with universally valid pure value-person-types. But besides these there are also other person-types which are not valid for all but only for certain individuals (*individual-gültige Wertpersontypen*).[19] The latter exist within the framework of universal types but emerge as models only from the concrete experience of history. In this context Scheler is calling for

[15] NACH, p. 268: ". . . die Wertsphäre des Nützlichen . . . oder der Zivilisationswerte. . . ."
[16] *Ibid.*, p. 268; also p. 262.
[17] NACH, p. 269.
[18] *Ibid.*, p. 262.
[19] FORM, p. 570.

a further elaboration and concretization of his general theory. We shall offer two examples of such explication later on in this chapter.

Value-person-types have also their negative counterparts (*Gegenbilder*). In his theory of resentment Scheler has presented an important example of how such negative images of man originate and how they are cultivated. As the positive model person is the most powerful influence for moral growth, likewise his negative counterpart is an extremely influential force in obstructing the moral development of man and in positively fostering evil.[20]

We shall now briefly characterize the five pure value-person-types. The highest among the exemplary types of persons is the saint. In describing the value modality of the holy, Scheler strongly emphasizes the uniqueness of this value which cannot be reduced to any other. Similarly, he stresses the uniqueness of the corresponding value-person-type of the saint. The saint is not a mere heightening or elevation of other exemplary types. He is "no mere raising or enhancement of the genius, the wise man, the good man or the righteous—nor any super-philanthropist or super-legislator. If a man were all these in one, he still would not create the impression of holiness."[21]

An important feature of the saint, in which he differs basically from other person-types, is the object of his creative activity. Whereas other person-types are concerned with extrinsic material or objects apart from themselves, the primary object of the saint's endeavor is the improvement and development of his own self. The saint

creates *himself* as the most perfect person possible in accordance with an ideal value-image which he has gradually acquired in the process of loving himself only "in God." The saint is the person most independent of extrinsic material, in that his "work" is none other than "himself" or the soul of another man who, in voluntary emulation, re-

[20] *Ibid.*, p. 579.
[21] VEIM, p. 312; *Eternal*, p. 316.

produces afresh his work's ideal content of value and meaning—that is, his own spiritual image.[22]

The hero lives on in and through his heroic deeds, and the genius through the external masterpieces of his creative work. The saint, however, lives in history among his followers through the splendor and radiance of his own person.[23]

> Thus, the eternal presence of the saint is actualized in a dynamic, unbroken chain of acts of following, so that he is, at each point in the history of his followers, the secret historicity of their history: the archetypal action which impels their history forward from one moment to the other.[24]

Scheler distinguishes different types of saints, for example, the original saint or founder of a religion, immediate followers, witnesses and martyrs, later followers of the original saint, and religious reformers. The prototype of all religious models is always the idea of God. Consequently, the image and likeness of God (*Gottähnlichkeit*) is the supreme standard and measure of all holiness.[25]

One cannot know a person by studying him from without. A person can be known only if he freely decides to disclose himself. A self-revelation of God is, therefore, essential for an original saint. For to be an original saint implies possessing a special knowledge of God.

Each person-type is guided by a "predominant direction of love." Whereas the life of other models is primarily directed toward this world, the prevailing love and concern of the saint is always basically tuned to the divine. But as the highest type of model person, the saint comprises also all other forms of human greatness. Thus, the positive dimensions of the genius and the hero are also, to a certain extent, contained in the pure value-

[22] VEIM, p. 217; *Eternal*, p. 222.
[23] NACH, pp. 281-282.
[24] *Ibid.*, p. 286.
[25] *Ibid.*, p. 277.

person-type of the saint. All other exemplars are constantly being nourished and enhanced by the supreme model of the saint.[26]

Emulating and following a saint as an exemplary person does
not mean simply copying him. Rather it is a "co-experience and
a re-living (*mit- und nacherleben*)" of the saint's life, and a living from the fountain of life of his personality. In a moving
description Scheler characterizes such following and exemplifies
it with the saints' following of Christ:

> I ask what is it, then, that the saints really wanted, expe-
> rienced and did when they, for instance, wanted to *follow*
> Christ? Certainly, they did not want to be psychically in-
> fected by one another. . . . Nor did they want to imitate Him
> as the misleading expression "imitatio Christi" suggests. Nor
> did they just want to copy Him, that is, live in Galilee, or
> agonize in Gethsemane, and die on the cross. Nor did they
> mean to commiserate with Him and share joy with Him
> in his glorification. They wanted, did and lived something
> different: they wanted in an act to *co-experience and re-
> live* (*mit- und nacherleben*) the life of His historically for-
> tuitous brief life of simplicity. . . . They wanted to permeate
> and leaven their . . . historical situations and their work . . .
> with the individual nature of His person and His mysterious
> life. This is like a unique jump into the core of a person, an
> intuitive appropriation of its source and fountain of life in
> order to live from this same source of life. . . . That is
> truly the great act of *following*. It is not an approach from
> without as the historian would have it. This knowledge of
> Christ in the above sense is something essentially different
> from the historical knowledge which theology transmits.
> But it is the fundamental and essential knowledge.[27]

The second value-person-type is the genius. He is correlated
to the modality of spiritual values. Scheler defines the genius as
the man who, without any previous rules or norms, creates some-

[26] *Ibid.*, p. 287.
[27] *Ibid.*, p. 285.

thing new and original that is of an exemplary nature.[28] Such
original creations are, for instance, Solon's legislation, Confucius' ethics,[29] Kant's *Critique of Pure Reason,* Beethoven's
Ninth Symphony, or Dante's *Divine Comedy.*[30] Creativity and
originality are the principal characteristics of the genius and his
performance. Scheler suggests that the word "creating" (*Schaf-
fen*) should be used exclusively in relation to a genius, whereas
"work" (*Arbeit*) should be the proper word for the performance
of ordinary people like businessmen and engineers.[31]

Scheler distinguishes different types of genius. A person can
be a genius in knowledge and value-perception, in art and literature, or in the field of legislation. The value-person-type of a
genius is, therefore, preeminently embodied in philosophers, art-
ists and legislators.

The genius turns his love toward the world as a whole. In
response to this love, the world opens itself, discloses its mysterious richness and reveals unceasingly a plethora of new values.[32] The genius does not adjust himself to the world but
rather creatively widens and expands the world.[33] This is especially true with regard to the realm of values. The philosopher-
genius, for example, is the discoverer of new values. He expands
the human consciousness and makes his fellow men aware of the
richness of values. The passion of his mind penetrates ever more
deeply into the essence of reality.

Every human being practices a certain love of this world, but
this love is usually intertwined with selfish interests and goals.
What distinguishes the genius from the ordinary man is that his
love for the world is a pure one, without concern for profit or
self-interest. This pure love enables him to discover more of
reality and to be more creative in his approach to the world.

The third value-person-type is the hero (*der Held*). The idea
of the hero is correlated to the modality of vital values. Scheler

[28] *Ibid.,* p. 326.
[29] *Ibid.*
[30] *Ibid.,* p. 323.
[31] *Ibid.,* p. 299.
[32] *Ibid.,* p. 308.
[33] *Ibid.,* p. 322.

characterizes the hero as a person-type who is primarily concerned with the "realization of the noble" or of pure vital values, and whose fundamental virtues are nobility of mind and magnanimity.[34] The hero is the very personification of the value "noble." [35] Furthermore, the hero is a person of great vitality and strength combined with extraordinary will power and self-control. The hero's "will to power" is joined with a singular sense of responsibility. He is generous and ready to sacrifice himself for others. Presence of mind, initiative, daring, as well as patience and strength in afflictions, are distinguishing features of the heroic type of man. Statesmen, military commanders, pioneers, discoverers and colonizers are prime examples of the heroic person-type.[36] However, on principle every individual person can cultivate the qualities of the hero type.[37]

Scheler calls the fourth value-person-type the leading spirit of civilization (der führende Geist der Zivilisation).[38] Scientists, engineers and economists usually embody the values of this person-type. Whereas the preceding three models are valuable as such, that is, as these particular person-types, the leading spirit of civilization is valuable primarily on account of his external performances and achievements. He dedicates himself mainly to the fostering of temporal values, not eternal ones. The progress of science, engineering and economy is his predominant concern.

The lowest rank within the hierarchy of value-person-types is occupied by the artist of enjoyment (Künstler des Genusses).[39] This person-type cultivates as a high art the enjoyment of pleasure-values. His basic principle consists in preferring the pleasant to the unpleasant. All values become for him mere objects of enjoyment. An extreme opposite to this person-type is the prosaic Philistine who, without pursuing higher values himself, still avoids the enjoyment of pleasure-values and instead culti-

[34] Ibid., p. 313.
[35] Ibid., p. 339: "Der Held ist die Personifizierung des 'Edlen.' "
[36] Ibid., pp. 311-314; 339-344.
[37] FORM, p. 573.
[38] NACH, pp. 315-316.
[39] Ibid., pp. 317-318.

vates feelings of resentment against the artist of enjoyment. Among the positive contributions of the artist of enjoyment is an expansion of mankind's sense of pleasure and luxury. The artist of enjoyment stimulates man's motivation for labor and teaches him to enjoy the fruits of his work.

In his discussion of model persons, Scheler refers to an analogous theory of Eduard Spranger and commends it as a corroboration of his own ideas.[40] In *Lebensformen*,[41] Spranger had established his theory of six basic types of men. He characterized them as theoretical man, economic man, esthetic man, social man, power man, and religious man.[42] Each basic type corresponds to one particular dimension of culture. The six types are, like Scheler's value-person-types, of an ideal nature. Actual historical men always embody various characteristics and traits and are, as "mixed" types, more complex than any of the basic exemplars.

The main value of Spranger's approach seems to lie in its function of widening our horizon toward a greater variety of potential "life-styles" (*Lebensformen*). It shows us new possibilities of molding our lives according to different possible models. Reflecting on Spranger's ideal types of person, man can discover and become aware of new dimensions of personhood and new options of creating and shaping his life in accordance with one or more of the ideal person types.[43]

Scheler refers several times to the Japanese idea of *bushido*

---

[40] *Ibid.*, p. 262; *Philosophische Weltanschauung*, p. 34.

[41] Eduard Spranger, *Lebensformen: Geisteswissenschaftliche Psychologie und Ethik der Persönlichkeit* (2nd ed. rev.; Munich: Siebenstern Taschenbuch Verlag, 1965). This book was first published in 1914. English translation: *Types of Men: The Psychology and Ethics of Personality* (Halle: Max Niemeyer Verlag, 1928).

[42] "Die idealen Grundtypen der Individualität: 1. Der theoretische Mensch. 2. Der ökonomische Mensch. 3. Der ästhetische Mensch. 4. Der soziale Mensch. 5. Der Machtmensch. 6. Der religiöse Mensch." Cf. *Lebensformen*, pp. 101-240.

[43] It is not surprising that Scheler and Spranger quote each other frequently. In their philosophy of man and in their views on the formation (*Bildung*) of man they are kindred spirits. There are, for example, frequent references to Scheler's philosophy in Spranger's *Lebensformen*. Cf. also Spranger's *Psychologie des Jugendalters* (17th ed.; Leipzig: Verlag Quelle & Meyer, 1925).

as an example of a model person.[44] He does not elaborate on it. It would seem that this idea of a model person in traditional Japanese culture provides a welcome illustration of the rich variety of possible human exemplars. The understanding of a model person in an oriental culture could expand the horizon of Western philosophy and open the mind to alternate approaches to the interpretation of human ideals.

Bushido, literally, "The Way of the Samurai," [45] signifies the feudal morality of the Japanese samurai class. Complete subordination and self-sacrificing loyalty to one's lord was placed at the apex of this value system. Although borrowing heavily from neo-Confucianism, the peculiar code of the warrior-aristocrat in Japan differed markedly from Chinese ethics by assigning obedience to parents and family loyalty a place far below that of loyalty to one's lord. In his classical work *Bushido: The Soul of Japan,* Inazo Nitobe characterizes the ethics of the Japanese samurai thus: "Feudal morality shares other virtues in common with other systems of ethics, with other classes of people, but this virtue—homage and fealty to a superior—is its distinctive feature." [46]

Besides loyalty, the virtues emphasized most strongly in the education of the samurai were self-control, justice, courage, sincerity, politeness, honor and benevolence. The samurai was expected to live a life of austerity and simplicity, always to put devotion to moral principles ahead of personal gain and advantage, and to be ready to meet death at any moment.[47]

"The Tale of the Forty-Seven Ronin," the great national epic

[44] FORM, p. 572; NACH, p. 273.
[45] "Bushi" means samurai or knight, "do" signifies way or code. Bushido is sometimes translated as "the code of chivalry."
[46] Inazo Nitobe, *Bushido: The Soul of Japan* (2nd ed. rev.; Tokyo: Charles E. Tuttle, 1969), p. 82.
[47] Some aspects of the bushido spirit are admirably captured in the chapter headings of Hajime Nakamura's classical work on the Japanese way of thinking: "Social relationships take precedence over the individual . . . unconditional belief in a limited social nexus . . . emphasis on rank and social position . . . absolute devotion to a specific individual. . . ." Cf. Hajime Nakamura, *Ways of Thinking of Eastern Peoples: India-China-Tibet-Japan* (3rd ed. rev.; Honolulu: East-West Center Press, 1968), pp. 407-530.

of Japan and the most popular play of the Japanese theater, is perhaps the most powerful historical example expressing the spirit of *bushido* as an absolute devotion to one's lord. The tale portrays the famous forty-seven samurai who entered upon a vendetta to restore the honor of their dead master, knowing well that this action entailed their own subsequent self-sacrifice through harakiri.

Although *bushido* is no longer taught as the quasi-official ideal image of man in Japan, the spirit and the virtues of *bushido* have in many ways survived the changes and developments of recent history.

III
EXEMPLAR AND FOLLOWING

The model (*Vorbild*), according to Scheler, is the most efficacious stimulus to good and the most important source of development and change in the moral cosmos.[48] "There is nothing on earth which prompts a person to become good as originally, immediately and necessarily as the insightful observation of a good person *in* his goodness."[49] It is more by following an exemplar than by following norms that a man is formed and molded in his moral behavior and being. An important difference between norm and model lies in the fact that the norm prescribes a mere *doing* whereas the model implies a new *being*. "Whoever follows a model tends to *become* like the model."[50] A moral norm presents an "ought-to-*do*," the exemplar is experienced as an "ought-to-*be*." In his "ontic" definition of the exemplar or model, Scheler again emphasizes the aspect of being rather than doing. He presents the exemplar as a "demand of ought-to-*be*" (*Sollseinsforderung*):

From the point of view of its constituents, the model is a value-structure belonging to the "form-unity" of the "per-

[48] FORM, p. 561.
[49] *Ibid.*, p. 560.
[50] Ibid., p. 559.

son-unity"—a determinate structured value-quality in the form of a person. From the point of view of the exemplarity of its contents, the model is the unity of a "demand of ought-to-*be*" (*Sollseinsforderung*) which is founded on the value-contents of this person.[51]

Historically and genetically, models have a fundamental priority over norms. Scheler suggests, therefore, that in the investigation and interpretation of moral systems in history one should always inquire into the ideal model persons predominant in that period. Since models are more fundamental than norms, they can illumine our understanding of moral norms and systems in a unique way.

How, then, does a model function in the moral cosmos, and how does he morally mold and transform people? The model acts on others not primarily by any particular volition or overt action, but simply by being what he is.

> The greatest effect of the good person upon the ethical cosmos is not based on his volition nor on his action; rather, it is based on his potential exemplary value (*Vorbildwert*) which he possesses exclusively by virtue of his *being* (*Sein*) and essence (*Sosein*) which are accessible to intuition and love.[52]

The exemplar or model person makes himself felt as an inviting and attractive ideal and goal. He attracts followers who in turn become aware that this exemplar ought to be followed and that it is right to follow him. Scheler then describes the effect of the model person from the point of view of the person who is attracted. He speaks here of "following" (*Folge, Nachfolge, Gefolgschaft*) [53] and explains it as a true moral transformation.

---

[51] *Ibid.*, p. 564: "Das Vorbild ist seinem Gehalt nach ein strukturierter Wertverhalt in der Einheitsform der Personeinheit, eine strukturierte Sowertigkeit in Personform, der Vorbildhaftigkeit des Gehalts nach aber die Einheit einer Soll*seins*forderung, die auf diesen Gehalt fundiert ist."

[52] *Ibid.*, p. 561.

[53] *Ibid.*, p. 565.

This following is not a mere imitation or obedience, but a genuine devotion to the exemplar. The whole person of the follower "grows into" the structure and traits of the model person. "Following" is thus a free abandonment or devotion to the value-content of the exemplary person.

The moral transformation of a person advances with his "growing into" the exemplar. "We become such *as* the exemplar is as a person, not *what* he is." [54] We learn to will and to act *as* the exemplar wills and acts but not *what* he wills and does. In this respect, "following" differs from imitation and obedience. In following an exemplar, our basic attitudes are changed and attuned to those we see in our prototype. This transformation of mind and attitudes concerns not only our volition and action but also our intuition of ethical values, our value preference, love and hatred. Such basic transformation of mind and attitude is brought about primarily by a change of the direction of love. We now love with the same love as the exemplary person, or our love follows the same direction and has the same quality as his love.[55] Ultimately, it is love for the value-content of a model person that inspires the follower in the formation of his moral being, and draws him toward the realization of his own ideal value structure. Love of an exemplar is more powerful and more effective than moral laws and norms. "There can be no respect for a norm or a moral law which is not based on respect for a person who posits it—and ultimately it is founded on love for the person as a model." [56]

In his essay "On the Forms of Knowledge and Education," [57] Scheler discusses once more the role of the model person, this time approaching it from an educational point of view. Here he raises the question of the most important influences in the education and formation (*Bildung*) of man. The most effective

[54] *Ibid.*, p. 566.

[55] *Ibid.* For a more detailed discussion of changes in the "direction of love," see the chapter on resentment (chapter V), especially the distinction between the views on love in ancient Greece, in Christianity and in modern humanism.

[56] *Ibid.*, p. 560.

[57] "Die Formen des Wissens und die Bildung" in Max Scheler, *Philosophische Weltanschauung*, pp. 16-48.

and forceful external stimulus, he says, is "the value-model (*Wertvorbild*) of a person who has won our love and admiration." [58] If man wants to be truly educated, he has to let himself be immersed into the wholeness, authenticity, freedom and nobility of such a model person. However, one does not choose a model. One is invited, attracted and captivated by it. The models may be saints, moral or artistic exemplars, national heroes, or exemplary members of a certain profession.

> Each individual, also each group, each profession, each period and its leaders possesses its own special and characteristic pattern of drives, i.e. a particular order of primary drives, as well as its own peculiar ethos. Therefore it also has its own special models.[59]

A model functions as a pioneer and trailblazer. He prepares the way for his follower and helps him to understand and clarify his own individual purpose and goal. Since every human being is unique, he should never blindly imitate or follow a model. "Models are precursors, enabling us to hear the call of our own particular person." [60] They are meant to free us to develop our own individuality and to pursue our own call and destiny.

Scheler's ideas on exemplar and following, and on the role of the model person in ethics have been widely appropriated by philosophers, psychologists and educators. Johannes Hessen, for example, devotes a whole chapter of his *Ethik* [61] to the meaning of the model person, and tries to demonstrate that it plays a more important role in ethics than do abstract norms:

> What an abstract norm cannot achieve, a concrete model often can: it transforms a man . . . helps him to conquer the negative tendencies of his nature and to achieve a higher and more ideal self-realization. It is precisely in this transforming effect that the power of the model discloses itself.[62]

[58] *Ibid.*, p. 33.
[59] *Ibid.*, p. 34; *Philosophical Perspectives*, p. 33.
[60] *Ibid.*
[61] Johannes Hessen, *Ethik* (Leiden: Brill, 1958), pp. 136-145: "VII Die Bedeutung des Vorbildes."
[62] *Ibid.*, p. 141.

Psychologist Theodor Müncker [63] reiterates Scheler's basic insight and substantiates it from a psychological point of view. He writes:

Moral values should never be presented to youth in an abstract manner, but preferably through exemplary persons to whom a youth will open his heart in love. In this way values will disclose themselves effectively and a youth will experience them as an obligation which makes its demand also on him. Empathy with the moral attitude of the model person will evoke feelings of sympathy, stir up motivation, and inspire the will to moral action. . . . Adults also grasp moral values primarily through exemplary persons. In fact, nobody can make the right value judgments without such model persons.[64]

Kurt Haase applied Scheler's ideas on the model person to education and developed it further within the framework of a philosophy of education.[65] He calls it one of Scheler's major achievements to have introduced into moral philosophy the ideal of the model person, and to have demonstrated the important role and function of the moral exemplar. Haase corroborates Scheler's theory with a wealth of data from the field of education. One of his historical examples is of particular interest here. The neo-humanist movement in German education developed an ideal image of man based on the great exemplary personalities of Greek history, similar to the attempt of Renaissance humanism which made Cicero the main prototype. Nevertheless, Haase contends, it was the living model person of Goethe who truly functioned as the ideal prototype in neo-humanist education. The living exemplar of Goethe was the real *Idealtypus* of neo-

---

[63] Theodor Müncker, *Die psychologischen Grundlagen der katholischen Sittenlehre* (Düsseldorf: Schwann, 1934).

[64] *Ibid.*, p. 279.

[65] Kurt Haase, "Das Wesen des Vorbilds und seine Bedeutung für die Erziehung," *Vierteljahrsschrift für wissenschaftliche Pädagogik*, III (Summer, 1927), pp. 243-273.

humanism, who gave inspiration and impetus to the whole movement.[66]

IV

HISTORY OF ETHICS AS HISTORY
OF VALUE-PERSON-TYPES

From his numerous writings Scheler emerges as a man who
was always intensely preoccupied with the meaning of history.
He raises this question in different contexts, in his discussion of
value-person-types, among others.

A system of values and ideals is hovering over each group of
men in any period of history. These values and ideals precede
the actual historical development of peoples and, in fact, largely
determine the course of history and the rise and fall of nations.
But if the course of history is determined by the particular values
and ideals that peoples are cherishing at the time, whence do
these values and ideals originate? Scheler sees the ultimate
source and origin of the value systems of any people and period
in the type of model persons which predominates in a particular
place and time. These model persons and the values embodied
in them determine the ethos of their epoch and bring about the
moral and socio-political developments and changes in history.[67] The guiding social and moral models may be living persons or even historical personalities that live on in the sagas
and myths of each nation:

The fate of peoples shapes itself through the modes of
thinking, viewing, and evaluating the world as expressed
in their myths—above all, however, in the model persons
embodied in these myths. What are, for the Greeks, Her-
akles, Orestes, and Ulysses; what, for the Teutons, the personal models of their sagas? [68]

[66] *Ibid.*, p. 270. For a more detailed discussion of this question see
Eduard Spranger, "Das deutsche Bildungsideal in geschichtsphilosophi-
scher Beleuchtung," *Erziehung*, I (January, 1921), pp. 15ff.

[67] NACH, pp. 319-321; 268-273.

[68] *Ibid.*, pp. 272-273.

Scheler intended to write an *Anthropologie*—a project his premature death did not allow him to carry out—in which he planned to propose a history of ideas about man in myth, religion and philosophy.[69] In this work he intended to portray a history of the ideal types of men and of the basic forms in which man had thought about himself and experienced himself. From this history of man's consciousness of himself, Scheler hoped to demonstrate that the growth, heightening and intensification of human consciousness of self is, indeed, the fundamental direction of history.[70]

Scheler exemplifies the historical function of model persons and of "leading types of men" in his reflections on the era of harmonization.[71] The dawning era of harmonization will be brought about not by a mere transformation of institutions but by a transformation of man himself. The very norms of judgment have to be changed, and this requires ultimately a refashioning of the prevailing image of man. History shows that man is a being of tremendous plasticity. Yet we are in constant danger of conceiving the idea of man too narrowly. We tend to restrict our concept of man and to reduce the richness of humanity to one particular historical form of manhood with which we happen to be familiar. The rich totality of manhood cannot be contained in such narrow concepts as *animal rationale, homo faber* or similar ideas. Preparing for the incipient era of harmonization, mankind has to become aware of all the plentiful concepts and models of man. Only then can we work for a convergence and harmonization of different types of men. "Apollonian" man and "Dionysian" man, Oriental man and Occidental man, as well as numerous other concepts of man must be harmonized and integrated to bring forth the fullness of total man. Model persons and different concepts of man thus play a paramount role in the historical process of bringing about the hoped-for era of harmonization.

[69] *Philosophische Weltanschauung*, p. 63.
[70] *Ibid*.
[71] "Der Mensch im Weltalter des Ausgleichs," in *Philosophische Weltanschauung*, pp. 89-118. For a detailed discussion of Scheler's ideas on the "era of harmonization" see chapter IX.

An understanding of model persons is, according to Scheler, of paramount importance for any comprehension and interpretation of history. Model persons are the primary vehicle of all change in history.

> The soul of all history is not the actual event, but rather the history of the ideals, value systems, norms and forms of ethos according to which men measure and evaluate themselves and their actions. It is only this soul of history that enables us to fully understand the factual events. Moreover, the history of model persons, their origin and transformation, is the innermost core of this soul of history.[72]

Value-person-types or model persons are thus at the core of all human history and development. The very meaning of history reveals itself in the continuously growing and developing concrete models of humanity.[73] Models attract and draw man to ever greater heights of self-realization, and they function thus as stepping-stones on man's road to his ultimate goal. Scheler describes this highest goal as the gradual unfolding of the image and likeness of God in man.[74]

[72] NACH, p. 268.
[73] *Ibid.*, p. 269.
[74] *Ibid.*

IX
Ethics and the "Era of Harmonization" (Weltalter des Ausgleichs)

In Scheler's later philosophy the idea of an emerging historical "era of harmonization" assumed the character of a unifying key concept and of a focal point for his philosophy of history, his epistemology, psychology, anthropology, political philosophy and ethics. Many isolated insights of Scheler's earlier period were now unified through this new insight, becoming, so to speak, integral parts of a monumental canvas illuminated by the new synthesis of the era of harmonization.

I
The "Era of Harmonization"

Before presenting Scheler's ideas in greater detail we must briefly discuss the English terminology. Oscar A. Haac, in his translation of Scheler's *Philosophical Perspectives*,[1] renders *Weltalter des Ausgleichs* as "era of adjustment." John Raphael Staude also uses the English term "adjustment."[2] Manfred Frings translates it as "age of balance" as well as "age of ad-

---

[1] Max Scheler, *Philosophical Perspectives*, trans. by Oscar A. Haac (Boston: Beacon Press, 1958), p. 94. (Hereinafter referred to as *Perspectives*.)

[2] John Raphael Staude, *Max Scheler* (New York: The Free Press, 1967), p. 203: "The Metaphysics of Adjustment."

justment." [3] Lewis A. Coser, in his introduction to the English translation of Scheler's *Ressentiment*,[4] refers to Scheler's essay as "Man in the Age of Harmonization." *Weltalter des Ausgleichs* then has such a rich meaning that no single translation suffices to express the breadth and depth of Scheler's thought. I would like to add as one further possible translation "era of convergence." [5] *Weltalter des Ausgleichs* signifies then: (1) era of adjustment, (2) era of balance, (3) era of harmonization, and (4) era of convergence.

[3] Manfred Frings, *Max Scheler* (Pittsburgh: Duquesne University Press, 1965), pp. 194-207.

[4] Max Scheler, *Ressentiment*, p. 9.

[5] Scheler uses the concept *Konvergenz* toward the end of his essay "Der Mensch im Weltalter des Ausgleichs" (*Philosophische Weltanschauung*, p. 118) and the verb *konvergieren* in *Die Wissensformen und die Gesellschaft*, pp. 187, 188. The term "convergence" also has the advantage of bringing out the close affinity between Scheler's insight and the parallel ideas that would later be developed by Teilhard de Chardin. A recent study presents the concept "convergence" as the focal point of Teilhard's basic thought structure: Alfred Glässer, *Konvergenz: Die Struktur der Weltsumme Teilhard de Chardin* (Kevelaer: Butzon & Bercker, 1969). See also Franz Michael Willam, "Teilhard de Chardin und Kardinal Newman (2)," *Orientierung*, January 31, 1970, pp. 25-28. Teilhard writes in *The Future of Man* (New York: Harper & Row, 1969), p. 171: "With and since the coming of Man, as we have seen, a new law of Nature has come into force—that of convergence. The convergence of the phyla both ensues from, and of itself leads to, the coming together of individuals within the peculiarly 'attaching' atmosphere created by the phenomenon of Reflexion. And out of this convergence, as I have said, there arises a very real social inheritance, produced by the synthetic recording of human experience." Again he writes in *Quelques réflexions sur la conversion du monde*, 1936, *Oeuvres*, IX, 161-162: "The world we know is not developing by chance, but is structurally controlled by a personal Centre of universal convergence." Henri de Lubac, in his Glossary of Teilhard's Vocabulary describes "convergence" this way: "Convergence—Synthetic movement toward an ultimate focus or meeting-point followed by the whole of evolving creation. After an initial stage of dispersion or divergence, convergence appears as an aggregation in elements and socialization in man. Even in the realm of intellectual disciplines (including religion) convergence occurs, since they all approach the same reality." Henri de Lubac, *Teilhard Explained* (New York: Paulist Press, 1968), pp. 84-85. Cf. also Henri de Lubac, S.J., *The Religion of Teilhard de Chardin*, Image Books (New York: Doubleday, 1968), pp. 146; 156-159; 239-241; 284. Christopher Mooney, S.J., *Teilhard de Chardin and the Mystery of Christ*, Image Books (New York: Doubleday, 1968), pp. 36; 39; 49-54; 60-63; 70; 120; 140; 163; 170; 174.

We will now offer a brief overview of the "era of harmonization." Scheler maintains that mankind is standing at the threshold of a new era which will be characterized by an integration and reconciliation of numerous tensions, differences and oppositions. There will be a world-wide redistribution and harmonization of various energies and forces—emotional, sexual, economic, social, political, and cultural, as well as intellectual and religious. The three types of knowledge—"control knowledge," essential knowledge and salvific knowledge—will no longer be considered as belonging to three different stages of history and as replacing one another (Comte) but rather as mutually complementing each other. A gradual balancing-out of different qualities and values prevalent in various societies and cultures will lead to a mutual enrichment and a fuller development of the enormous psychological, ethical, social, political and religious potential in mankind.

II
THREE TYPES OF KNOWLEDGE IN THE
"ERA OF HARMONIZATION"

History Moving toward a Balanced
Complementation of the Three
Types of Knowledge

In the dawning "Era of Harmonization," all one-sidedness of thought, emotion and valuation will be transcended in a new balanced synthesis of mutual complementation. The areas of complementation are manifold, and we will now examine in somewhat greater detail the different kinds of harmonization that Scheler expects to emerge in the dawning epoch of history. The first one that deserves a careful scrutiny is the balanced complementation of the three types of knowledge—"control knowledge" (*Herrschaftswissen*), essential knowledge (*Wesenswissen*), and salvific knowledge (*Erlösungswissen*). Alois Dempf, Paul L.

Landsberg, Alfred Schutz and other competent students of Scheler's philosophy consider this doctrine of the three kinds of human knowledge and their hierarchical order to be at the heart of Scheler's philosophical anthropology; some even consider this theory to be Scheler's greatest achievement.[6]

Scheler starts his reflections on the three types of knowledge as a dialogue with and a critique of the pragmatic concept of knowledge, or more explicitly, as a creative response to Auguste Comte's law of the three stages. Comte maintains—and this is the framework into which he fits his whole philosophy—that "every branch of our knowledge necessarily has to pass through three successive theoretical states: the theological or fictitious state, the metaphysical or abstract state, and the scientific or positive state." [7] Scheler would agree with Comte that we must distinguish different types of knowledge. His basic disagreement concerns the assertion of Comte that these kinds of knowledge supersede each other in successive periods of history. For Scheler, one type of knowledge does not replace the other in a gradual evolution of the human mind. This would mean reducing the richness of possible human knowledge to a one-dimensional model, ignoring and excluding thereby essential aspects of the total reality. According to Scheler, the three types of knowledge do not correspond to three successive stages of history; they rather present three co-existent modes of knowledge which correspond to three different aspects of reality.[8] Developing one type of knowledge at the expense of the other two would lead to reductionism and to an impoverishment of the human mind and of man's cognitional activity.

The last centuries have been characterized by precisely such reductionist tendencies. Consequently, there now exists a great

[6] Alfred Schutz, *Collected Papers*, Vol. III: *Studies in Phenomenological Philosophy*, ed. by I. Schutz (The Hague: Martinus Nijhoff, 1966), pp. 140, 150.

[7] Auguste Comte, *Considerations philosophiques sur les savants*. Quoted in Henri de Lubac, S.J., *The Drama of Atheist Humanism*, trans. by Edith M. Riley, Meridian Books (New York: The World Publishing Company, 1966), p. 79.

[8] SOZ, p. 30.

need for developing harmoniously and in a balanced way all three mutually complementary kinds of knowledge. The "Era of Harmonization" presents us with the task of achieving this kind of balanced synthesis. In order to better understand the hoped for harmonization, we have to take a closer look at each of the three types of knowledge. We shall consider them in the following order: (1) "control knowledge" (*Herrschaftswissen*); (2) essential knowledge (*Wesenswissen*); (3) salvific knowledge (*Erlösungswissen*).

Characterization of the Three
Types of Knowledge

"Control Knowledge" (Herrschaftswissen)

Scheler's elaboration of the concept of "control knowledge" (*Herrschaftswissen*) represents "a highly original and bold attempt to comprehend the underlying structure and historical significance of the modern natural sciences." [9] Although Scheler never gives a systematic exposition of this important notion, references to it can be found scattered throughout many of his works. The two principal sources are the essays, *Probleme einer Soziologie des Wissens* (written 1921-1924; first published in 1924) [10] and *Erkenntnis und Arbeit* (1926). [11]

Before presenting Scheler's ideas on control knowledge in greater detail, it might be advisable to consider briefly a linguistic problem. It is difficult to find an accurate and graceful English equivalent of the German concept *Herrschaftswissen*. Wilhelm Leiss suggests that this term ought to be left untranslated for lack of an appropriate English word. [12] Oscar A. Haac, in his translation of Scheler's *Philosophische Weltanschauung*, renders the term as "knowledge of control." [13] Manfred Frings

[9] William Leiss, "Max Scheler's Concept of Herrschaftswissen," *The Philosophical Forum*, II (Spring, 1971), 317.
[10] GES, pp. 15-190.
[11] *Ibid.*, pp. 191-382.
[12] Leiss, p. 329.
[13] *Perspectives*, p. 3.

speaks of "knowledge of control and achievement." [14] Hans Meyerhoff, the translator of Scheler's *Die Stellung des Menschen im Kosmos,* uses the phrase "knowledge of domination." [15] John Raphael Staude, in his book *Max Scheler,* translates it as "knowledge of domination or control of nature." [16] Since in Scheler's *Herrschaftswissen* control (*Herrschaft*) is not the object of knowledge (*Wissen*) but rather its motive and goal, the above translations are misleading or can at least be easily misunderstood. By *Herrschaftswissen* Scheler means a knowledge that is born of a desire to achieve control over nature. "Control knowledge" seems, therefore, to be the most appropriate translation.

In his book *Philosophische Weltanschauung,* Scheler describes *Herrschaftswissen* as the knowledge which "serves our ability to exercise power over nature, society, and history. It is the knowledge of the specialized experimental sciences." [17] The main objective of this knowledge is to discover the laws of nature in space and time. We are, however, not interested in these laws for their own sake, but rather because they enable us to achieve control over the world. "Only what recurs according to laws can be predicted; only the predictable can be controlled." [18]

Scheler acknowledges the importance of "control knowledge" within its proper bounds. Man has to struggle with nature and achieve mastery over the surrounding environment in order to secure and maintain his own human existence. "Control knowledge," or the development of various techniques for subjecting the environment to the ends of man, is a necessity for his survival and development.

Scheler's critique is directed against those who would make "control knowledge" the only valid type of knowledge. In his essay *Erkenntnis und Arbeit,* which presents a critique of prag-

[14] Manfred Frings, *Max Scheler,* p. 189.

[15] Max Scheler, *Man's Place in Nature,* trans. by Hans Meyerhoff (New York: The Noonday Press, 1962), p. xxiii.

[16] Staude, *Max Scheler,* p. 209.

[17] Max Scheler, *Philosophische Weltanschauung,* Dalp Taschenbücher (3rd ed. rev.; Bern: Francke Verlag, 1968), p. 7. (Hereinafter referred to as PHIL.) *Perspectives,* p. 3.

[18] PHIL, p. 7; *Perspectives,* p. 4.

matism, Scheler attempts to show that the pragmatic notion of knowledge is accurate with respect to only *one* type of knowledge, namely "control knowledge." Failure to recognize the existence of other types of knowledge—essential knowledge (*Wesenswissen*) and salvific knowledge (*Erlösungswissen*)—constitutes a basic error of the pragmatic concept of knowledge.[19]

Modern scientific knowledge views itself as being free of all value-judgment and value-determination. In a similar vein, the objects of scientific inquiry are considered to be value-free. In a poignant critique of these assumptions, Scheler points to the implicit value-judgments underlying the new science: "Although men conceive the world as value-free, nevertheless they conceive of it this way because of a value, that is, the vital value of mastery and power over things."[20] Scheler borrows here an insight of Nietzsche, namely that the will to power (*Wille zur Macht*) is a primary value underlying the positive sciences in their approach to the world. Modern science is a concrete expression of this will to power, bent on increasing the power of man over the environment and on converting all of nature into a field of operation for his own human purposes. Scientific knowledge as conquest and domination of nature constitutes, therefore, a definite option for a particular set of values. In a sense, Scheler tries to "demythologize" the myth of a value-free science by pointing up the primacy of valuation in the cognition of the world that also underlies the basic approach of modern sciences.

After these more fundamental reflections on "control knowledge," Scheler enters into a discussion of distinct stages in the development of the will to power as expressed in "control knowledge." He again takes up the idea of changing types of ethos according to which the state of the positive sciences varies and changes from one historical epoch to another. In particular, Scheler deals with the transition from the medieval to the modern period in European history and its underlying fundamental value-transformation.[21] The power drive (*Machttrieb*) of the

[19] GES, p. 205.
[20] *Ibid.*, p. 122.
[21] *Ibid.*, p. 257.

Middle Ages was essentially directed toward the exercise of domination over men, whereas the power drive of the new ethos concentrates on power over things.[22] Man's way of looking at nature and his basic attitude toward it have radically changed. In the Middle Ages, man showed a loving dedication (*liebevolle Hingabe*) [23] to nature and was satisfied with a merely conceptual ordering of her phenomena. In sharp contrast, the overriding interest of the new ethos with its new power drive is the domination of nature and the transformation of things into valuable goods. The search for the other types of knowledge—essential knowledge and salvific knowledge—are now subordinated to the primacy of "control knowledge," of achievement and of the will to power over nature.[24]

Essential Knowledge (Wesenswissen)

Scheler calls the second type of knowledge *Wesenswissen* (essential knowledge) or *Bildungswissen* (knowledge directed to the cultivation of the person). The two concepts are used interchangeably.[25] Essential knowledge is the knowledge of essences attained through eidetic intuition (*Wesensschau.*) In *Philosophische Weltanschauung* it is defined as "the knowledge of all forms of being and of the essential structure of all that is." [26] In his essay "Vom Wesen der Philosophie" Scheler describes the mental attitude which underlies all philosophical thinking, i.e. all essential knowledge, as "a love-determined movement by which the inmost center of a finite human person participates

[22] *Ibid.*, pp. 124-125.
[23] *Ibid.*, p. 125.
[24] It would be a fruitful enterprise to apply Scheler's insights on the one-sided development of "control knowledge" and on the new ethos of nature conquest to the present-day discussion on ecology and environmental protection. Though lacking the statistical data that are available to us today, Scheler foresaw with amazing accuracy the grave dangers inherent in an approach to nature which is characterized by domination and exploitation.
[25] PHIL, p. 7: ". . . Wesens- oder Bildungswissen. . . ." *Perspectives,* p. 3.
[26] PHIL, p. 9: ". . . die Wissenschaft von den Seinsweisen und der Wesensstruktur alles dessen, was ist." *Perspectives,* p. 5.

in the essence of all possible reality." [27] Toward the end of the same treatise Scheler offers this tentative definition of philosophy:

In essence philosophy is strictly self-evident insight, which cannot be augmented or nullified by induction and which has *a priori* validity for all contingent existence: insight into all such essences and essential interrelations of beings as are accessible to us from available instances, in the order and hierarchy as they stand in relation to absolute being and its essence.[28]

In an essay which he published only two weeks before his death, Scheler delineated in a more detailed manner the main characteristics of essential knowledge: [29]

1. First, to gain essential knowledge man must make an effort to bracket out all desires and drives of the senses. A loving attitude which seeks out the basic phenomena (*Urphänomene*) and ideas of the world must replace man's orientation toward domination and control.

2. Essential knowledge requires a bracketing out of the real existence (*reales Dasein*) of things. Only the essence (*Wesen, essentia*) is the object of this type of knowledge.

3. Essential knowledge precedes induction, observation and measurement. Although it is "not independent of all experience, it is independent of the *quantum* of experience or of so-called "induction.' " [30] Thus, it resembles the propositions of pure mathematics which obtain a priori necessary relations before real nature is investigated and measured.

4. Essential knowledge and the knowledge of essential relationships are valid above and beyond that limited realm of the world

[27] VEIM, p. 68: "Liebesbestimmter Aktus der Teilnahme des Kernes einer endlichen Menschenperson am Wesenhaften aller möglichen Dinge." *Eternal*, p. 74.

[28] VEIM, p. 98; *Eternal*, p. 104.

[29] "Philosophische Weltanschauung," *Münchener Neueste Nachrichten*, May 5, 1928. Reprinted in *Philosophische Weltanschauung*, pp. 5-15. Our references are to the latter edition. Cf. *Perspectives*, pp. 1-12.

[30] PHIL, p. 10; *Perspectives*, p. 6.

230 PROCESS AND PERMANENCE IN ETHICS

which is accessible to us through sense experience. Thus, it has a transcendental dimension and is valid for being as such.[31]

5. Essential knowledge is the true knowledge of reason (*Vernunft*) to be distinguished from such knowledge as we gain from conclusions of practical understanding (*Verstandesschlüsse*). The latter ability must also be attributed, in different degrees, to higher animals. Essential knowledge reveals itself as specifically human when it applies a priori contents to the fortuitous facts of experience and when it is concerned with the objective order of values, with wisdom and the moral ideal.

6. Essential knowledge can be applied in two ways. First, it circumscribes the ultimate assumptions of each field of the experimental sciences and furnishes each science the "axioms of its essential nature" (*Wesensaxiomatik*). Secondly, in the area of metaphysics essential knowledge functions as "the window into the absolute" (Hegel); it discloses the essential structure of world and man and relates this to absolute being; that is, to the supreme ground of both world and man.[32]

In several essays, Scheler refers to the three types of knowledge but uses the term *Bildungswissen* (knowledge directed to the cultivation of a person) instead of *Wesenswissen*.[33] Here he emphasizes that whereas control knowledge is concerned with a limited field of knowledge, *Bildungswissen* must always be concerned with the cultivation of the total person (*allseitige Bildung*).[34] Furthermore, "*Bildung* is not possible without value judgments and the commitment of the whole man to a definite set of values of one distinct historical period." [35] Without such a commitment a man would be an irresponsible intellectual adventurer, not a cultivated and responsible human being.

The finality of any knowledge is, according to Scheler, a "be-

[31] PHIL, p. 10: ". . . für das Seiende, wie es an sich selbst und in sich selbst ist." *Perspectives*, p. 7.

[32] PHIL, pp. 9-12; *Perspectives*, pp. 5-9.

[33] "Erkenntnis und Arbeit," in GES, pp. 205-207. "Probleme einer Soziologie des Wissens," in GES, p. 60.

[34] "Universität und Hochschule," in GES, p. 394.

[35] *Ibid.*

coming or a transformation" (*ein Werden—ein Anderswer-
den*).[36] *Bildungswissen* has as its particular finality the "becoming and development of the person." [37] In his reflections
on the reform of the German universities, Scheler speaks of the
cultivation of mental attitudes, of the will, of the heart and the
soul as goals of genuine *Bildung*.[38] *Bildungswissen,* or "knowledge born of a desire to cultivate and refine the personality," [39]
is at present being neglected in favor of a one-sided emphasis
on control knowledge and must be restored to its proper place
if Western man wants to return to a balanced education and
formation of man.

Scheler's theory of cognition is also distinguished by a strong
emphasis on the moral prerequisites for achieving essential
knowledge.[40] Value-deception and blindness to true values are
common phenomena among men and they originate mainly
from a way of life which is not in harmony with the objective
order of morality. If a man does not live a moral life, his sense
of values and of the proper hierarchy of values is impaired and
reduced to the level of his actual moral behavior. A continuous
self-deception may eventually lead to total blindness with regard
to moral values.

Essential knowledge and the cognition of the moral good
involves the whole man, not just his rational faculty. Therefore,
to achieve this kind of knowledge, man must first prepare himself both on the theoretical and on the practical-moral level. "A
man first has to learn in a more or less blind way to will and act
rightly and well, objectively speaking, before he is in a position
to apprehend the good as good, and to will and actualize the
good with discernment." [41]

A moral upsurge (*moralischer Aufschwung*) [42] becomes an

---

[36] "Erkenntnis und Arbeit," in GES, pp. 204-205.

[37] *Ibid.,* p. 205: ". . . Werden und Entfaltung der Person. . . ."

[38] "Universität und Volkshochschule," in GES, p. 408: ". . . Gesin-
nungs-, Willens-, Herzensbildung . . . Wachstum der Seele. . . ."

[39] This is Werner Stark's description of Scheler's *Bildungswissen.* Cf.
Stark, *The Sociology of Knowledge,* p. 117.

[40] VEIM, pp. 78-79, 85, 89-90; *Eternal,* pp. 84-85, 90-91, 95-96.

[41] VEIM, p. 79; *Eternal,* p. 85.

[42] VEIM, pp. 83-90; *Eternal,* pp. 89-98.

integral part of that upward movement through which the in-most personal self strives to participate in the essence of being by knowledge. The breadth and depth of man's essential knowl-edge depends, ultimately, on the degree of man's moral eleva-tion. Scheler, however, distinguishes his own view from Fichte's proposition that "one's philosophy is governed by the kind of man one is." [43] According to Scheler, the moral character is not simply responsible for the content or result of one's philosophy. The moral attitude directly influences man's total upward move-ment; that is, the degree, purity and dynamism of the transcend-ing upsurge, which first opens to man the realm of essences.

Scheler characterizes three basic moral acts as fundamental predispositions for essential knowledge: (1) the love of the whole spiritual person for absolute value and being; (2) humil-ity of the natural self and ego; (3) self-control involving es-pecially the mastery over the instinctual impulses of life.[44]

Each of these three basic moral acts fulfills a special prepara-tory function in the complex process of achieving essential knowledge. Love of absolute values takes us beyond objects which exist only relatively to our being and leads us in the direction of absolute being. Humility overcomes our natural pride and leads us away from contingent things toward pure es-sences. Self-control enables us to restrain and objectify the in-stinctual impulses and leads us from inadequate knowledge toward full adequacy of cognitive insight.

Scheler maintains that there exists an essential connection between these three moral attitudes and the possibility of any advance in essential knowledge. In systematic interaction, these moral acts lead the person out of the realm of relative being onto the threshold of the higher sphere of pure essences and of ab-solute being. After this basic moral preparation, it is in an act of self-giving or "devotion" [45] that man can achieve a cognitive participation in the realm of the absolute.

---

[43] VEIM, p. 85: ". . . die Philosophie, die man habe, richte sich danach, was für ein Mensch man sei." *Eternal*, p. 91.

[44] VEIM, pp. 89-90; *Eternal*, pp. 95-96.

[45] VEIM, p. 92; *Eternal*, p. 98.

Salvific Knowledge (Erlösungswissen)

The third type of knowledge is called *Erlösungswissen* or *Heilswissen* (salvific knowledge). The ultimate origin of this highest form of knowledge and the motivation for pursuing it is rooted in the "irresistible urge" of all persons to seek deliverance and salvation and "to establish contact on the level of knowledge with a reality intuited as supremely powerful and holy and at the same time the highest good and the universal ground of being." [46] In contrast, essential knowledge (*Wesenswissen*) has its origin in the "intentional emotion of wonderment (*thaumazein*)," [47] and control knowledge is motivated by man's desire to control and dominate nature.[48]

Salvific knowledge is, according to Scheler, an essential and necessary dimension of the human mind. But how can one then explain the situation of a man who rejects the existence of God and closes his mind to the realm of the holy and divine? Scheler responds that "since the religious act is an essential endowment of the human mind and soul, there can be no question of whether a man performs it or not. The question can only be of whether he finds its adequate object." [49] A great number of people do, indeed, reject God and the realm of the holy; but they choose instead finite and contingent objects which function as the surrogate of a positive religion. "Every finite spirit believes either in God or in idols." [50]

The finite mind does not have the choice of believing in something or not believing in anything. Any man who examines himself or his fellow men will find that he identifies himself, or they identify themselves, with a particular good or kind of good in such a way that his (or their) personal relationship to that good may be summarized in these

[46] Scheler, "Probleme einer Soziologie des Wissens," in *Die Wissensformen und die Gesellschaft*, p. 65.
[47] *Ibid.*
[48] *Ibid.*, p. 66.
[49] VEIM, p. 261; *Eternal*, p. 267.
[50] *Ibid.*

words: "Without thee, in which I believe, I cannot be, I will not be, I ought not to be. We two, I and thou good, stand and fall together." [51]

There exists an infinite variety of goods and objects that are "deified" and take the place of God. Some men idolize power, others put art in the place of God. There are State-worshippers who make the State the supreme good, and there are servants of Mammon for whom the pursuit of money turns into a surrogate religion. The idea of an ideal future state has become the Messianic religion of Marxism. The Faustian men make limitless knowledge the absolute goal, and the Don Juan types are enamoured by the idea of ever new conquests of women.[52]

All the numerous instances of idolizing and deification have this one characteristic in common: that a finite goal occupies the place of God, and that a human being is chained to an idol and behaves "as if" the idol were God himself.[53]

For many people the way to develop genuine salvific knowledge and a genuine understanding of God will lead through a process which Scheler calls a "shattering of idols" (*Zerschmetterung der Götzen*).[54] The path from unbelief to belief does not lead directly to God. Rather, man must first become aware that he has interposed an idol between himself and God. The religious development leads through a process where man gradually discovers that he has become enamoured of a finite object (*sich "vergafft" hat*). He must then remove the veil which conceals the idea of God and must restore the jumbled and inverted order of reality. Once a man's faith in his idols is shaken, and he has become disillusioned, a great void opens up in his mind and heart. This new void yearns to be filled and the formerly misdirected religious acts can now find their real fulfillment in turning to their proper object, i.e. the idea of the true God.

[51] VEIM, pp. 398-399; *Eternal*, p. 399.
[52] VEIM, pp. 261-263, 398-399; *Eternal*, pp. 267-269, 398.
[53] VEIM, p. 263; *Eternal*, p. 268-269.
[54] VEIM, p. 262; *Eternal*, p. 267.

Scheler sums up his reflections on the necessity of performing religious acts: "Thus man believes either in God or in an idol. There is no third course open." [55] In other words, "you cannot choose between having or not having a good of this kind. You can only choose whether your absolute sphere will be inhabited by God, as the one good commensurate with the religious act, or by an idol." [56]

For Scheler, knowledge is always closely linked to love, and the higher the form or object of knowledge, the greater the role of love in the cognitional process. Man's love and hate determine which objects he selects and focuses upon. His axiological view-points (*Wertgesichtspunkte*) which originate from his *ordo amoris* divide objects into significant and non-significant, and focus the mind's interest and attention to those materials of knowledge which are considered as important. If love is a pre-requisite for any type of human knowledge, it is all the more essential in the sphere of man's salvific knowledge. God can be known only through love. In his approach to God, man discovers that his own love is but a response to a pre-existent love in God which is directed toward man. This love in God is the ultimate condition of the possibility of any salvific knowledge in man.

Salvific knowledge is characterized by one more important dimension, namely its moral prerequisite. "Of all kinds of cognition, knowledge of God is most intimately linked to moral progress." [57] Every religious act includes also an act of moral value apprehension; namely, the cognition of God as the good. Martin Luther wrongly contended that moral volition and conduct are mere consequences of religious faith. On the contrary, Scheler asserts, that any cognitive advance into the full breadth and depth of God presupposes morally good volition and conduct.

Good will and conduct do more than reflect religious awareness: at every step they widen and deepen one's con-

[55] VEIM, p. 399; *Eternal*, p. 399.
[56] VEIM, p. 263; *Eternal*, p. 269.
[57] VEIM, p. 259; *Eternal*, p. 265.

crete knowledge of God. They bring about a genuine penetration of His volitional aspect, a heightened participation
of the person in His internal dynamic, even where there is
no conscious reflection that such is the nature of the process. And since knowledge of values is the foundation for
knowledge of being, this kind of penetration is also a pre-
condition of knowing God's being.[58]

The fact that God is a person is the ultimate reason why he
cannot be known through mere speculation. The person in his
deepest essence is not naked being, but value and love. Therefore, it is only personal love that enables man to know the value
of a person and to discover the personal God.

When Scheler speaks of the love of God as a prerequisite of
knowing him, he does not mean love "for" God (*Liebe "zu
Gott"*) in which case God would be the object of our love.[59]
A person can never be disclosed to us as an "object." "Persons
cannot be objectified, in love or any other genuine act, not even
in cognition." [60] This is precisely the point where a person differs from any thing which can become an object. We can know
a person only by our joining in the performance of his acts. The
love of God in its highest form consists, therefore, in partici-
pating (*Mitvollzug*) in his love for the world (*amare mundum
in Deo*) and for himself (*amare Deum in Deo*).[61]

Here Scheler clearly asserts a primacy of loving over knowing.
It is only in "co-loving" (*Mit-lieben*) and in the participation
in and emulation of God's infinite action of love toward himself
and his creatures,[62] that we can ascertain genuine knowledge
of God. The co-realization (*Mitvollzug*) of God's own love, is
then for Scheler the deepest essence of man's religious act. A

[58] *Ibid.*
[59] SYM, p. 177; *Sympathy*, p. 164.
[60] *Ibid.*
[61] VEIM, pp. 220, 223; *Eternal,* pp. 226, 229. SYM, pp. 177, 181;
Sympathy, pp. 164, 168.
[62] VEIM, p. 220: ". . . Mitvollzug und Nachvollzug des unendlichen
Liebesaktes Gottes zu sich selbst und zu seinen Geschöpfen. . . ." Cf.
Eternal, p. 226.

grandiose vision of the essence of religion! Yet Scheler considers his own insights only as a retrieve and a modern restatement of the great medieval tradition in which scholastics and mystics spoke of this same love as *amare in Deo*.[63]

In light of the preceding discussion, we are now in a position to offer a definition of what Scheler means by salvific knowledge. It is that type of knowledge by which man endeavors to participate with the innermost core of his person in the very life and love of the supreme person of God.[64]

Harmonization of the Three
Types of Knowledge

In his brilliant critique of Comte's "law of three stages" (*Dreistadiengesetz*) and in the development of his own theory of forms of knowledge, Scheler is concerned with two basic issues. First, he wants to establish the autonomy and irreducible uniqueness of both philosophical and religious knowledge against the reductionist claims of modern positivism which acknowledges none but "control knowledge." Secondly, by way of a cultural criticism, he wants to demonstrate that the one-sidedness of positivism is at the root of many ills in contemporary society and that only a harmonious development of all three types of knowledge can remedy the present situation and restore a proper balance in Western culture.

Religious thought, metaphysical thought and the thinking of the positive sciences are not three historical stages in the development of human knowledge as people like Comte, Mill, Spencer,

[63] SYM, p. 177; *Sympathy,* p. 164.

[64] In his later years Scheler modified his concept of salvific knowledge. As a result of his development from a theistic toward a pantheistic position, salvific knowledge, which he then also called metaphysical knowledge (*metaphysisches oder Erlösungswissen;* cf. *Philosophische Weltanschauung,* pp. 7, 12), signified that knowledge by which the supreme ground of being knows itself, redeems itself and "becomes" itself (cf. "Erkenntnis und Arbeit" in *Die Wissensformen und die Gesellschaft,* pp. 205-206). However, it is significant that Scheler never rejected the profound insights of his early and middle periods which we have delineated above.

Mach and Avenarius contend. Rather, they are "essential, perennial attitudes of the mind and forms of knowledge (*Erkenntnisformen*) which are given with the essence of the human mind itself. None of them can ever replace the other or substitute for it." [65] The three types of thinking correspond to three different, equally original tasks of man, namely to understand the world as proceeding from personal causes, to understand the essential and eternal relations of ideas (metaphysics), and to discover, to order and classify in their mutual dependence the various appearances of nature.

In his defense of religion, metaphysics and positive science as three autonomous approaches to reality with three corresponding types of knowledge, Scheler offers a perceptive analysis of six criteria which reveal the irreducible uniqueness and the characteristic differences of the three basic endeavors of the human mind. Religion, metaphysics and the positive sciences differ basically, and the uniqueness of each is shown forth in the differences of the following six dimensions: (1) motives, (2) acts, (3) goals, (4) personality types, (5) social groups, and (6) types of historical movements (*geschichtliche Bewegungsformen*).[66]

1. Motives: [67] There are three entirely different motives leading to three types of knowledge and three basic human endeavors. Religion has its motive in man's yearning for salvation by a personal, holy, world-guiding power. Metaphysics is based on an ever new sense of wonder that something "is" rather than "is not." The motive for positive science is the desire and need to control nature, society and the human psyche.

2. Acts: [68] The characteristic acts of religion are spiritual acts like love, hope, fear, willing and knowing, which cannot find their fulfillment in the experience of finite objects but only

[65] Max Scheler, "Uber die positivistische Geschichtsphilosophie des Wissens (Dreistadiengesetz)," in SOZ, p. 30: ". . . essentielle, dauernde, mit dem Wesen des menschlichen Geistes selbst gegebene Geisteshaltungen und 'Erkenntnisformen.' "

[66] *Ibid.*, pp. 31-35.

[67] *Ibid.*, p. 31.

[68] *Ibid.*

through the correlates of the holy and divine. The acts of metaphysics consist in the intellectual intuition of essences (*wesensschauende Vernunft*). The positive sciences are practiced through the acts of observation, experimentation, induction and deduction.

3. Goals: [69] The goal of religion is the salvation of the person and the group. Metaphysics sees its goals in the highest development of the person through wisdom. The positive sciences pursue as their goal the establishment of a world-view in mathematical symbols for the purpose of controlling and dominating nature.

4. Personality types: The saint or the *homo religiosus* is the leading personality type of religion. Charismatic qualities are characteristic of this type of man. The priest is another personality type of religion. He is the cult leader and the ecclesiastic official who derives his authority from the charismatic quality of the founder of the religion, the church or the sect. The sage, or the wise man (*der Weise*), is the leading personality type of metaphysics. He is the one who is concerned with essences and with the world as a whole, not with the specialized knowledge of the natural sciences. In the positive sciences, it is the research man (*Forscher*) who represents the leading personality type. The researcher is not concerned with the whole or with a system, but rather with advancing the limitless process of scientific inquiry in one particular area.

5. Social groups: The three types of knowledge and the three basic functions of the human mind are correlated to three different social groups or forms. Churches, sects, and religious communities are the social forms of religion. The "school," in the classical sense, is the appropriate social form of metaphysics, and the international scientific republic with its organizations (universities, learned societies, academies, etc.) is the social form of the positive sciences.

6. Types of historical movements (*geschichtliche Bewegungsformen*): Three different forms of historical manifestations

[69] *Ibid.*

correspond to the three basic forms of knowledge. Religious knowledge is retrospective and completed. Since religion is based on the free acceptance of divine revelation, development and progress in religious knowledge consists not in completely new discoveries but rather in a deeper penetration and understanding of the content of past revelation. Religious renewal and reform does not mean acquiring new knowledge but a retrospective "return to the sources" (*ein "Zurück zu den Quellen"*).[70] Metaphysics is the expression of individual creativity. Metaphysical systems which develop through the intuition of essences, are complete in themselves. They are closely linked to the person of their originator, and they recur at different stages of scientific progress. Metaphysical systems are deeply rooted in and closely bound to a specific cultural matrix. Metaphysics does not show a cumulative progress (*kumulativer Fortschrift*), but at the same time it also does not suffer the negative counterpart of such progress, namely devaluation and historical obsolescence. The positive sciences exhibit an entirely different form of historical manifestation. The sciences are impersonal, without close personal links to the scientists. They develop in a cumulative progression, and previous achievements often become obsolete. There is a division of labor, and one person can often be replaced by another. The research is international, and the cultural matrix is less important than in religion and metaphysics.

The analysis of these six different dimensions in religion, metaphysics and positive science corroborates and substantiates Scheler's thesis that each of the three basic mental functions as well as each of the three types of knowledge is, indeed, autonomous, essentially different and irreducible. Religion, metaphysics and positive science represent three basic challenges and tasks for man, each one original, different and of essential importance for the full development of man's humanity. The fundamental moral imperative emerging out of these reflections on the essence of man and the types of his knowledge is a call to overcome the one-sidedness, reductionism and impoverishment

---

[70] *Ibid.*, p. 32.

of positivism, and to develop harmoniously the whole richness of man's potential knowledge. The task at hand is to rediscover religion, metaphysics and positive sciences as three mutually complementary endeavors which together enable man to develop the fullness and depth of his humanity.

III
HARMONIZATION OF THE EMOTIONAL
POWERS IN MAN

Another important area of harmonization concerns the balanced cultivation of all the various emotional powers in man. In an important chapter of *Wesen und Formen der Sympathie*,[71] Scheler demonstrates that different historical periods and diverse civilizations within the same historical period stressed one or another emotional function to the neglect of the balanced and harmonious development of all the rich emotional potentialities of man. "If man is to achieve the total realization of his ideal capacities and of his full humanity, all his various emotional powers must be cultivated, and not just one or another of them." [72]

Scheler distinguishes five basic sympathetic functions (*sympathetische Funktionen*): [73] (1) Identification (*Einsfühlung*); (2) Vicarious feeling (*Nachfühlung*); (3) Fellow-feeling (*Mitgefühl*); (4) Benevolence (*Menschenliebe*); (5) Non-cosmic personal love (*akosmistische Personliebe*).

1. Identification (*Einsfühlung*) is the experience in which a person identifies his own self with nature, with another person or with a group, and feels an emotional unity.[74] Identification does not occur on the level of intellectual consciousness but is rather confined to the sphere of vital consciousness (*Vitalbewusstsein*). It is an automatic, i.e. involuntary, operation.[75]

[71] SYM, pp. 112-143: "VII. Die Kooperation der sympathetischen Funktionen." *Sympathy*, pp. 103-129.
[72] SYM, p. 113; *Sympathy*, p. 103.
[73] SYM, p. 112; *Sympathy*, p. 103.
[74] SYM, pp. 105-107; *Sympathy*, pp. 96-98.
[75] SYM, p. 105; *Sympathy*, p. 97.

2. Vicarious feeling (*Nachfühlung*) is a more highly developed emotional power. It takes place on a higher level of consciousness and is a free act. In it we feel the other person's feeling.[76]

3. Fellow-feeling (*Mitgefühl*) fulfills the important metaphysical function of helping man to transcend his natural illusion of egocentricity, i.e. the illusion of taking his own world to be the world itself.[77] "It is the very office of true fellow-feeling to dissipate the solipsistic illusion by apprehending the equivalent reality-status of the other person *as* such." [78] Fellow-feeling, be it compassion or co-rejoicing, is something "undergone" (*ein "Leiden"*), not a spontaneous act. In this point it differs from love. Love is a spontaneous action, not a reaction.[79]

4. Benevolence (*Menschenliebe*), or a general love of humanity, regards individuals as lovable qua "specimens" of the human race. It does not direct its attention to the person as an individual, unique human being.[80]

5. Non-cosmic personal love (*akosmistische Personliebe*) is the very essence of the Christian love of neighbor. This type of love is "general" in the sense that it is extended to *all* men, not to man's general essence but to the individual center of being in every spiritual person.[81]

These five emotional powers or forms of sympathy represent a hierarchy of five stages.[82] The sense of vital unity with the cosmos (*kosmisch-vitale Einsfühlung*) is the first and lowest stage, the non-cosmic love of persons the last and highest. If man wants to ascend this scale he cannot take the second step before he has made the first. The full development of the higher forms of emotional energy presupposes the prior cultivation of the lower forms.

In the past, the people of India and Greece, for example, have

[76] SYM, p. 5; *Sympathy*, p. 9.
[77] SYM, pp. 62-63; *Sympathy*, pp. 58-59.
[78] SYM, p. 71; *Sympathy*, p. 65.
[79] SYM, p. 73; *Sympathy*, p. 67.
[80] SYM, pp. 108-109; *Sympathy*, pp. 99-100.
[81] SYM, p. 142; *Sympathy*, p. 128.
[82] SYM, p. 143; *Sympathy*, p. 129.

over-emphasized the cultivation of a sense of unity with the universe or of a cosmo-vital identification.[83] Christianity, on the other hand, has tried to cultivate and develop the higher forms of man's emotional life, benevolence and non-cosmic personal love. In the process of shifting the attention from nature to the person, the Judeo-Christian tradition has developed a one-sided conception of nature as a mere instrument and object of human domination.[84] Early Christianity, the Franciscan movement, Goethe and the romantic philosophy of Nature, all attempted to fight against the stream of the prevailing Western ethos but could not change its course. The lack of a cosmo-vital identification with nature and the domination-oriented approach to nature in modern Occidental civilization have become forces destructive of man's natural environment. Here is one concrete example where the need for a reciprocal adjustment or harmonization (*Ausgleich*) of emotional energies is evident. The West has to cultivate again the sense of unity with nature or the cosmo-vital identification (*kosmovitale Einsfühlung*). The East, on the other hand, ought to develop the non-cosmic love of persons.[85]

[83] SYM, p. 113; *Sympathy,* p. 104.
[84] SYM, p. 114; *Sympathy,* p. 105.
[85] SYM, p. 115; *Sympathy,* p. 105. In recent years many studies have been published which reiterate Scheler's point and show in greater detail the desirability and fruitfulness of such harmonization between Eastern and Western ideas, moral systems and religions. Here are a few examples: Junyu Kitayama, *West-Östliche Begegnung* (3rd ed.; Berlin: Walter de Gruyter, 1942). Heinrich Dumoulin, *Östliche Meditation und christliche Mystik* (Freiburg: Verlag Karl Alber, 1966). William Johnston, *The Still Point—Reflections on Zen and Christian Mysticism* (New York: Fordham University Press, 1970). Maurus Heinrichs, *Katholische Theologie und asiatisches Denken* (Mainz: Grünewald Verlag, 1963). Hugo Enomiya-Lassalle, S.J., *Zen: Way to Enlightenment* (New York: Taplinger Publishing Co., 1968). Peter Kreeft, "Zen Buddhism and Christianity: An Experiment in Comparative Religion," *Journal of Ecumenical Studies,* VIII (Summer, 1971), 513-538. Kreeft writes on p. 519: "The two are not strange bedfellows, not because they are alike but because they are different: like a man and a woman. Zen teaches no dogma and Christianity no practical psychology of Enlightenment. But each needs the other (like a man and a woman): Zen may be the most efficient method ever discovered for reaching the psychological state sought by the Christian mystic; and Christianity may be the revelation of the ultimate meaning of that state attained by Zen."

The history of Europe teaches us the important lesson that, in the long run, if man cultivates the higher forms of human emotions and ignores the lower ones, this one-sidedness proves destructive of man and nature alike. The higher forms of emotional power can be fully developed only if they are firmly grounded on the foundations of fully-developed lower stages in man's emotional life. To achieve the much-needed balance and harmonization, Scheler offers this advice to Western civilization:

> Like Goethe, Novalis and Schopenhauer, we must learn once more "to look upon Nature as we look into the heart of a friend" and to limit the scientific-mechanistic investigation of her, indispensable as it is for technology and industry, to the "artificial" specialist attitude of the physicist, chemist, etc.[86]

Since women and children have a greater natural capacity for experiencing a vital unity and identity with nature (*Einsfühlung*), they have suffered most in our reductionist utilitarian civilization. Childhood possesses an irreplaceable value of its own, yet in our civilization children exist for no other reason than to become adults. Despite the fact that womanhood with its special power of identification (*einsfühlende Kraft*) possesses an intrinsic value of its own, nevertheless in our male-dominated and achievement-oriented civilization the potentialities of women cannot be properly cultivated and developed.[87]

The cosmo-vital identification, the cultivation of which is a prime task of Western man today, should not be misunderstood as being exclusively concerned with man's relation to external nature.

A decisive factor in cultivating a capacity for identification with the cosmos is that sense of immersion in the total stream of life (*die Einsfühlung in den Allebensstrom*),

---

[86] SYM, pp. 114-115; *Sympathy*, p. 105. The phrase "wie in den 'Busen eines Freunds' zu schauen" refers to Goethe's *Faust*, I, line 3220.
[87] SYM, p. 117; *Sympathy*, p. 107.

which is first aroused and established among men with respect to their mutual status as individual centres of life.[88]

Because man can experience the life of the cosmos most profoundly in another man, the "Dionysian ecstasy of emotional union between man and man" [89] is also man's point of entry into the experience of unity with cosmic life.

The adjustment and harmonization of the various emotional powers in man which we have briefly sketched above must be seen within the framework of a multi-leveled convergence and harmonization which will, according to Scheler, take place in the emerging "era of harmonization."

IV

CONVERGENCE OF PROTESTANTISM AND CATHOLICISM

In 1920, Scheler delivered a moving lecture on peaceful cooperation between Catholics and Protestants,[90] in which he claimed that the time had come for a convergence and harmonization (*Ausgleich*) of the distinctive characteristics of the two Christian denominations. There were, he felt, four moral imperatives which demanded a peaceful working together of all Christians. First, the commandment of love which requires that we love all our neighbors, not only those of our own faith. Second, the ancient Christian principle that we should not only combat errors but show understanding and loving concern for those who err (*Interficite errores, diligite homines*). The third source of unity is the natural law which provides a common unifying bond for people of all faiths and even for non-believers. We ought to acknowledge and respect the natural rights also of those who profess another faith. Fourth, in matters of faith we ought never to allow ourselves to be merely reacting in pro-

[88] SYM, p. 118; *Sympathy*, p. 108.
[89] *Ibid*.
[90] "Der Friede unter den Konfessionen," in *Schriften zur Soziologie und Weltanschauungslehre*, pp. 227-258.

test or counter-protest—a source of continued mutual enmity since the Reformation—but rather should act positively out of faith.[91]

Scheler views the history of European Churches since the 16th century as one of particularization and of a narrowing of religious energies. In sharp contrast, the coming era will possess an essentially different character, for it will be an era of synthesis and of unification. Both on the intellectual and on the practical level, people of different faiths will try to bring about a convergence of their different traditions.[92] The work for the unity of Christians is now emerging as a moral and religious duty.[93]

Scheler singles out two areas where a convergence and harmonization between Protestantism and Catholicism is presently emerging. The first area concerns the roles of the individual and of community. Protestantism has, in the past, encouraged the fullest development of the freedom and individuality of the single person, but has neglected the equally important dimensions of community and solidarity. Catholicism, on the other hand, has instilled in its followers a strong social awareness but has not sufficiently developed the dimensions of individuality, spontaneity and personal conscience. In a process of healthy self-criticism, both Protestants and Catholics now ought to discover their own strengths and weaknesses and try to achieve a balanced position by integrating the values they judge more highly developed in the other denomination.[94]

A second type of convergence is taking place in a new harmonization between the rational and the mystical dimensions of religion. Catholic theology is being enriched by the scientific studies and biblical research of modern Protestant scholars. A renaissance of mysticism, on the other hand, is presently emerging in Protestant circles, for traditional Catholic mysticism fas-

[91] *Ibid.*, pp. 230-233.
[92] *Ibid.*, p. 243.
[93] *Ibid.*, p. 245.
[94] *Ibid.*, pp. 246-247.

cinates numerous Protestants today.[95]

The new harmonization of Protestantism and Catholicism constitutes one instance of a large-scale general convergence of different ideologies, values and approaches to reality which is emerging all around the world and will be the outstanding characteristic of the coming era of human history.

V
CONVERGENCE OF RUSSIA AND WESTERN EUROPE

One of the harmonizations which Scheler describes, and for which he hopes, is a new synthesis between the spirit of Russia and that of Germany. He believes that "rich fruits" would result from a complementary blending of the Slavic sense of community with Germanic individualism.[96] Russia and the Slavic countries have cultivated mysticism, contemplative devotion and a sense of the free flowing of human life. Germany has, in the past, emphasized the complementary dimensions of intellect, activity and discipline. What is needed now is a mutual cultural interpenetration (*Kulturdurchdringung*) between East and West. Thus, Russia could enrich the German culture with its spiritual techniques, mysticism, contemplation, and with the spirit of community and solidarity while Germany could offer Russia science, technology and the spirit of active Christian love. Striving for the new synthesis, Germany could then also play a mediating role between East and West by bringing the riches of the East to the other Western nations.

In his essay "Über östliches und westliches Christentum," [97] Scheler characterizes in greater detail the contrasting features of Christianity in Russia and in Western Europe. There is a

[95] *Ibid.*, p. 249. Scheler explicitly mentions Rudolf Otto's book *Das Heilige,* and Friedrich Heiler's *Der Katholizismus* as turning points which indicate that Protestantism is moving from rationalism to a new understanding of the mystical dimension of Christianity.

[96] VEIM, pp. 430-431; *Eternal,* p. 431.

[97] Max Scheler, "Über östliches und westliches Christentum," in *Liebe und Erkenntnis,* pp. 73-90.

different emphasis within the concept of redemption. The Western Churches stress redemption from sin, the Eastern redemption from death and transiency in general.[98] This objective distinction between two different dimensions of redemption leads to a difference in the subjective attitude of Christians. In the West they want to be freed from sin, in Russia they appropriate Christianity through meditative immersion into the mystery of the Incarnation and contemplative anticipation of future heavenly bliss.[99] While Western Christians strive for the salvation of their individual souls, Russian Christians endeavor to enter more deeply into the community of the faithful which, as a community, moves toward the eternal goal of heaven.

From such differences on the doctrinal level, there result basic differences on the practical level of life-ideals and religio-moral behavior. The passive virtues of endurance and humility are cultivated in the East, the active virtues, especially active love, are held in higher esteem in the West. Christians in Russia have developed great strength and patience in the face of suffering. Evil is not seen as something one should fight against, but rather something to be suffered and endured, a mentality expressed in Tolstoy's doctrine of "non-resistance against evil." A sense of the tragic element in life is highly developed in the East where the basic attitude toward God is one of fear and reverence, whereas the West encourages an intimate love of the heavenly Father.

Scheler sees the most fundamental difference between Eastern and Western Christianity in the distinction between the Hellenistic theology of Clement and Origen which exercised a decisive influence on the Eastern Churches, and the theology of St. Augustine which molded Christianity in the West. The Hellenistic approach, under the influence of the Platonic concept of eros, sees God not as the source of all love, but rather as the goal toward which all creatures are striving. St. Augustine and Western theology emphasize the twofold movement of descent and ascent, of God's creative self-disclosure in love and the creature's

[98] *Ibid.*, p. 76.
[99] *Ibid.*, pp. 77-78.

loving response. The twofold commandment of love of God and love of neighbor as one dynamic act became the very soul of Western Christianity.

Russia and Western Europe have both cultivated important dimensions of religion, ethics and culture, and each can enrich the other by sharing its specific insights. The intercultural adjustment (*Ausgleich*) or harmonization envisaged for the future would actualize the manifold potentialities of human nature which are now lying dormant, and eventually bring about a proper balance of culture in both East and West.

Scheler did not live to witness the new hostility that would soon emerge between Russia and Germany instead of the hoped for harmonization. But Scheler's idea of convergence between Russia and the West has continued to fascinate philosophers, sociologists and economists on both sides. On the political and economic level, for example, two émigré Russian sociologists, Pitrim Sorokin and Nikolai Timasheff, strongly advocated a convergence theory according to which Russia would gradually develop into a less repressive and more democratic country whereas the non-Communist countries would emphasize more central planning and economic control by the state. The fact that today Russian newspapers keep denouncing any convergence theory as a major heresy would seem to indicate that this "heretical doctrine" continues to be tossed around among Russian intellectuals. Jan Tinbergen, the Dutch economist and Nobel prizewinner, is an enthusiastic defender of the convergence theory. John Kenneth Galbraith, in *The New Industrial State,* speaks of "convergent tendencies of industrial societies, however different their popular or ideological billing." [100] According to Galbraith, modern industrial systems have built-in imperatives of their own which will, even within different ideological frameworks, eventually prove to be convergent in their development. [101] On the religious level, Scheler's prophetic vision is, at

[100] John Kenneth Galbraith, *The New Industrial State* (New York: The New American Library, 1968), p. 396.
[101] *Ibid.,* pp. 396-398. Cf. also the *Time* essay, "Convergence: The Uncertain Meeting of East and West," *Time,* January 12, 1970, pp. 18-19.

least to a certain degree, realized in the intensive ecumenical movement of our time.[102] The renaissance of the works of Wladimir Soloviev, a great Russian philosopher and theologian of convergence, might be interpreted as a new interest in the intellectual harmonization of Russia and the West as well as in the convergence between the Orthodox and Catholic forms of Christianity.[103]

VI
"MAN IN THE ERA OF ADJUSTMENT":
THE NEW "TOTAL MAN" (ALLMENSCH)

In 1927, in a lecture at the anniversary celebration of the German College for Political Sciences in Berlin,[104] Scheler presented his most systematic treatment of the question of harmonization and adjustment. The lecture, entitled "Man in the Era of Adjustment" (*Der Mensch im Weltalter des Ausgleichs*), was later published as part of the book *Philosophische Weltanschauung*.[105] Scheler expressed his firm conviction that a new era was dawning, in which the idea of harmonization or adjustment would play a dominant role: "Were I to inscribe on the gate of the era opening to us a name that would pinpoint its dominant trend, only one would suffice: 'era of adjustment.' " [106] Although he never doubts that this era of adjustment is already on the horizon, his explanation as to how this adjustment might be achieved, is ambiguous. On the one hand, the tendency toward adjustment is "not something we choose; it

---

[102] Robley Edward Whitson, *The Coming Convergence of World Religions* (New York: Newman Press, 1971). Cf. also the recent cooperation and doctrinal agreements between the Orthodox and Catholic Church.

[103] Helmut Dahm, *Solov'ev und Max Scheler* (Munich: Anton Pustet, 1971).

[104] Jahresfeier der Deutschen Hochschule für Politik am 5. November, 1927.

[105] PHIL, pp. 89-118; *Perspectives*, pp. 94-126.

[106] PHIL, p. 97; *Perspectives*, p. 102.

is an inescapable fate." [107] Yet, on the other hand, Scheler never tires of exhorting politicians, intellectuals and, indeed, all mankind to work and strive for harmonization and adjustment. Having called adjustment an "inescapable fate of mankind," Scheler continues in the very next sentence:

> Even so, it is the task of the intellect and of the will to guide and direct this adjustment of group qualities and forces in such a way that the species will gain in value while the adjustment takes place. This is also a task of all politics, indeed, it concerns primarily politics.[108]

History did not start out with a united mankind. Racial and cultural unity and harmony of all men, is, rather, a goal-direction (*Zielrichtung*) of the historical process.[109] In an interesting comparison, Scheler likens the structure of history and the trend toward harmonization to a river system:

> The structure of history resembles a river system in which a great number of rivers continue their particular courses for centuries but, nourished by innumerable tributaries, finally tend to converge ever more directly and to unite in one great river.[110]

The individual rivers that move toward convergence signify here the different cultures and civilizations of mankind as well as all the multiple philosophies and value systems. This comparison, although an illuminating image of the gradual process of rapprochement and harmonization in history, brings out once again the basic ambiguity as to whether and how far the adjustment is achieved by necessary "fate" or through free human endeavor.

In his Berlin lecture, "Man in the Era of Adjustment," Scheler

[107] PHIL, p. 97; *Perspectives*, p. 103.
[108] PHIL, p. 98; *Perspectives*, p. 103.
[109] PHIL, p. 99; *Perspectives*, p. 105.
[110] *Ibid.*

is concerned with the whole spectrum of harmonizations which will include a transformation of institutions, social structures, concepts of arts and sciences and of man's attitude toward nature. His reflections culminate in the idea of the adjustment and harmonization of man himself. What concerns Scheler most deeply is

> a transformation of man himself, of the nature of his internal constitution in body, drives, soul, and spirit. It is not only a change in his actual being, but in his standards of judgment.[111]

In order to achieve his own transformation, man must first become aware that he is a being of tremendous plasticity with the freedom to develop himself.[112] This freedom allows man to "shape that infinitely plastic segment of his nature which can be influenced directly or indirectly by the spirit and the will." [113] Man, in fact, may be characterized as "a creature whose very essence is the open decision on what he wants to be and to become." [114]

Throughout history there have been many images and ideas of man. The greatest danger has always been to conceive the idea of man too narrowly by assuming that one particular historical image of him contains all that there is in man. Scheler enumerates several images of man which have been prevalent in the past, all of which suffer from being too narrow and restricted: the idea of the *animal rationale* of classical times; the *homo faber* of the positivists; the "Dionysian man" of Nietzsche; man as a "disease of life" in the panromantic doctrines; the "superman"; the *homo sapiens* of Linné; *l'homme machine* of Lamettrie; man solely as "power" as expounded by Machiavelli; libido-man of Freud; economic man of Marx; finally, the God-created, fallen Adam of the Judeo-Christian tradition.[115] All of these images

[111] PHIL, p. 91; *Perspectives*, p. 97.
[112] PHIL, pp. 95-96; *Perspectives*, p. 101.
[113] PHIL, p. 95; *Perspectives*, p. 101.
[114] PHIL, p. 96; *Perspectives*, p. 101.
[115] PHIL, p. 96; *Perspectives*, pp. 101-102.

and ideas of man present partial aspects but none of them encompasses the whole of man.

The ideal man which hopefully will emerge in the dawning "era of adjustment" is the new "total man" (*Allmensch*) [116] who transcends narrow limitations and strives to achieve a balanced harmonization of all the different potentialities inherent in man. "Total man" is, however, not meant in the absolute sense, i.e. as the man who has realized all his essential capabilities. This is beyond the power of any human being. What is possible is a relatively total man (*relativer Allmensch*) who has realized "the maximum of total humanity which is accessible to him, a relative maximum of participation in the highest forms of human existence." [117]

Scheler sketches in somewhat greater detail one particular example of adjustment, namely the harmonization between "Apollonian" and "Dionysian" man.[118] The "total man" (*Allmensch*) emerging in the coming era of adjustment will be, among other things, a synthesis combining the "Apollonian" and "Dionysian" dimensions of humanity. In past philosophical thought, rationalism and irrationalism or a philosophy of ideas and a philosophy of life have represented these two contrasting images of man.

Occidental cultures have, Scheler contends, developed a one-sided type of man which is characterized by over-intellectualization, asceticism, spiritualization and sublimation.[119] First came the patristic asceticism of the early Church, then a reinforcement of this ascetical ideal in the monastic lifestyle of the Middle Ages. Protestantism continued this trend, although as an "innerworldly" type of asceticism. This was followed by a capitalist "asceticism of the golden idol" (Karl Marx) of modern industrial society. In this way, Occidental man has constantly sublimated his vital energies in a one-sided manner and has cultivated an extremely dualistic, spirit-centered consciousness. The

116 PHIL, p. 96; *Perspectives*, p. 101.
117 PHIL, p. 96; *Perspectives*, p. 102.
118 PHIL, pp. 100-105; *Perspectives*, pp. 106-112.
119 PHIL, pp. 102-105; *Perspectives*, pp. 108-112.

result is an overdeveloped "Apollonianism" which suppresses the "Dionysian" dimensions in man.

In order to bring forth the new "total man," the past movement of constant sublimation has now to be balanced by a process of re-sublimation (*Prozess der Re-Sublimierung*).[120] This re-sublimation is defined as the "process of consciously limiting the amount of accumulated energy which the organism transfers to the brain or the intellect, the apparent locus of all purely intellectual activity, i.e. of all acts of ideation." [121] This re-sublimation is already taking place in Western civilizations. It manifests itself in a diminished appreciation of the spirit and the intellect and in a rediscovery of the body. The rationalism of the past is transcended by a new appreciation of myths. A systematic revolt of man's drives is putting an end to one-sided sublimation and exaggerated intellectualism. A redistribution of man's total energy between the cortex and the rest of his organism brings about a new balance within man.

One important instance of the new adjustment is the harmonization between the male and female principles in mankind. Religion, like most areas of life, manifests a lack of balance between these two principles today. Once there existed the cult of mother earth, but now the Occidental concept of God has become one-sidedly masculine and virile. In the West, everything is measured according to the male standards of value. Etymologically, in many languages, the term for "human being" (*Mensch*) goes back to the word "man" (*Mann*). The new appreciation of the values and the power of women in recent years signals a re-emergence of a "Dionysian" phase in our era. This development must be seen as part of the larger process of a general re-sublimation.[122]

---

[120] PHIL, p. 101; *Perspectives,* p. 107.

[121] PHIL, p. 101: "Ich verstehe unter Resublimierung jenen Vorgang einer—selbst geistgewollten—Begrenzung des Masses der Kraftzufuhr der vom Organismus aufgenommenen Energie zum Gehirn, beziehungsweise zur Intelligenz, in die alle rein geistige, d.h. ideenerfassende Tätigkeit eingebettet erscheint." Cf. *Perspectives,* pp. 106-107.

[122] Karl Stern has later taken up and systematically explored the problem of the de-feminization and de-humanization of Western civilization during the scientific revolution of the past 300 years. Cf. Karl

Scheler does not expect an instant harmonization between the "Apollonian" and "Dionysian" dimensions of man. In fact, he is quite realistic in his appraisal that temporarily the pendulum might swing to the other extreme, i.e. to irrationalism and anti-intellectualism. In this context he quotes Luther's earthy observation that man finds his way to God only like a drunken peasant, reeling to the right and left.[123] Nevertheless, Scheler is confident that the present movement is a healthy process of correction which will eventually lead to a new harmonious synthesis.

We will conclude this chapter on the "Era of Harmonization" with some reflections on the significance of Scheler's insights for our contemporary world. Scheler has heightened our awareness that there are different "eras" in the moral history of man and that each generation of men has to confront the basic question as to what the specific ethical imperative of the present epoch may be.

Let us illustrate this point and its importance by a concrete example. A politically inclined Italian or German in the early 19th century could scarcely have thought of working for a United States of Europe as a moral imperative. Both of them would rather have thought of uniting their own respective countries as the task of the time. For both the Italian and German, unifying their own countries was probably a necessary step before they could effectively build a closer union transcending national borders.

But reflecting today on the evils of past nationalism, on the yearning of mankind for unity, on the real opportunities of realizing at least partially this lofty ideal, and on the immense good that could result from unifying the nations of Europe, it might well be that a politician in today's Italy, Germany or France

---

Stern, *The Flight from Woman* (New York: The Noonday Press, 1966). According to Stern, a rejection of the feminine is at the bottom of a profound disharmony in our Western culture and society. He writes, "If we equate the one-sidedly rational and technical with the masculine, there arises the ghastly spectre of a world impoverished of womanly values."

[123] PHIL, p. 102; *Perspectives*, p. 108.

would come to consider it a genuine moral imperative to work for a United States of Europe.

We might expand this idea even further on a worldwide scale. Mankind has now reached, for the first time in history, the possibility of total self-destruction. Since mankind has now entered this new stage in its historical development, incomparable with any period of past history, international relations would seem to have acquired new ethical dimensions. Whereas in the past it made sense to talk of "just wars," which at that time and in the context of that world, might possibly, in the long run, produce greater good than the necessary evil inherent in any warfare, today one may rightly ask the question whether in our historical period the risks involved have not reached a proportion that would seem to make the morality of any warfare extremely doubtful. As the late President Kennedy put it, "Either man puts an end to war or war puts an end to man."

To pose the problem in more positive terms: since we are commissioned to build the earth and not to destroy it, and since today anything short of positive cooperation of all mankind runs a grave risk of eventual war and possible self-destruction, one may rightly ask whether working for the unification of all countries and peoples does not become in our age a genuine moral imperative—and not merely a laudable enterprise of some romantic idealists, as might have been the case in past centuries. Today, we cannot afford to do less than seek the common interests of all mankind and, putting aside all secondary disagreements, cooperate in building a united family of man.

Scheler's insights on harmonization, convergence and complementation would seem to be of eminent value for the endeavor of working for a unification of mankind. They also open up new vistas for the nations of Asia and Africa that are struggling today to achieve a new synthesis between their own traditional cultures and the civilization of the West. More than half of mankind is presently involved in this gigantic process of cultural harmonization and adjustment.

The example of Japan can illustrate both the problems of cultural conflict and the extraordinary relevancy of Scheler's ideas in the search for a viable solution. Ever since the opening of Japan to Western influences at the time of the Meiji Restoration (1868), the task of harmonizing the conflicting cultures of East and West has been one of the major preoccupations of the Japanese intellectuals. This has become a predominant theme in modern Japanese literature, philosophy and the social sciences. Modernization which means, to a large extent, Westernization, has been accepted as an inevitable process. But how far can or should one preserve the native cultural tradition and attempt to harmonize it with the civilization of the West?

The profound differences of the two cultures make such balancing an eminently difficult endeavor. Some basic differences are: Greek versus Confucian thought; Christianity versus Shintoism and Buddhism; individualism versus collective group consciousness; logic versus esthetics; the scientific versus the emotional approach; reason versus intuition; abstract versus concrete thinking; the merit system versus the seniority system; horizontal versus vertical relationships; individual freedom and democracy versus feudalism.[124]

Natsume Soseki (1867-1916), the foremost Japanese novelist of the 20th century, has thematized in his literary works the alienation and isolation of the modern Japanese who is uprooted from his old traditions and cannot feel at home in the modernized and Westernized Japan of the Meiji and post-Meiji era. Soseki, who called himself an ethical writer or a moralist, viewed the socio-cultural dilemma of 20th-century Japan as an impossible hybrid of Oriental and Occidental civilization. Keenly aware of Japan's failure to achieve a genuine synthesis between the two cultures, Soseki became disillusioned and pes-

---

[124] Hajime Nakamura, *Ways of Thinking of Eastern Peoples: India-China-Tibet-Japan* (3rd ed. rev.; Honolulu: East-West Center Press, 1968), pp. 345-587. Charles A. Moore, ed., *The Japanese Mind. Essentials of Japanese Philosophy and Culture* (Honolulu: East-West Center Press, 1967). Robert J. Smith and Richard K. Beardsley, eds., *Japanese Culture* (London: Methuen & Company, 1963). Wm. Theodore de Bary, ed., *Sources of Japanese Tradition* (New York: Columbia University Press, 1958). Marius B. Jansen, ed., *Changing Japanese Attitudes toward Modernization* (Princeton, N.J.: Princeton University Press, 1965). Chie Nakane, *Japanese Society* (Berkeley: University of California Press, 1970).

simistic, ending his life in suicide. His great novels are poignant monuments to the painful intellectual struggle of men caught between two civilizations.[125]

To these basic problems of Japan and of the other countries of Asia and Africa, Scheler's ideas concerning harmonization and cultural adjustment would seem to provide some highly valuable and helpful responses. First, Scheler offers a profound analysis of the problems involved. Secondly, he provides the proper framework within which the questions can be dealt with appropriately, namely the historicity of man and of cultures. Thirdly, he views the historical process not as a simple transition from one culture to another whereby the old tradition would be replaced by a new one, but rather as a dialectical process whereby the positive elements of all cultural traditions are preserved in the emerging new world culture. Fourthly, Scheler's approach to harmonization avoids simplification and impoverishing reductionism and is always oriented toward fullness and growth. The basic orientation is toward mutual complementation and an all-embracing cosmopolitan value system. Finally, Scheler's approach is characterized by a transcendence of all national and cultural bias and by a humble openness to the full richness of all possible cultural values, a point of considerable importance in today's so-called Third World.

With his creative reflections on the "Era of Harmonization," Scheler has accomplished an essential preparatory work capable of meeting one of the major challenges confronting mankind today. His ideas may not offer a perfect blueprint for a harmonization of cultures and a unification of mankind. They do, however, offer a considerable number of valuable building-stones for the ethical, social and cultural foundation of a future world civilization.

[125] Natsume Soseki, *Kokoro,* trans. by Edwin McClellan (Chicago: Henry Regnery, 1957). Natsume Soseki, *Grass on the Wayside (Michikusa),* trans. by Edwin McClellan (Chicago: The University of Chicago Press, 1969). Natsume Soseki, *Three-Cornered World* (London: Owen, 1965). Soseki Natsume, *The Wayfarer,* trans. by Beongcheon Yu (Tokyo: Charles E. Tuttle, 1970).

Bibliography

I. Works by Max Scheler

Scheler, Max. *Frühe Schriften. Gesammelte Werke.* Edited by Maria Scheler and Manfred S. Frings. Vol I. Bern: Francke Verlag, 1971.

——. *Der Formalismus in der Ethik und die materiale Wertethik. Gesammelte Werke.* Edited by Maria Scheler. Vol. II. 5th ed. revised. Bern: Francke Verlag, 1966.

——. *Vom Umsturz der Werte. Gesammelte Werke.* Edited by Maria Scheler. Vol. III. 4th ed. revised. Bern: Francke Verlag, 1955.

——. *Vom Ewigen im Menschen. Gesammelte Werke.* Edited by Maria Scheler. Vol. V. 5th ed. revised. Bern: Francke Verlag, 1968.

——. (Eng. trans. of above) *On the Eternal in Man.* Translated by Bernard Noble. New York: Harper & Brothers, 1960.

——. *Schriften zur Soziologie und Weltanschauungslehre. Gesammelte Werke.* Edited by Maria Scheler. Vol. VI. 2nd ed. revised. Bern: Francke Verlag, 1963.

——. *Die Wissensformen und die Gesellschaft. Gesammelte Werke.* Edited by Maria Scheler. Vol. VIII. 2nd. ed. revised. Bern: Francke Verlag, 1960.

——. *Schriften aus dem Nachlass.* Band I: *Zur Ethik und Erkenntnislehre. Gesammelte Werke.* Edited by Maria Scheler. Vol. X. 2nd ed. revised. Bern: Francke Verlag, 1957.

——. *Wesen und Formen der Sympathie.* 5th ed. revised. Frankfurt: Verlag G. Schulte-Bulmke, 1948.

——. (Eng. trans. of above) *The Nature of Sympathy.* Translated by Peter Heath. With a general introduction to Max Scheler's work by Werner Stark. London: Routledge and Kegan Paul, 1958.

259

————. *Philosophische Weltanschauung.* Dalp-Taschenbücher. 3rd ed. revised. Bern: Francke Verlag, 1968.

————. (Eng. trans. of above) *Philosophical Perspectives.* Translated by Oscar A. Haac. Boston: Beacon Press, 1958.

————. *Die Stellung des Menschen im Kosmos.* Bern: Francke Verlag, 1966.

————. (Eng. trans. of above) *Man's Place in Nature.* Translated, and with an Introduction, by Hans Meyerhoff. New York: The Noonday Press, 1962.

————. *Liebe und Erkenntnis.* Dalp-Taschenbücher. Bern: Francke Verlag, 1955.

————. *Die Idee des Friedens und der Pazifismus.* Berlin: Der Neue Geist Verlag, 1931.

————. *Deutschlands Sendung und der katholische Gedanke.* Berlin: Germania, 1918.

————. *Der Genius des Krieges und der deutsche Krieg.* 3rd ed. revised. Leipzig: Verlag der Weissen Bücher, 1917.

————. *Krieg und Aufbau.* Leipzig: Verlag der Weissen Bücher, 1916.

————. *Ressentiment.* Edited, with an Introduction by Lewis A. Coser. Translated by William W. Holdheim. New York: The Free Press of Glencoe, 1961.

————. "Soziologische Neuorientierung und die Aufgabe der deutschen Katholiken nach dem Krieg." *Hochland,* XIII (January, 1916), 385-406; (March, 1916), 682-700; (May, 1916), 188-204; (June, 1916), 257-294.

————. "Die deutsche Philosophie der Gegenwart." *Deutsches Leben der Gegenwart.* Edited by Philipp Witkop. Berlin: Wegweiser-Verlag, 1922.

————. "Idealismus-Realismus." *Philosophischer Anzeiger,* II (Fall, 1927), 255-324.

————. "Problems with a Sociology of Knowledge." Translated by Ernest Ranly. *Philosophy Today,* XII (Spring, 1968), 42-70.

II. Secondary Sources

Alpheus, Karl. *Kant und Scheler: Phänomenologische Untersuchungen zur Ethik zwecks Entscheidung des Streites zwischen der formalen Ethik Kants und der materialen Wertethik Schelers.* St. Georgen im Schwarzwald: Buchdruckerei J. Huss, 1936.

Altmann, Alexander. *Die Grundlagen der Wertethik: Wesen, Wert, Person. Max Schelers Erkenntnis- und Seinslehre in kritischer Analyse.* Berlin: Reuther & Reichard, 1931.

Bahr, Herman. "Max Scheler." *Hochland,* XIV (April, 1917), 35-44.

Bassenge, Friedrich, "Drang und Geist: Eine Auseinandersetzung mit Schelers Anthropologie." *Zeitschrift für philosophische Forschung,* XVII (Summer, 1963), 385-418.

Becker, Howard, and Dahlke, Otto. "Max Scheler's Sociology of Knowledge." *Philosophy and Phenomenological Research,* II (March, 1942), 310-322.

Berger, Peter, and Luckmann, Thomas. *The Social Construction of Reality: A Treatise in the Sociology of Knowledge.* New York: Doubleday, 1967.

Blessing, Eugen. *Das Ewige im Menschen: Die Grundkonzeption der Religionsphilosophie Max Schelers.* Stuttgart: Schwabenverlag, 1954.

Bochenski, I. M. *Europäische Philosophie der Gegenwart.* 2nd ed. revised. Bern: Francke Verlag, 1951.

Boelen, Bernard. "The Question of Ethics in the Thought of Martin Heidegger." *Heidegger and the Quest for Truth.* Edited by Manfred S. Frings. Chicago: Quadrangle Books, 1968.

Bollnow, Otto Friedrich, *Einfache Sittlichkeit.* 3rd ed. Göttingen: Vandenhoeck & Ruprecht, 1962.

―――. *Wesen und Wandel der Tugenden.* Frankfurt: Ullstein, 1958.

―――. "Konkrete Ethik. Vorbetrachtungen zu einer philosophischen Tugendlehre." *Zeitschrift für Philosophische Forschung,* VI (Winter, 1952), 321-339.

Buber, Martin. "The Philosophical Anthropology of Max Scheler." *Philosophy and Phenomenological Research,* VI (December, 1946), 307-321. Reprinted in Martin Buber. *Between Man and Man.* New York: The Macmillan Company, 1968.

Cantius, P. "Max Scheler's Ethik als Personalisme." *Bijdragen,* VII (January, 1946), 36-59.

Cassirer, Ernst. " 'Spirit' and 'Life' in Contemporary Philosophy." *The Philosophy of Ernst Cassirer.* Edited by Paul Arthur Schilpp. Evanston: The Library of Living Philosophers, 1949.

Chang, Matthieu. "Valeur, personne et amour chez Max Scheler." *Revue Philosophique de Louvain,* LXIX (February, 1971), 44-72; (May, 1971), 216-249.

Clarke, Mary Evelyn. "A Phenomenological System of Ethics." *Philosophy,* VII (October, 1932), 414-430; VIII (January, 1933), 52-65.

Closs, Lothar. *Sittlicher Relativismus und Schelers Wertethik.* St. Ottilien: Eos Verlag, 1955.

Collins, James. "Catholic Estimates of Scheler's Catholic Period." *Thought,* XIX (December, 1944), 671-704.

―――. "Scheler's Transition from Catholicism to Pantheism." *Philosophical Studies in Honor of the Very Reverend Ignatius Smith.* Edited by John K. Ryan. Westminster: Newman, 1952. Reprinted under the title "Roots of Scheler's Evolutionary Pantheism," in James Collins, *Crossroads in Philosophy.* Chicago: Regnery, 1969.

―――. "Scheler, Max, The Moral Philosophy of." *Encyclopedia of Morals.* Edited by Vergilius Ferm. New York: Philosophical Library, 1956.

Commentator, George, E. "The Phenomenology of Love in Max Scheler." Unpublished Ph.D. dissertation, Boston College, 1970.

Crumbaugh, James. "The Relation of Kairos to Encounter in Psychotherapy." *Review of Existential Psychology and Psychiatry,* III (Winter, 1963), 35-38.

Curtius, Ernst Robert. *Französischer Geist im neuen Europa.* Berlin: Deutsche Verlags-Anstalt, 1925.

Dahm, Helmut. *Vladimir Solov'ev und Max Scheler.* Munich: Anton Pustet, 1971.

————. "Zur Sowjetischen Rezeption der Phänomenologie Schelers." *Studies in Soviet Thought,* XI (September, 1971), 159-181.

D'Arcy, M. C. *The Mind and Heart of Love.* The Fontana Library. London: Collins, 1962.

Deininger, Dieter. *Die Theorie der Werterfahrung und der Begriff der Teilhabe in der Philosophie Schelers.* Frankfurt: Goethe-Universität, 1966.

Denninger, Erhard. *Rechtsperson und Solidarität: Ein Beitrag zur Phänomenologie des Rechtsstaates unter besonderer Berücksichtigung der Sozialtheorie Max Schelers.* Frankfurt: Alfred Metzner Verlag, 1967.

Diemer, Alwin. *Edmund Husserl: Versuch einer systematischen Darstellung seiner Phänomenologie.* 2nd ed. revised. Meisenheim am Glan: Anton Hain, 1965.

Driscoll, Giles. "Heidegger's Ethical Monism." *The New Scholasticism,* XLII (Autumn, 1968), 497-510.

Dupuy, Maurice. *La Philosophie de Max Scheler. Son évolution et son unité.* 2 vols. Paris: Presses Universitaires, 1959.

————. *La Philosophie de la Religion chez Max Scheler.* Paris: Presses Universitaires, 1959.

Eklund, Harald. *Evangelisches und Katholisches in Max Schelers Ethik.* Uppsala: Lundequitska Bokhandeln, 1932.

Emad, Parvis. "Die philosophische Anthropologie Max Schelers." Unpublished Ph.D. dissertation, University of Vienna, 1966.

————. "The Great Themes of Scheler." *Philosophy Today,* XII (Spring, 1968), 4-12.

————. "Max Scheler's Notion of the Process of Phenomenology." *The Southern Journal of Philosophy,* X (Spring, 1972), 7-16.

————. "Max Scheler's Phenomenology of Shame." *Philosophy and Phenomenological Research,* XXXII (March, 1972), 361-370.

Esser, Albert. *Das Phänomen Reue.* Cologne: Jakob Hegner, 1963.

Eschweiler, Karl. "Religion und Metaphysik. Zu Max Schelers 'Vom Ewigen im Menschen.'" *Hochland,* XIX (December, 1921), 303-313; (January, 1922), 470-489.

Farber, Marvin. "Max Scheler on the Place of Man in the Cosmos."

Philosophy and Phenomenological Research, XIV (March, 1954), 393-399.

Farre, Luis. "El Sistema de Valores de Max Scheler comparado con Aristoteles." *Kantstudien,* XLVIII (Summer, 1956), 399-403.

Feretti, Giovanni. "Rassegna di studi scheleriani in Lingua tedesca." *Rivista di Filosofia Neo-Scolastica,* LVII (July, 1965), 483-498; (November, 1965), 808-847.

————. "Sviluppe E Struttura della Filosofia della Religione in Max Scheler." *Rivista di Filosofia Neo-Scolastica,* LXII (July, 1970), 398-432; (September, 1970), 668-707.

Filippone, Vincenzo. *Società e Cultura a nel Pensiero di Max Scheler.* Milan: Dott. A. Giuffré, 1964.

Franke, Erich. "Max Schelers Gesellschafts-und Geschichtsphilosophie." *Welt und Wort,* XIV (July, 1959), 207-212.

Frick, Paul. *Der weltanschauliche Hintergrund der Materialen Wertethik Max Schelers.* Stuttgart: Adler-Druckerei, 1933.

Fries, Heinrich. *Die katholische Religionsphilosophie der Gegenwart. Der Einfluss Max Schelers auf ihre Formen und Gestalten.* Heidelberg: Kerle Verlag, 1949.

Frings, Manfred S. *Max Scheler. A Concise Introduction into the World of a Great Thinker.* Pittsburgh: Duquesne University Press, 1965.

————. *Person und Dasein: Zur Frage der Ontologie des Wertseins.* Den Haag: Martinus Nijhoff, 1969.

————. *Zur Phänomenologie der Lebensgemeinschaft: Ein Versuch mit Max Scheler.* Meisenheim: Verlag Anton Hain, 1971.

————. "Non-Formal Ethics of our Time." *Philosophy Today,* IX (Summer, 1965), 85-93.

————. "Max Scheler's Theory of Social Economy with Special Attention to its Ethical Implications." *Review of Social Economy,* XXIII (September, 1965), 127-142.

————. "Der Ordo Amoris bei Max Scheler. Seine Beziehungen zur materialen Wertethik und zum Ressentimentbegriff." *Zeitschrift für Philosophische Forschung,* XX (January, 1966), 57-76.

————. "Max Scheler: On the Ground of Christian Thought." *Franciscan Studies,* XXVII (Spring, 1967), 177-189.

————. "Heidegger and Scheler." *Philosophy Today,* XII (Spring, 1968), 21-30.

————. "Max Scheler: Rarely Seen Complexities of Phenomenology." *Phenomenology in Perspective.* Edited by F. J. Smith. Den Haag: Martinus Nijhoff, 1969.

————. "Insight-Logos-Love (Lonergan-Heidegger-Scheler)." *Philosophy Today,* XIV (Summer, 1970), 106-115.

————. "Bericht über die Sachlage am philosophischen Nachlass Max Schelers." *Zeitschrift für philosophische Forschung,* XXV (Summer, 1971), 315-320.

Frondizi, Risieri. *What is Value? An Introduction to Axiology.* 2nd ed. revised. LaSalle, Ill.: Open Court, 1971.

Funk, Roger. "Ethics and Emotion: A Study in the Philosophy of Max Scheler." Unpublished Ph.D. dissertation, Northwestern University, 1968.

Furstner, H. "Schelers Philosophie der Liebe." *Studia Philosophica,* XVII (Spring, 1957), 23-48.

Getzeny, Heinrich. "Um die Religionsphilosophie Max Schelers." *Hochland,* XXI (March, 1924), 583-594.

———. "Zur Soziologie der Religion." *Hochland,* XXII (August, 1925), 519-529.

Grooten, Johan. "L'augustinisme de Max Scheler." *Augustinus Magister. Congrès International Augustinien Paris, September, 1954.* 3 vols. Paris: Etudes Augustiniennes, 1954. II, 1111-1120.

Gründel, Johannes. *Wandelbares und Unwandelbares in der Moraltheologie.* Düsseldorf: Patmos-Verlag, 1967.

Guthrie, Hunter. "Max Scheler's Epistemology of the Emotions." *The Modern Schoolman,* XVI (March, 1939), 51-54.

Gutwenger, Engelbert. *Wertphilosophie mit besonderer Berücksichtigung des ethischen Wertes.* Innsbruck: Felizian Rauch, 1952.

Haase, Kurt. "Das Wesen des Vorbilds und seine Bedeutung für die Erziehung." *Vierteljahrsschrift für Wissenschaftliche Pädagogik,* III (Summer, 1927), 243-273.

Haecker, Theodor. *Metaphysik des Fühlens.* Munich: Kösel Verlag, 1958.

———. "Geist und Leben. Zum Problem Max Scheler." *Hochland,* XXIII (May, 1926), 129-155. Reprinted in Theodor Haecker, *Christentum und Kultur.* Munich: Kösel Verlag, 1946.

Hafkesbrink, Hanna. "The Meaning of Objectivism and Realism in Max Scheler's Philosophy of Religion: A Contribution to the Understanding of Max Scheler's Catholic Period." *Philosophy and Phenomenological Research,* II (March, 1942), 292-308.

Hammer, Felix. *Theonome Anthropologie? Max Schelers Menschenbild und seine Grenzen.* Den Haag: Martinus Nijhoff, 1972.

Häring, Bernhard. *Das Heilige und das Gute: Religion und Sittlichkeit in ihrem gegenseitigen Bezug.* Munich: Wewel Verlag, 1950.

Hartmann, Nicolai. *Ethik.* 4th ed. Berlin: Walter de Gruyter, 1962.

———. (Eng. trans. of above) *Ethics.* Translated by Stanton Coit. 3 vols. 3rd ed. New York: The Macmillan Company, 1958-1963.

———. "Max Scheler." *Kantstudien,* XXXIII (Spring, 1928), 9-16. Reprinted in Nicolai Hartmann, *Kleinere Schriften.* Vol. III. Berlin: Walter de Gruyter, 1958.

Hartmann, Wilfried. *Max Scheler: Bibliographie.* Stuttgart-Bad Canstatt: Friedrich Fromann Verlag, 1963.

————. *Die Philosophie Max Schelers in ihren Beziehungen zu Eduard von Hartmann.* Düsseldorf: Triltsch, 1956.

————. "Max Scheler's Theory of Person." *Philosophy Today,* XII (Winter, 1968), 246-261.

————. "Max Scheler and the English-speaking World." *Philosophy Today,* XII (Spring, 1968), 31-41.

Haskamp, Reinhold J. *Spekulativer und Phänomenologischer Personalismus. Einflüsse Fichtes und Euckens auf Schelers Philosophie der Person.* Freiburg: Karl Alber, 1966.

Heber, Johannes. *Das Problem der Gotteserkenntnis in der Religionsphilosophie Max Schelers.* Naumburg: Lippert & Co., 1931.

Heidegger, Martin. *Sein und Zeit.* Tübingen: Niemeyer Verlag, 1953.

Hengstenberg, Hans-Eduard. *Grundlegung der Ethik.* Stuttgart: Kohlhammer Verlag, 1969.

————. *Philosophische Anthropologie.* 3rd. ed. rev. Stuttgart: Kohlhammer Verlag, 1966.

Héring, Jean. "De Max Scheler à Hans Reiner. Remarques sur la Théorie des Valeurs Morales dans la Mouvement Phénomenologique." *Revue D' Histoire et de Philosophie Religieuse,* XL (Summer, 1960), 152-164.

Herrman, Joachim. *Die Prinzipien der formalen Gesetzesethik Kants und der materialen Wertethik Schelers: Beitrag zum Problem des Verhältnisses zwischen Psychologie und Ethik.* Breslau: Schelesny, 1928.

Herzfeld, Hans. *Begriff und Theorie vom Geist bei Max Scheler.* Leipzig: Druckerei der Werkgemeinschaft, 1930.

Hessen, Johannes. *Max Scheler. Eine kritische Einführung in seine Philosophie.* Essen: H. V. Chamier, 1946.

————. *Ethik. Grundzüge einer personalistischen Wertethik.* Leiden: E. J. Brill, 1958.

————. *Religionsphilosophie.* 2 vols. 2nd ed. rev. Munich: Ernst Reinhardt, 1955.

————. *Lehrbuch der Philosophie.* Vol. I: *Wertlehre.* Munich: Ernst Reinhardt, 1959.

Hildebrand, Dietrich von. *Das Wesen der Liebe. Gesammelte Werke.* Edited by Dietrich von Hildebrand Gesellschaft. Vol. III. Regensburg: Josef Habbel, 1971.

————. *Die Idee der sittlichen Handlung. Sittlichkeit und ethische Werterkenntnis.* (Nachdruck aus *Jahrbuch für Philosophie und phänomenologische Forschung,* 1916 and 1922). Darmstadt: Wissenschaftliche Buchgesellschaft, 1969.

————. *Die Menschheit am Scheideweg. Gesammelte Abhandlungen und Vorträge.* Edited by Karla Mertens. Regensburg: Habbel, 1954.

————. *Christian Ethics.* New York: David McKay Company, 1952.

————. "The Role of Affectivity in Morality." *Proceedings of the*

American Catholic Philosophical Association, XXXII (1958), 85-95.

――――. "Die geistigen Formen der Affektivität." *Philosophisches Jahrbuch,* LXVIII (Summer, 1960), 180-190.

――――, and Hildebrand, Alice von. *Morality and Situation Ethics.* Chicago: Franciscan Herald Press, 1966.

Holl, Adolf. "Max Scheler's Sociology of Knowledge and his position in relation to Theology." *Social Compass,* XVII (Summer, 1970), 231-241.

Hollenbach, J. M. "Urleidenschaft und natürliche Gotteserkenntnis. Zu Max Schelers Fundierung des religiösen Bewusstseins." *Der beständige Aufbruch.* Edited by Siegfrid Behn. Nuremberg: Glock und Lutz, 1959.

Hölzen, Edmund. *Max Scheler: Les grands courants de la pensée mondiale contemporaine.* Paris: Librairie Fischbacher, 1964.

Hügelmann, Hildegard. *Max Schelers Persönlichkeitsidee unter Berücksichtigung der Gemeinschaftsprobleme.* Leipzig: Helen & Torton, 1927.

Hund, William B. "The Distinction between Ought-to-be and Ought-to-do." *The New Scholasticism,* XLI (Summer, 1967), 345-355.

Hürlimann, Kaspar. "Person und Werte. Eine Untersuchung über den Sinn von Max Schelers Doppeldevise: 'Materiale Wertethik' und 'Ethischer Personalismus'." *Divus Thomas,* XXX (September, 1952), 273-298; (December, 1952), 385-416.

――――. "Axiologische Fundierung des sittlichen Sollens." *Studia Philosophica,* XVII (Spring, 1957), 87-100.

Husserl, Edmund. *Logische Untersuchungen.* 3 vols. Halle: Max Niemeyer, 1921-22.

――――. *Ideen zu einer reinen Phänomenologie und phänomenologischen Philosophie.* 3 vols. Edited by Walter Biemel and Marly Biemel. The Hague: Martinus Nijhoff, 1950-52.

――――. *Cartesianische Meditationen und Pariser Vorträge.* Edited by S. Strasser. The Hague: Martinus Nijhoff, 1950.

――――. *Phenomenology and the Crisis of Philosophy: Philosophy as Rigorous Science and Philosophy and the Crisis of European Man.* Translated with notes and an introduction by Quentin Lauer. New York: Harper & Row, 1965.

Ishizeki, Keizoo. *Jisshitsuteki Kachirinrigaku no Kenkyu* ("Studies on Material Value Ethics"). Tokyo: Maeno Shoten, 1960.

Jaspers, Karl. *Philosophie.* 3 vols. 3rd ed. Berlin: Springer Verlag, 1956.

Kant, Immanuel. *Kritik der Praktischen Vernunft.* Hamburg: Felix Meiner, 1963.

Kanthack, Katharina. *Max Scheler: Zur Krisis der Ehrfurcht.* Berlin: Minerva Verlag, 1948.

Keen, Ernest. "Scheler's View of Repentance and Rebirth and its

Relevance to Psychotherapy." *Review of Existential Psychology and Psychiatry,* VI (Winter, 1966), 84-87.

Kockelmans, Joseph., ed. *Phenomenology: The Philosophy of Edmund Husserl and its Interpretation.* New York: Doubleday, 1967.

Koehle, Eckhard. *Personality. A Study according to the Philosophies of Value and Spirit of Max Scheler and Nicolai Hartmann.* Newton, N.J.: Privately printed, 1941.

Koestenbaum, Peter. "Scheler, Max." *The Encyclopedia of Philosophy.* 1967. Vol. VII.

Kraft, Julius. *Von Husserl zu Heidegger: Kritik der phänomenologischen Philosophie.* Leipzig: Hans Buske, 1932.

Kränzlin, Gerhard. *Max Schelers phänomenologische Systematik.* Leipzig: Hirzel, 1934.

Kreppel, Friedrich. *Die Religionsphilosophie Max Schelers.* Munich: Kaiser Verlag, 1926.

———. "Max Scheler und das Philosophieren." *Zeitschrift für Religions- und Geistesgeschichte,* XI (Fall, 1959), 383-386.

Kron, Helmut. *Ethos und Ethik. Der Pluralismus der Kulturen und das Problem des ethischen Relativismus.* Frankfurt: Athenäum Verlag, 1960.

Kühler, Otto. *Wert, Person, Gott. Zur Ethik Max Schelers, N. Hartmanns und der Philosophie des Ungegebenen.* Berlin: Juncker & Dünnhaupt, 1932.

Kuhn, Helmut. "Max Scheler im Rückblick." *Hochland,* LI (April, 1959), 324-338.

———. "Scheler, Max." *Staatslexikon.* 6th ed. Vol. VI.

Kürth, Herbert. *Das Verhältnis von Ethik und Ästhetik bei Max Scheler.* Leipzig: Werkgemeinschaft, 1929.

Kuroda, Sen. "Shinjoo no Chitsujoo" ("On the 'Ordo Amoris' "). *Risoo,* XLIV (March, 1970), 20-27.

Lauer, Quentin. *Phenomenology: Its Genesis and Prospect.* New York: Harper & Row, 1965.

———. *Phénoménologie de Husserl. Essai sur la genese de l'intentionalité.* Paris: Presses Universitaires de France, 1955.

———. "The Phenomenological Ethics of Max Scheler." *International Philosophical Quarterly,* I (May, 1961), 273-300.

———. "The Subjectivity of Objectivity." *Edmund Husserl 1859-1959.* The Hague: Martinus Nijhoff, 1959.

Leiss, William. "Max Scheler's Concept of Herrschaftswissen." *The Philosophical Forum,* II (Spring, 1971), 316-331.

Lenk, Kurt. *Von der Ohnmacht des Geistes. Kritische Darstellung der Spätphilosophie Max Schelers.* Tübingen: Hopfer, 1959.

———. "Die Mikrokosmosvorstellung in der philosophischen Anthropologie Max Schelers." *Zeitschrift für philosophische Forschung,* XII (Fall, 1958), 408-415.

268   BIBLIOGRAPHY

Lennerz, Heinrich. *Schelers Konformitätssystem und die Lehre der katholischen Kirche*. Münster: Aschendorff, 1924.

Lenz, Joseph. "Das personale Menschenbild in der Sicht christlicher Lebensphilosophie." *Ekklesia. Festschrift für Dr. Matthias Wehr*. Edited by Theologische Fakultät Trier. Trier: Paulinus-Verlag, 1962.

Lenz-Medoc, Paulus. "Max Scheler und die französische Philosophie." *Philosophisches Jahrbuch*, LXI (Fall, 1951), 297-303.

Lieber, Hans-Joachim. *Wissen und Gesellschaft*. Tübingen: Niemeyer, 1952.

Linfert, Carl. "Philosophie des Ewigen und des Flüchtigen in unserer Zeit—Das Lebenswerk Max Schelers." *Universitas*, XIX (March, 1964), 285-291.

Llambias de Azevedo, Juan, *Max Scheler*. Buenos Aires: Editorial Nova, 1966.

Lorscheid, Bernhard. *Max Schelers Phänomenologie des Psychischen*. Bonn: H. Bouvier, 1957.

————. "Zur philosophischen Erhellung des menschlichen Miteinanderseins." *Ekklesia. Festschrift für Dr. Matthias Wehr*. Edited by Theologische Fakultät Trier. Trier: Paulinus-Verlag, 1962.

Lotz, Johannes Baptista. "Sein und Wert. Das Grundproblem der Wertphilosophie." *Zeitschrift für Katholische Theologie*, LVII (October, 1933), 557-613.

Löwith, Karl. "Max Scheler und das Problem einer philosophischen Anthropologie." *Theologische Rundschau*, VII (Winter, 1935), 349-372.

Lubac, Henri de. *The Drama of Atheist Humanism*. Meridian Books. New York: The World Publishing Company, 1966.

Luther, Arthur. *Persons in Love: A Study of Max Scheler's Wesen und Formen der Sympathie*. The Hague: Martinus Nijhoff, 1972.

————. "Scheler's Interpretation of Being as Loving." *Philosophy Today*, XIV (Fall, 1970), 217-228.

————. "Hocking and Scheler on Feeling." *Philosophy Today*, XII (Summer, 1968), 93-99.

Lützeler, Heinrich. *Der Philosoph Max Scheler*. Bonn: H. Bouvier, 1947.

————. "Zu Max Schelers Persönlichkeit." *Hochland*, XXVI (January, 1929), 413-418.

Maliandi, Ricardo-Guillermo. *Wertobjektivität und Realitätserfahrung*. Bonn: H. Bouvier, 1966.

Malik, Josef. "Wesen und Bedeutung der Liebe im Personalismus Max Schelers." *Philosophisches Jahrbuch*, LXXI (Spring, 1963), 102-131.

————. "Das personale und soziale Sein des Menschen in der Philosophie Max Schelers." *Theologie und Glaube*, LIV (November, 1964), 401-436.

Mandelbaum, Maurice. *The Phenomenology of Moral Experience.* Baltimore: The Johns Hopkins Press, 1969.

Martin-Izquierdo, Honorio. *Das religiöse Apriori bei Max Scheler.* Bonn: Weyler, 1964.

Maxsein, Anton. *Philosophia Cordis: Das Wesen der Personalität bei Augustinus.* Salzburg: Otto Müller Verlag, 1966.

McGill, V. J. "Scheler's Theory of Sympathy and Love." *Philosophy and Phenomenological Research,* II (March, 1942), 273-291.

Mengüsoglu, Takiyettiu. "Der Begriff des Menschen bei Kant und Scheler." *Proceedings of the XIth International Congress of Philosophy, Brussels, 1953.* 14 vols. Amsterdam: Nauwelaerts, 1953. VII, 28-37.

Merleau-Ponty, Maurice. "Christianity and Ressentiment." *Review of Existential Psychology and Psychiatry,* IX (Winter, 1968), 1-22.

Messner, Johannes. *Das Naturrecht.* 5th ed. revised. Innsbruck: Tyrolia-Verlag, 1966.

————. *Kulturethik mit Grundlegung durch Prinzipienethik und Persönlichkeitsethik.* Innsbruck: Tyrolia-Verlag, 1954.

————. *Widersprüche in der menschlichen Existenz.* Innsbruck: Tyrolia-Verlag, 1952.

Metzger, Arnold. *Phänomenologie und Metaphysik.* Pfullingen: Neske, 1966.

Meurers, Joseph. "Wissenschaft und Ehrfurcht. Zum 30. Todestage Max Schelers." *Philosophia Naturalis,* V (Winter, 1959), 377-412.

Muller, Philippe. *De la Psychologie a L'Anthropologie: A Travers L'Oeuvre de Max Scheler.* Neuchâtel: Imprimerie Centrale, 1946.

Muth, Carl. "Begegnungen. Max Scheler." *Hochland,* XLVI (October, 1953), 10-19.

Nakamura, Hajime. *Ways of Thinking of Eastern Peoples: India-China-Tibet-Japan.* 3rd ed. revised. Honolulu: East-West Center Press, 1968.

Newe, Heinrich. *Max Schelers Auffassung von der religiösen Gotteserkenntnis und ihrem Verhältnis zur metaphysischen.* Würzburg: Becker Universitäts-Druckerei, 1928.

Nietzche, Friedrich. *Also sprach Zarathustra.* Munich: Goldmann, 1966.

————. *Jenseits von Gut und Böse.* Munich: Goldmann, 1966.

————. *Zur Genealogie der Moral.* Munich: Goldmann, 1966.

Nota, John, S.J. *Max Scheler. Een Worstelen om het Wezen van den Mens.* Utrecht: Het Spectrum, 1947.

————. "De Rol van de Liefde in Max Schelers Ethica." *Bijdragen,* XXVII (Summer, 1966), 245-253.

————. "Max Scheler's Philosophy of History." *Proceedings of the*

XIVth International Congress of Philosophy, Vienna, September 1968. 4 vols. Vienna: Herder, 1969, IV, 572-580.

Oesterreicher, John M. *Five in Search of Wisdom.* Notre Dame: University of Notre Dame Press, 1967.

Ogura, Sadahide. *Makusu Shera—Hito to sone Shisoo* ("Max Scheler—The Man and his Thought"). Tokyo: Kooshobo, 1969.

———. *Kachi Rinrigaku Kenkyu* ("Studies on Value Ethics"). Tokyo: Risoosha, 1968.

Ortega y Gasset, José. "Max Scheler. Un Embriagado de Esencias." *Obras Completas,* Vol. IV. Madrid: Revista de Occidente, 1957.

Owens, Thomas J. "Scheler's Emotive Ethics." *Philosophy Today,* XII (Spring, 1968), 13-20. Reprinted from *Cross Currents,* XVI (Spring, 1966), 143-152.

Pape, Ingetrud. "Das Individuum in der Geschichte: Untersuchung zur Geschichtsphilosophie von Nicolai Hartmann und Max Scheler." *Nicolai Hartmann. Der Denker und sein Werk.* Edited by Heinz Heimsoeth and Robert Heiss. Göttingen: Vandenhoeck & Ruprecht, 1952.

Passweg, Salcia, *Phänomenologie und Ontologie: Husserl-Scheler-Heidegger.* Zürich: Hertz, 1939.

Pivcevic, Edo. "Scheler's Anthropology." *Husserl and Phenomenology.* London: Hutchinson University Library, 1970.

Plack, Arno. *Die Stellung der Liebe in der materialen Wertethik.* Landshut: Isar-Post Verlag, 1962.

———. *Die Gesellschaft und das Böse. Eine Kritik der herrschenden Moral.* Munich: Paul List Verlag, 1967.

Plessis, Samuel Ignatius Marinus du. *Die Mensbekoning van Max Scheler.* Pretoria: University of Pretoria, 1951.

Plessner, H. "Scheler, Max." *Handwörterbuch der Sozialwissenschaften.* Vol. IX.

Pöll, Wilhelm. *Wesen und Wesenserkenntnis. Untersuchungen mit besonderer Berücksichtigung der Phänomenologie Husserls und Schelers.* Munich: Reinhardt, 1936.

Przywara, Erich, S. J. *Religionsbegründung. Max Scheler—J. H. Newman.* Freiburg: Herder, 1923.

———. "Zu Max Schelers Religionsauffassung." *Zeitschrift für katholische Theologie,* XLVII (January, 1923), 24-49.

Quiles, Ismael. "La Antropologia Filosofica de Max Scheler." *Estudos,* LXVI (January, 1941), 13-26.

———. "Observationes a la Filosofia de la Religion de Scheler." *Ciencia y Fe,* I (January, 1944), 41-76.

Ranly, Ernest. *Scheler's Phenomenology of Community.* The Hague: Martinus Nijhoff, 1966.

———. "Ethics in Community." *Proceedings of the American Catholic Philosophical Association.* Edited by George F.

McLean, O.M.I. Washington: The Catholic University of America, 1968.
Recaséns-Siches, Luis. "Der Sinn der Objektivität der Werte. Ihre Lebens- und Situationsbedingtheit." *Sinn und Sein.* Edited by Richard Wisser. Tübingen: Max Niemeyer Verlag, 1960.
Reding, Marcel. "Scheler, Max." *Lexikon der Pädagogik.* 1954. Vol. III.
Reinach, Adolf. *Was ist Phänomenologie?* Munich: Kösel Verlag, 1951.
————. "What is Phenomenology?" *The Philosophical Forum,* I (Winter, 1968), 231-256.
Reiner, Hans. *Pflicht und Neigung. Die Grundlagen der Sittlichkeit erörtert und neu bestimmt mit besonderem Bezug auf Kant und Schiller.* Meisenheim/Glan: Westkulturverlag Anton Hain, 1951.
————. *Die philosophische Ethik. Ihre Fragen und Lehren in Geschichte und Gegenwart.* Heidelberg: Quelle & Meyer, 1964.
————. *Gut und Böse. Ursprung der sittlichen Grundunterscheidungen.* Freiburg: Bielefelds Verlag, 1965.
Reuter, Otfried. *'Sittlichkeit und ethische Werterkenntnis' nach Dietrich von Hildebrand im Zusammenhang mit der Tugend der Klugheit.* Regensburg: Verlag Josef Habbel, 1966.
Richardson, William J. *Heidegger: Through Phenomenology to Thought.* The Hague: Martinus Nijhoff, 1963.
Rohner, Anton. "Thomas von Aquin oder Max Scheler." *Der Mensch als Bild Gottes.* Edited by Leo Scheffczyk. Darmstadt: Wissenschaftliche Buchgemeinschaft, 1969.
Rothacker, Erich. *Schelers Durchbruch in die Wirklichkeit.* Bonn: H. Bouvier, 1949.
————. *Geschichtsphilosophie.* Munich: R. Oldenbourg, 1934.
Rüssel, Herbert. "Max Scheler und die Probleme der deutschen Politik." *Hochland,* XXVII (September, 1930), 518-529.
Rutishauser, Bruno. *Max Schelers Phänomenologie des Fühlens. Eine kritische Untersuchung seiner Analyse von Scham und Schamgefühl.* Bern: Francke Verlag, 1969.
Sadler, William A. *Existence and Love: A New Approach in Existential Phenomenology.* New York: Charles Scribner's Sons, 1969.
Scheler, Maria. "Bericht über die Arbeit am Philosophischen Nachlass Max Schelers." *Zeitschrift für Philosophische Forschung,* II (Winter, 1948), 597-602.
Schillp, Paul Arthur. "Max Scheler 1874-1928." *The Philosophical Review,* XXXVIII (November, 1929), 574-588.
Schneider, Marius. *Max Scheler's Phenomenological Philosophy of Values.* Washington: Catholic University of America Press, 1951.

Schoeck, Helmut. *Der Neid. Eine Theorie der Gesellschaft.* Freiburg: Alber Verlag, 1966.

Schoeps, Hans-Joachim. *Was ist der Mensch. Philosophische Anthropologie als Geistesgeschichte der neuesten Zeit.* Göttingen: Musterschmidt-Verlag, 1960.

Schöllgen, Werner. *Die soziologischen Grundlagen der katholischen Sittenlehre.* Düsseldorf: Patmos-Verlag, 1953.

————. "Ethik und Ethos." *Aus Theologie und Philosophie. Festschrift für Fritz Tillmann.* Edited by Theodor Steinbüchel und Theodor Müncker. Düsseldorf: Patmos-Verlag, 1950.

————. "Wertethik und Kultursoziologischer Pluralismus." *Die Rolle der Werte im Leben. Festschrift für Johannes Hessen.* Edited by Cornel J. Bock. Cologne: Wienand Verlag, 1969.

Schorer, Edgar. *Die Zweckethik des Hl. Thomas von Aquin als Ausgleich der formalistischen Ethik Kants und der materialen Wertethik Schelers.* Vechta: Albertus-Magnus Verlag, 1937.

Schubart, W. "Russische Züge in der Philosophie Max Schelers." *Kyrios,* II (Fall, 1937), 175-187.

Schutz, Alfred. "Scheler's Theory of Intersubjectivity and the General Thesis of the Alter-Ego." *Philosophy and Phenomenological Research,* II (March, 1942), 323-347. Reprinted in Alfred Schutz, *Collected Papers.* Vol. I: *The Problem of Social Reality.* Edited by Maurice Natanson. The Hague: Martinus Nijhoff, 1962.

————. "Max Scheler's Philosophy." *Collected Papers.* Vol. III: *Studies in Phenomenological Philosophy.* Edited by Ilse Schutz. The Hague: Martinus Nijhoff, 1966.

————. "Max Scheler's Epistemology and Ethics." *Review of Metaphysics,* XI (December, 1957), 304-314, and XI (March, 1958), 486-501. Reprinted in Alfred Schutz, *Collected Papers.* Vol. III: *Studies in Phenomenological Philosophy.* Edited by Ilse Schutz. The Hague: Martinus Nijhoff, 1966.

Spiegelberg, Herbert. *The Phenomenological Movement.* 2 vols. The Hague: Martinus Nijhoff, 1965.

Spranger, Eduard. *Lebensformen. Geisteswissenschaftliche Psychologie und Ethik der Persönlichkeit.* Munich: Siebenstern Taschenbuch Verlag, 1965.

————. *Types of Men: The Psychology and Ethics of Personality.* Halle: Niemeyer Verlag, 1928.

Stallmach, Josef. "Das Problem sittlicher Eigengesetzlichkeit des Individuums in der philosophischen Ethik." *Theologie und Philosophie,* XLII (Spring, 1967), 22-50.

Stark, Werner. *The Sociology of Knowledge.* Glencoe, Ill.: The Free Press, 1958.

Staude, John Raphael. *Max Scheler: An Intellectual Portrait.* New York: The Free Press, 1967.

Stegmüller, Wolfgang, *Haupströmungen der Gegenwartsphilosophie.*
4th ed. revised. Stuttgart: Kröner Verlag, 1969.

Ströker, Elizabeth. "Der Tod im Denken Max Schelers." *Man and World,* I (May, 1968), 191-207.

Strolz, Walter. "Max Schelers tragische Wendung." *Wort und Wahrheit,* X (November, 1955), 768-771.

Sweeney, Robert Daniel. "A Study of Max Scheler's Philosophy of Value." Unpublished Ph.D. dissertation, Fordham University, 1962.

Temuralp, Takiyettin. *Über die Grenzen der Erkennbarkeit bei Husserl und Scheler.* Berlin: Max Schmersow, 1937.

Troeltsch, Ernst. *Der Historismus und seine Probleme. Gesammelte Schriften.* Vol. III. 2nd ed. Aalen: Scientia Aalen, 1961.

Uchiyama, Minoru. *Das Wertwidrige in der Ethik Max Schelers.* Bonn: H. Bouvier, 1966.

Watsuji, Tetsuro. *Ningen no gaku to shite no Rinrigaku* ("Ethics as Anthropology"). Tokyo: Iwanami, 1964.

———. *Rinrigaku* ("Ethics"). Tokyo: Iwanami, 1963.

———. *Fuudo* ("A Climate"). Tokyo: Iwanami, 1963.

———. *A Climate.* Tokyo: Japanese National Commission for UNESCO, 1961.

Weymann-Weyhe, Walter. *Das Problem der Personeinheit in der ersten Periode der Philosophie Max Schelers.* Emsdetten: Heinrich & Lechte, 1940.

Wilhelm, Sigrid. *Das Bild des Menschen in der Philosophie Max Schelers.* Dresden: Bufra Verlag, 1937.

Williams, Richard Hays. "Scheler's Contributions to the Sociology of Affective Action with special Attention to the Problem of Shame." *Philosophy and Phenomenological Research,* II (March, 1942), 348-358.

Wittmann, Michael. *Max Scheler asl Ethiker.* Düsseldorf: Schwann, 1923.

Wust, Peter. "Max Scheler. Zum Tode des Philosophen." *Gesammelte Werke von Peter Wust.* Vol. VII. Münster: Regensburg, 1966.

———. "Max Schelers Lehre vom Menschen." *Gesammelte Werke von Peter Wust.* Vol. VII. Münster: Regensburg, 1966.

Index of Names

Adam, Karl, 5
Anesaki, Masaharu, 100n.
Apollo, 219, 253ff.
Aquinas, Thomas, 40
Aristotle, 102
Augustine, St., 34f., 38, 42f., 188, 203, 248
Aurelius, Marcus, 154

Bacon, Francis, 77
Balthasar, Hans Urs von, 91n., 167
Beethoven, Ludwig van, 104, 209
Bergson, Henri, 20, 26, 92n.
Bernard, St., 38, 172
Binswanger, Ludwig, 39
Bochenski, I. M., 1
Boelen, Bernard, 122n.
Bollnow, Otto Friedrich, 19f., 97, 99
Bonaventura, St., 38
Brunner, Emil, 81
Buber, Martin, 81

Calvin, 105, 120
Cassirer, Ernst, 4
Cicero, 217
Coit, Stanton, 28n.
Comte, August, 153, 223f., 237
Confucius, 209, 257
Coser, Lewis A., 87, 222
Crumbaugh, James, 128f.

Dahm, Helmut, 250n.
Dante, Alighieri, 38, 209
D'Arcy, Martin C., 189f.
Dempf, Alois, 4, 5, 223
Denninger, Eberhard, 204n.
Descartes, René, 26f.
Dilthey, Wilhelm, 5-7, 26, 96
Dionysus, 219, 245, 252-255
Dostoievsky, Fyodor, 153
Downs, Ray, 108n.
Driscoll, Giles, 122n.

Dumoulin, Heinrich, 243n.
Dupuy, Maurice, 177n.
Durckheim, Emile, 72, 76.

Ebner, Ferdinand, 81
Einstein, Albert, 78
Esser, Albert, 168f.
Eucken, Rudolf, 5f.

Fagothey, Austin, 40
Fichte, Johann Gottlieb, 102, 232
Finance, Joseph de, 127
Fletcher, Joseph, 129n.
Francis, St., 104-106, 243
Frederick the Great, 103, 203
Freud, Sigmund, 252
Fries, Heinrich, 4
Frings, Manfred S., 4, 69f., 122n., 124n., 138n., 169n., 170n., 177n., 221f., 225f.
Fuchs, Josef, 127f.

Galbraith, John Kenneth, 249
Glässer, Alfred, 222n.
Goethe, Johann Wolfgang von, 32, 114, 153, 217, 243f.
Goodhue, William, 37n.
Gordon, Elizabeth, 110f.
Grooten, Johann, 35n.
Gründel, Johannes, 79-84
Guardini, Romano, 5, 37f., 81
Guilead, Reuben, 122n.

Haac, Oscar, 221, 225
Haase, Kurt, 217f.
Hansen, Warren, 105n.
Häring, Bernard, 4, 18, 47n., 127
Harnack, Adolf von, 35
Hartmann, Eduard von, 102
Hartmann, Nicolai, 4, 17-18, 22-23, 28-29, 57-58, 97-99, 121, 191-192
Heath, Peter, 18n.

Spiegelberg, Herbert, 46n., 92n.
Spranger, Eduard, 97, 191, 211, 218n.
Stark, Werner, 5n., 45n., 74, 96n., 185-186, 231n.
Staude, John, 221, 226
Stein, Edith, 1
Steinbüchel, Theodor, 81, 127
Stern, Karl, 254n.

Teilhard de Chardin, Pierre, 222n.
Tertullian, 145
Tillich, Paul, 9, 125-126

Timasheff, Nikolai, 249
Tinbergen, Jan, 249
Tolstoy, Leo, 248
Troeltsch, Ernst, 20

Vogel, Ezra, 111n.

Watanabe, Shoko, 101n.
Watsuji, Tetsuro, 97, 103n.
Whitson, Robley Edward, 250n.
Wilhelm, Sigrid, 163
Wurst, Peter, 5

Subject Index

according to Crumbaugh, 128-129

according to Heidegger, 122-124

according to Rahner, 124-125

according to Schillebeeckx, 126-127

according to Tillich, 125-126

and World War I, 117-121

Knowledge,

types of, 77, 196, 225-241

control knowledge, 225-228

essential knowledge, 228-232

salvific knowledge, 233-237

by connaturality, 40-41

sociological character of, 75-79, 95-96

moral prerequisites, 231-232, 235

harmonization of types of, 237-241

relation to love, 10, 32-33, 67-68, 185-188, 235-236

Labor theory of value, 156-157

Leading spirit of civilization, 205-210

Life-styles, 97, 211-213

Love, 10, 17-18, 42-44, 53, 177-198

according to Jaspers, 191-195

amare in Deo, 17-18, 68, 195-198

as a dynamic movement, 10, 91, 181-192

as existential communication, 193-195

Christian idea of, 149-152, 155, 195-198

creative role of, 10, 181

forms of, 195-198

humanitarian, 151-156

"loving strife", 193-195

man as an ens amans, 10, 187

ordo amoris, 10, 177-186

primacy of love over knowledge, 10, 32, 186-189

relation to knowledge, 10, 32-33, 67-68, 185-191, 235-236

spontaneity of, 181-182

Man, see also Anthropology, Value-person-types

according to K. Rahner, 124-125

"Apollonian" man, 219, 253-255

"Dionysian" man, 219, 245, 253-255

historical nature of man, 80-84, 91, 163-175, 181-195, 219-220

"total man", 250-255

Marxism, 22, 76

Meaning,

of past deeds, 10, 163-175 passim

of history, 86, 94, 218, 220-223, 251

Microcosm, 10

Models, 93-94, 199-220

Moral prerequisites for knowledge, 231-232, 235

Mother-in-law, 143-145

Natural law, 80, 87-88, 128

Nichiren, 100-101

Nomos, 123

Nomos agraphos, 33

Objectivity, 10, 15-17, 57, 177, 184

Obligation, 52, 70, 84, 115-117, 213-214

Ordo amoris, 10, 177-186; see also Love

distortion of, 179-181

Participation, 10, 17, 76, 79, 86, 185-186, 195-198

Peak experience, 40

Permanence, 7-8, 38, 49, 52-53; see also Objectivity, Values

Person, 25, 68, 81, 124-125, 127, 199-220 passim, 230, 236; see also Anthropology, Man

Personalism, 10, 18, 25, 91, 199, 201

Perspectivism, 8-9, 71-79, 87-89

Phenomenology, 2-5, 20, 31, 189, 229-232

Philosophy of the heart, 34-38

Philosophy of history, 11, 25, 94, 100-102, 220-225

Philosophy of life, 26-27

Philosophy of religion, 4-6, 18, 71-73, 61-65, 195-198

DATE DUE

MAR 1 '79			

GAYLORD PRINTED IN U.S.A.